Learning DaVinci Resolve 12.5

A step-by-step guide to editing and color grading

By Dion Scoppettuolo

1st Edition

Learning DaVinci Resolve 12.5
Dion Scoppettuolo
Copyright © 2016 by Dion Scoppettuolo
www.learning-paths.com
To report errors, please send a note to support@learning-paths.com.

ISBN 978-0-9961528-1-5

Acknowledgements:
Many thanks to Leo Bechtold, Taryn Jayne Glass Blowing, Patty Montesion,
Kent Oberheu, Paul Saccone and Alexis van Hurkman.

How to Begin

Welcome to Learning DaVinci Resolve 12.5, a step-by-step guide to editing and color grading. Learning to communicate with media is just as important as learning any computer skill. If you can communicate with images, you can speak to potentially hundreds of millions of people across the globe. That's a powerful skill to master!

Throughout this book we'll explore how Resolve can help you effectively communicate with pictures and sound. You'll learn how to create atmosphere and emotional impact through color, and then deliver your visual story in the perfect format.

We'll use a complete project to organize clips, edit timelines, color grade scenes and output various files in DaVinci Resolve 12.5. To follow along you'll need a Mac or Windows computer, Blackmagic Design's DaVinci Resolve 12.5 software, and the training media that accompanies this book. Information about these requirements are found below.

About DaVinci Resolve 12.5

Blackmagic Design's DaVinci Resolve is widely known as a fantastic color grading and finishing application for feature films, TV shows, and commercials. Its ability to import native RAW files captured from digital cinema cameras and process them in a high precision colorspace has made it popular with colorists world wide. Now, with the release of DaVinci Resolve 12.5, Blackmagic Design has added a very deep set of editing tools so you can also begin assembling and refining your projects using the same application you use to finish them. Best of all, Blackmagic Design offers a free version of the software, which you can use to follow the exercises in this book.

Content Overview

This book takes a complete project from start to finish. Although the chapters are designed to be followed in the order they are written, there are sections to the book that allow you to jump in at chapters 6 or 11.

Chapter 1 through Chapter 5 build upon each other, so you must complete each lesson in sequential order. In them, you'll learn to prepare your media, work with metadata, create Smart bins as well as how to edit and move clips around in the timeline.

Chapter 6 begins with restoring an archived project that contains material you will use in Chapter 6 through 10. These are focused on trimming, audio, speed changes and graphics.

I

The Color grading chapters (11-15) use an Adobe Premiere XML file that is imported in chapter 11. If you are only interested in color grading in Resolve, you can start on chapter 11.

System Requirements

This book is based on DaVinci Resolve 12.5 for OS X and Windows. If you have an older version of DaVinci Resolve, you will need to upgrade to follow along with this book.

Blackmagic Design publishes a Configuration Guide, which can be downloaded from their support web site for the latest operating requirements.

Download DaVinci Resolve 12.5

DaVinci Resolve 12.5 can be downloaded from the Blackmagic Design website:

1. In a web browser, go to www.blackmagicdesign.com/products/davinciresolve.

2. On the DaVinci Resolve page, click the Download button.

After completing the software installation, follow the instructions in the next section to download the media for the exercises in this book.

Download the Training Project

The R12_5 Training Project must be downloaded to your OS X or Windows computer to perform the exercises in this book. The download requires at least 15Gb of free hard disk space. Downloading can take up to 1 hr using a standard broadband connection.

To download the content, you must use the password provided below.

Password: davinciresolve12

To Download and Install the R12_5 Training Project:

1. Open a web browser and go to www.learning-paths.com

2. Click Download to open the DaVinci Resolve download web page.

3. Enter the password listed above.

4. On the Learning-Paths DaVinci Resolve web page, read the instructions and click the Download button to begin downloading the zip file.

5. After downloading, open your Downloads folder and uncompress or unzip it.

6. Drag the unzipped R12_5 Training Project.dra folder from the Downloads folder to your Documents folder.

You are now ready to begin chapter 1.

Ch.1: Starting a Project
Settings, Importing and the Media Page

To get started, you should have taken the time to read the How to Begin chapter, installed Resolve on your computer, downloaded the training project for this book and copied the project folder to your Documents folder.

Producing film and video content is a very creative and exciting process. However, before you can dive into the creative side of things, you need to build a foundation that will allow you to construct a project and try out new ideas efficiently.

This chapter starts you off by configuring the settings for a project appropriately, and importing media that you'll use throughout this book. To begin, we'll start from scratch and learn how to log into the application.

Logging in with a User Profile

You open Resolve just as you open any other application on your computer, for instance, open it from the Dock on OS X or the Start Screen on Windows.

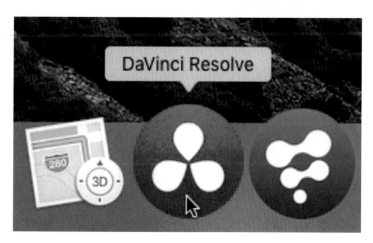

The DaVinci Resolve icon in the OS X Dock.

1. Click the Resolve icon by doing one of the following:

    - On OS X, click the Resolve icon in the Dock.

    - On Windows, click the Resolve icon from the Start Screen.

    Once the application is open, there are two possible windows that appear first.

If you have never opened Resolve before now, you won't see the login window described below. You'll be presented with one of Resolve's main windows. If that is the case with your screen, you can skip the next three steps below (steps 2-4).

If you previously installed an earlier version of DaVinci Resolve, a login window will appear. The login window is used to create and manage user accounts, which are helpful if you share your computer with other editors or colorists.

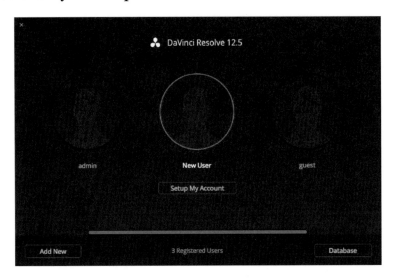

The login window manages multiple users and determines the projects you can open.

2. Double-click the New User icon in the center of the login window.

3. Enter a user name and optionally, a password to protect the account. Then, click the Setup New User button.

4. Click the Login button in the login window.

NOTE: *Even if you have a user account, create a new account for the purposes of this book.*

This multi-user capability allows multiple people using the same computer to customize the application's settings and keyboard shortcuts how they like. Most importantly, each login also determines the projects that you can open. The logged in user can only open projects that they have created.

TIP: *You can enable multi user login by opening a project in Resolve and choosing DaVinci Resolve > Preferences. In the Systems category, click the multi user login check box.*

Once you log in you'll be presented with the Project Manager. The Project Manager window lists all the projects belonging to the logged in user account.

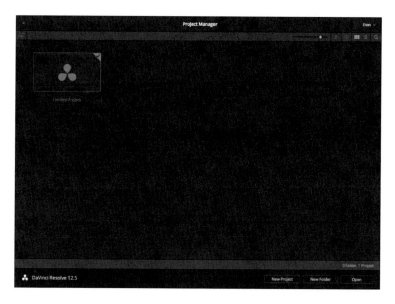

The Project Manager displays all the projects created by the logged in user.

By default, Resolve includes an empty Untitled project thumbnail displayed in the Project Manager. You can use this Untitled project and rename it later or create your own project using the New Project button in the lower right corner of the window.

Any new project you create is added to the Project Manager as a thumbnail. Double-clicking the thumbnail will open the project.

5. In the Project Manager window, double-click the untitled project to open it.

A project represents a single job. It contains the clips that link to the media on your hard drives and any edited timelines you create.

Overview of Pages

Resolve is divided into four different screens called Pages. The four pages are accessible using the buttons (Media, Edit, Color and Deliver) at the bottom of the main window. Each page organizes the various tools you'll use during different stages while making a program.

The four page buttons reconfigure the toolset and interface for different tasks.

1. Click the Edit button to view the Edit page.

    The Edit page is where you assemble clips together into a complete program.

2. Click the Color button to view the Color page.

    The Color page is used to modify the brightness and color of your program.

3. Click the Deliver button to view the Deliver page.

   The Deliver page is used to output your program.

4. Click the Media button to view the Media page.

The Media page is the first page you'll generally use and that is where we will start as well.

Importing Clips

The primary purpose of the Media page is to import video and audio clips from your hard drives. You can also perform other tasks here, such as adding metadata to clips, syncing separate picture and sound clips together, and troubleshooting clips that appear offline.

Media Storage browser is divided into two sections.
A list of hard drives on the left and the hard drive contents on the right.

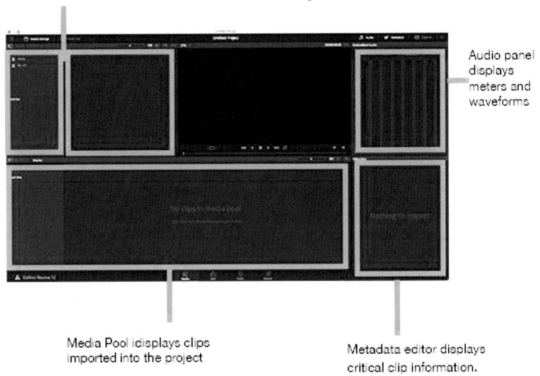

Audio panel displays meters and waveforms

Media Pool displays clips imported into the project

Metadata editor displays critical clip information.

The Media page is primarily used to bring clips into a project.

The Media Storage browser, in the upper left of the Media page, is used to navigate to any folder or hard drive where you keep your video and audio files.

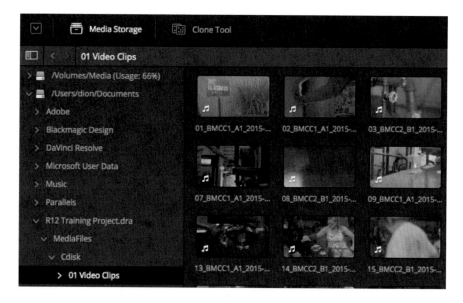

To find clips on your hard drives, use the Media Storage browser.

1. In the Media Storage browser sidebar, click the icon for your computer's hard drive.

2. Navigate through your hard drive to your Documents folder.

NOTE: *This book assumes you have copied the R12_5 Training Project folder to your Documents folder. If you copied the files to a different location, use that substitute location.*

3. In the Documents folder, double-click the R12_5 Training Project folder.

4. Double-click the MediaFiles > 01 Video Clips folder.

    The browser is divided into two sections. The left side displays a list of all your hard drives and the right side displays the video and audio files on those hard drives. Video and audio files are displayed as thumbnail-sized images called clips.

    You import clips to a project by dragging them from the Media Storage browser, into the Media Pool in the lower half of the Media page.

5. Click any clip in the browser, then choose Edit > Select All to select all the clips displayed in the browser, or press Command-A (OS X) or Ctrl-A (Windows).

6. In the Media Storage browser, drag any clip down into the Media Pool to import the clips into your project.

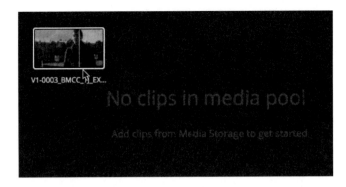

Drag clips from the Media Storage browser to the Media Pool to import them.

When you import clips into a project, they are stored in bins in the Media Pool. Resolve includes a Master bin as the default location for all imported clips. Clips that you add to the Media Pool are not copied or moved from their original location, nor are they transcoded to another format. The clips or media, are unaltered and left in the current hard drive location.

TIP: *You can drag clips to the Media Pool from the OS X Finder or Windows File Explorer.*

Importing Folders

You can drag an entire folder of clips into the Media Pool. Dragging a folder creates a separate bin in the Media Pool side bar using the folder's name.

1. In the upper area of the Media Storage browser, click the Back arrow to view the the R12_5 Training Project > MediaFiles folder.

2. Drag the 02 Audio Clips folder to an empty area below the word Master in the Media Pool bin list.

You can drag entire folders of clips into the bin list area of the Media Pool.

The folder is added as a bin inside the Master bin. All the clips contained in the 02 Audio Clips folder are imported along with the new bin.

Reviewing and Scrubbing Clips

Once clips are imported into your project, you'll want to play them to review their contents.

1. In the Media Pool bin list, select the Master bin.

2. Click any clip thumbnail to load it into the viewer.

   Clicking a clip thumbnail in the Media Pool loads that clip into the viewer, where you can see a larger version of the thumbnail. Once a clip is loaded into the viewer, you can then play and shuttle through the clip using the jog bar and transport controls.

Clicking a clip in the Media Pool loads it into the viewer, where it can be played.

3. Drag the jog bar playhead to fast forward and rewind quickly through the clip.

4. Under the viewer, click the Play button or press the spacebar.

5. Click the Stop button or press the spacebar again to stop playback.

   To become familiar with the content you will be using, you should always watch each source clip. Although this may seem time consuming, skipping it will only waste time later while editing. Once you complete this chapter, take time to review the clips.

Reviewing Audio Clips

When you load an audio-only clip, the viewer displays the file's audio waveform.

1. In the Media Pool bin list, select the 02 Audio Clips bin.

2. Click any audio clip thumbnail to load it into the viewer.

At the top of the viewer is a zoomed out view showing the entire mixed down audio file. At the bottom is a detailed view showing the audio that immediately surrounds the red playhead. The playhead is used to identify the current position in the clip.

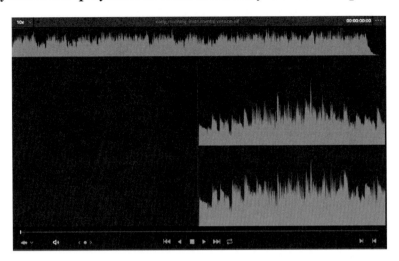

An audio clip loaded into the viewer, displays a detailed waveform view.

The top, zoomed out display can be used to navigate to any portion of the clip by dragging the red playhead.

3. At the top of the Audio viewer, in the zoomed out waveform, drag the red playhead to scrub through the clip.

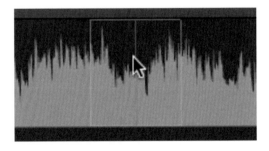

Use the small red playhead at the top of the audio viewer to move to a different area in the clip.

As you scrub through the audio clip, snippets of sound are played to give you an idea of where you are in the clip. Because there are times when this scrubbing sound can be annoying, it can be enabled and disabled using a keyboard short cut.

4. To disable the digital audio scrubbing sound, press Shift-S, then drag the red playhead to a new location.

5. Press Shift-S, again to enable the scrubbing sound.

Manually Syncing Picture with Sound

When on set, some productions choose to have a sound person responsible for recording the audio. The camera person may or may not record rough or back up audio on the camera, but the main audio is recorded on a separate device. This double-system set up has been common in feature film productions for years because separate audio recording devices can record a greater dynamic range than audio recording in most digital film cameras. Using a double system set up means you must sync the video clips with their matching audio.

Resolve includes three different ways to sync these clips. Two are automatic and one takes a bit more effort. If the audio and video clips use the same timecode you can choose to auto sync the audio based on timecode. If the camera person recorded some rough camera audio and you also have high quality audio files, audio can be automatically synced by analyzing the two audio recordings. Both options are available by right-clicking on the selected clips.

```
Auto-sync Audio Based on Timecode
Auto-sync Audio Based on Timecode and Append Tracks
Auto-sync Audio Based on Waveform
Auto-sync Audio Based on Waveform and Append Tracks
```

The right-click contextual menu options for auto-syncing audio and video clips.

TIP: *Timecode is a time stamp signal inserted into each frame of audio or video, which is used to identify a precise location. Timecode is made up of a series of two-digits representing hours:minutes:seconds:frames (such as HH:MM:SS:FF or 01:00:00:00).*

In our Master bin, I've created a real challenge for you. Although three of the interview clips have the good audio already synced for you, the last audio clip does not. To makes matters worse, (because that's just the way film and video productions are) the last clip doesn't even have a clapper! To sync this clip, you'll use the manual method in Resolve. This is done by manually lining up the video and audio files on the same frame and linking them together.

1. From the Master bin, select 04_BMCCA_TJ_EXT video clip to load it in the viewer.

2. In the viewer, move the playhead to the frame when the woman begins to say the word "different". This is at timecode number 15:38:15:05.

3. To fine tune the position of the playhead, use the left and right arrow keys on the keyboard to move one frame forward or backwards, as necessary.

Use the timecode number above the viewer to move the playhead to 15:38:15:05.

Without a clapper recorded, you need to locate a point that is easy to hear. Words that start with B or D are the best places to try and sync, because they clearly start on a specific frame. Now, you need to locate the same D on the higher quality audio clip.

4. Click the Waveform tab in the Audio panel.

The Audio panel can display meters or waveforms for audio clips.

This lets you view and scrub the waveform of audio clips you select in the Media Pool.

5. Select the 02 Audio Clips bin and click 04_AUDIO_TJ_EXT.

The audio clip loads into the Waveform display of the Audio panel. The clip is a recording of the entire interview, where as the video clip is just a small portion of the interview. So, the same frame on the audio clip is located near the end.

6. Below the Audio panel, drag the scrubber bar to move the playhead to 15:33:51:03. Again, use the left and right arrow keys if necessary.

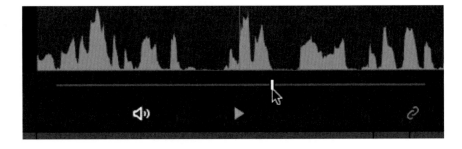

Use the scrubber bar to move the playhead to 15:33:49:15.

7. When both clips are at the start of the word "different", click the Link/Unlink Audio button 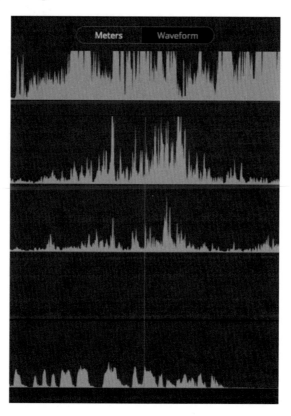 located in the bottom right of the audio panel.

The new audio is now linked into the video clip. If you find the audio is a frame or two off, click the Link/Unlink button and try to sync them again.

Configuring Audio Channels

Audio files recorded in camera or on external devices can contain two or more channels of audio. It's not always the case that each audio channel will be useful. Often the different channels come from different microphones. One particular mic may be the primary recording, while the others are just back ups. That's the case we have with our newly synced interview audio file. It has two audio channels recorded from built in stereo mics on the audio recording device and one, very clear audio channel on channel 4, from a lavaliere mic fastened to the woman speaking.

Three channels of an audio clip loaded into the viewer.

If you have no plans to use the alternative channels, you can modify the audio file so Resolve only uses the primary channel.

1. Select the 04_BMCCA_TJ_EXT clip from the Master bin.

Select the 04_BMCCA_TJ_EXT clip in the Master bin.

2. Right-click the clip, and choose Clip Attributes.

    The Clip Attributes window includes an Audio panel that is used to modify channels. These settings affect which channels are used, and how they appear in the timeline.

The Audio panel in the Clip Attributes window.

3. Click the Audio panel tab at the top of the Attributes window.

4. Click the Mono button to change the audio file to a mono file.

5. The best sounding audio is only on one audio channel. To make sure we use this channel when we edit, in the Audio Tracks entry box replace 4 with a 1. This will cause only one audio track to be created when you edit this clip into the timeline.

6. Below the Audio Tracks entry box, from the Source Channel pop-up menu, change the Embedded Channel 1 to Linked Channel 4 to use the best sounding channel.

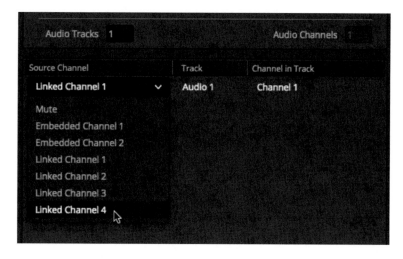

Choose Linked Channel 4 from the Source Channel popup menu.

7. Click OK to accept the changes.

TIP: *You can update the attributes at anytime. However, segments already in a timeline will not update. Only newly edited segments will contain the new attributes settings.*

8. Play the clip to hear the higher quality audio.

   With some work under our belt, it might be a smart idea to save our project.

9. From the Media page, choose File > Save Project.

10. In the dialog, type the project name R12_5 Starting Project, then click Save.

Setting up a New Project

When you open a new project, you should define the resolution and playback frame rate your program will use. This is typically based on the eventual output format. You can do this using the Project Settings dialog accessed under the File menu.

1. Choose File > Project Settings (Shift-9) to open the Project Settings dialog.

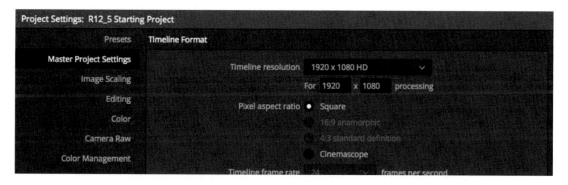

Use the Master Project settings category to set the timeline resolution.

The Timeline Resolution and Timeline Frame rate pop-up menus define the resolution and frame rate for the timelines you create in the current project.

2. From the Timeline resolution pop-up menu, choose 1280 x 720 HD 24p.

3. At the bottom of the Project Settings dialog, click Save and return to the Media page.

TIP: You can change the resolution setting at anytime during your project.

That is one piece of house cleaning that needs to be done before you can begin putting your program together. There are two others that you should be aware of as well.

Setting a Scratch Disk

This section is mostly intended for educational purposes. There is no need to set the Scratch Disk for this book. However, you should learn about setting the scratch disk for your own projects. Throughout the duration of a project, Resolve will occasionally create media that needs to be saved to a hard drive. These types of media may include rendered files, still frames and optimize media for better playback performance. These files get saved to the first hard drive you add to the Scratch Disks list of the Preferences Media Storage panel.

1. Choose DaVinci Resolve > Preferences.

2. Click the Media Storage panel in the Preferences window.

The Media Storage panel in the Resolve Preferences.

It's nearly always advisable to set your first scratch disk to the largest, fastest hard drive available to your computer. If you don't set a Scratch disk, your System disk is used. Not really a good idea! Your internal system disk probably lacks the space and speed needed to be a Scratch disk.

NOTE: Do not follow the steps below for this book. However, be aware you should set a Scratch disk for your own projects.

3. Click the Add button.

4. Navigate to the hard drive you want use as a Scratch disk, then click Open.

5. Click Save at the bottom of the Preferences window to close it.

TIP: You can only set the Scratch Disk before beginning a project. Changing a scratch disk after beginning to edit may cause you to lose audio waveforms, stills and other files.

What is Color Space

Every digital camera tries to reproduce the real world colors seen by the human eye, using custom palettes of colors. These palettes called color spaces dictate how cameras map real world colors to the smaller range of colors a camera can record. HD video cameras use the HD color space called Rec. 709. So cameras only need to follow the specification to produce images that can be broadcast on television and look relatively good.

Advances in imaging sensors have resulted in the creation of digital film cameras, that can now capture higher resolution images. These cameras produce more "filmic" images with a greater tonal range (the range from shadows to highlights). To do this, digital film cameras save images using a logarithmic gamma curve, which cause images to appear flat or low contrast on computer displays and HD monitors.

Images using Linear, Rec.709 and Log gamma curves.

To appear correct on a monitor or computer display, the gamma curve needs to be corrected for your display. To make matters a bit more difficult, each digital film camera manufacturer uses its own unique gamma curve to redistribute tonal levels. So the process of correcting these non linear gamma curves is unique for each camera model.

Most editing and color grading applications use lookup tables or LUTs to convert from one color space into another. Lookup Tables are configured in the Color Management section of the Project Settings. They allow for very specific and custom color conversions. However, Resolve also provides a much simpler yet in some ways more advanced, color management system, and that's the route we will take.

Setting Up Project Color Management

The clips we are using were recorded with a Blackmagic digital film camera, which records images using a non-linear gamma curve to capture more detail. So you may have noticed that they appear low in contrast.

To correct for the differences between the camera's color space and your output color space, you can use Resolve's Color Management project setting. To set up a color managed project you enable the type of color science you want to use. This is less scary than it sounds.

15

1. Choose File > Project Settings or press Shift-9.

2. In the Master Project Settings category, click the Color Science pop-up menu.

3. Choose DaVinci YRGB Color Managed.

The Color Science menu allows you to choose between ACES, DaVinci color management or LUTs.

Unless you are on a film that has standardized on an ACES workflow, you should always choose DaVinci YRGB Color Managed.

The DaVinci YRGB Color Managed setting is a project wide setting that allows you set color profiles based on what camera you used (Input) and where it will be displayed (Output). This is done in the Color Management category of the Project Settings

4. In the Project Settings' list of categories, click Color Management.

The first step is setting the color profile for the incoming source clips.

5. Click the Input Colorspace menu to view the source color space choices.

The menu includes common profiles for digital cameras. You must select the correct profile for your camera. Our clips came from a Blackmagic Design camera.

6. From the Input Colorspace menu, choose Blackmagic Design 4.6K Film v3.

The Color Management setting configures the input, output and timeline color space.

The Output Colorspace is typically set to Rec.709 for HD programs.

7. Set the Timeline Colorspace and Output Colorspace to Rec.709 Gamma 2.4.

    The Timeline Colorspace is a more specialized setting. In most cases, you'll set the Timeline Colorspace to match the Output Colorspace. However, if you are a colorist who prefers to grade in a specific color space, you might set it differently.

    If you are on OS X, you have the option to use Apple's Color Sync Color management software to have the viewers in Resolve simulate an external broadcast monitor or 4K projector. For the purposes of this book, let's assume you have not calibrated your OS X display to Rec 709 or P3 and we will disable this setting.

8. On OS X, disable the check box for Use Mac Color Display Profiles for viewers.

9. Click Save to close the dialog.

10. To see the color and contrast update, press Space bar to play the clip.

    When the viewer updates, the clip that is loaded reflects the new color space with greater contrast. Even though the clips look better, they are not color corrected in the traditional sense. You have just corrected the gamma curve for an HD monitor.

TIP: *The viewers in Resolve are not meant to be color accurate.*

Setting Input Color Space Per Clip

On most productions there is a primary camera, but different cameras maybe used on one day, or you may be using some stock footage. Whatever the reason, you will need a way to change the Input color profiles for the odd clip or two.

1. Select the Master bin and right click over the MVI_9787 clip.

The MVI-9787 clip uses an sRGB color space.

This clip was captured using a Canon DSLR, which uses the sRGB color space, so the Project Input color profile of Blackmagic Design 4K Film is incorrect.

2. From the contextual menu choose Input Color Space > sRGB.

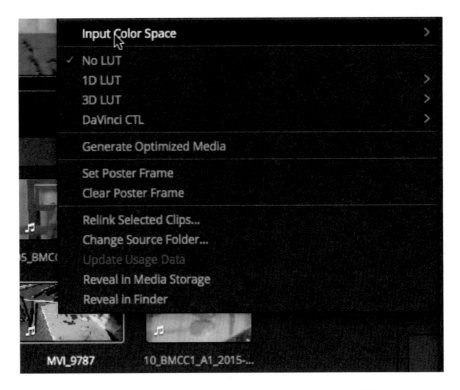

Right-click over a clip in a bin and choose a new Input Color Space.

Saving and Auto Saving a Project

Resolve includes an Autosave feature that you can rely on in case of accidents, but you also need to save your work periodically.

1. Choose File > Save Project or press Command-S (OS X) or Ctrl-S (Windows).

2. Choose File > Project Settings, then select the Auto Save category in the side bar.

3. Make sure the setting is enabled by clicking the On radio button.

4. Below the radio button, change the 10min pop-up menu to something to frequency you feel more comfortable with for the Autosave . This is a personal choice and the default is fine if you do not want to change anything.

5. Click Save to keep the configuration and close the Project Settings dialog.

You'll be using this project over the next 4 chapters, so it is important to save the work you do at the end of each chapter.

Chapter 1 Test Questions

Q1: What are the four main pages of Resolve?

Q2: What is the primary purpose of the Media page?

Q3: Which panel in the Media page is used to navigate the drives connected to your computer, the Media Storage browser or the Media Pool?

Q4: After you import clips into a bin, where are the original media files located?

Q5: True or False: The Clip Attributes window is used to change the clip's colorspace?

Ch. 2: Bringing Order to Clips
Bins, Smart Bins and Metadata

All the clips needed for the next few exercises in this book were imported in the previous chapter. Since you can have hundreds of clips in a project, you need to be organized about where clips are located and the information you attach to them. You primarily keep a project organized by adding valuable information to each clip called metadata, making clips easier to locate. Then, based on the metadata, you categorize the clips into bins. This chapter will introduce you to the ways to add metadata and how to create bins based on that metadata.

Working with Metadata

Clips can contain information, called metadata, which includes all the settings captured by the camera as well as any custom information you choose to add. Essentially, it is everything that isn't the image itself. Metadata can help you organize your projects more efficiently so Resolve includes a dedicated place called the Metadata editor.

1. If necessary, open Resolve and the R12_5 Starting Project.

2. Make sure you are on the Media page , then select a clip from the Master bin.

   The metadata for a selected clip is shown in the lower-right corner of the Media page.

The Metadata editor displays information about a selected clip.

Since a production can include an enormous amount of metadata for every clip, a pop-up menu in the upper right corner of the Metadata editor lets you choose from multiple groupings of metadata.

3. In the Master bin, select the 01_BMCCA_TJ_EXT clip thumbnail.

    The Metadata editor displays information about the 01_BMCCA_TJ_EXT clip.

4. In the upper-right corner of the Metadata editor, from the Groups pop-up menu, choose Shot Scene.

The Groups pop up menu allows you to display different sets of metadata for a clip.

A lot of metadata can be captured by the camera, but adding your own custom metadata can make it easier to find clips based on their content. The Shot Scene group allows you to add variety of custom information including tags or keywords.

Our media contains four interview clips that you'll be using. Adding a keyword to each of these interview clips will make it easier to locate them when we need them.

5. In the Keyword field of the Metadata editor, enter interview.

    This adds the keyword metadata to the one clip we have selected.

6. To add the same keyword to multiple clips, in the Master bin, select the 02_BMCCA_TJ_EXT clip, hold the Command key (OS X) or Ctrl key (Windows) and select the two remaining interview clips (03_BMCCA_TJ_EXT and 04_BMCCA_TJ_EXT.)

Select the three remaining interview clips in the Master bin.

7. In the Metadata editor, enter interview. A list of commonly used and previously entered keywords appears and you can select interview from the list.

    Selecting from the list helps to ensure spelling is consistent with keywords.

8. Click Save at the bottom of the Metadata editor.

Metadata added here can be used throughout Resolve in unique ways that we will explore later in this chapter.

Viewing Metadata in a List

Clips can be displayed as thumbnails or in a list view, to better view all of the metadata. The buttons and slider in the upper right corner of the Media Pool control the viewing options.

The controls above the Media Pool are for the size of thumbnails, thumbnail view, list view and search.

1. In the upper right corner of the Media Pool, click the list view button .

Clicking the list view button displays clips in a list with the various metadata shown in columns. You can sort the order of clips by clicking the header of a column.

2. Click the heading for File Name so a small arrow next to the name points up.

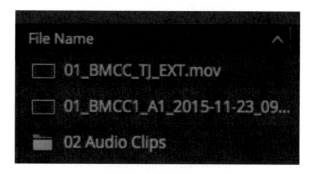

Click a column header to sort the bin in ascending or descending order.

Clicking the File Name heading sorts the column based on the name of each clip.

3. Click the heading for File Name again to reverse the sort order.

A small arrow pointing down is shown next to the column heading name to indicate that it is sorted in descending order (Z-A or larger numbers at the top).

TIP: *Thumbnail view sorts clips based on the sort order you select in list view. The first clip in the list view is placed as the first clip on the left in thumbnail view.*

Although you can sort the columns, the truth is that some of the columns will be more important than others, so it helps that you can hide and show columns in this view.

4. Right-click any column heading to display a contextual menu of all the headings.

The contextual menu lists all the columns that can be displayed in a bin. The headings with a check mark are currently displayed. Clicking a check mark to remove it will hide the column in the bin.

5. In the menu, uncheck all the column headings except Start TC, End TC and Duration.

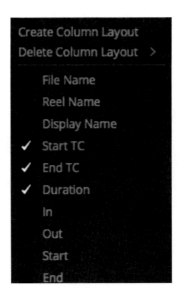

Right-clicking a column header allows you to select which columns are displayed in list view.

6. In the menu, add checks next to Display Name, Description, Scene and Take.

7. Click in an empty space in the bin to hide the contextual menu.

Most of these headings are easy to understand but the Display Name is not as obvious. Display Name is a useful column used to customize the name of a clip in the bin. Where File Name is the name of the file on your hard drive, Display Name is the name of the clip used in Resolve. We'll use the Display Name column in a bit, but right now we'll learn how to save the customized list view we have created.

Saving Bin Views

Once you have the columns you want displayed in the bin, you can save views and recall them throughout a project. This allows you to have different sets of metadata displayed in the bin at different times.

1. Right-click over the headings area again, and then choose Create Custom Layout.

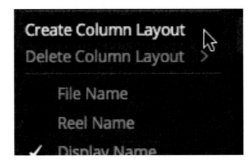

Create custom views for the list view using Create Custom Layout.

2. In the Create Custom Layout dialog type Basic View for the name, then click OK.

You can save as many layouts as you like and recall them using the contextual menu.

Importing Metadata

Now that we have Description, Shot and Take fields in our bin, you'll need to fill in those fields with metadata. However, instead of typing it in, metadata can also be added by importing a csv file. Being able to export and import metadata makes it easy to bring in metadata created in other applications or in another Resolve project. For our purposes I've already created a CSV file that contains additional metadata about the interview clips.

NOTE: *CSV files are text based files that separate each value using a comma.*

1. Select the four interview clips in the bin (01_BMCC_TJ_EXT, 02_BMCC_TJ_EXT, 03_BMCC_TJ_EXT, 04_BMCC_TJ_EXT).

04_BMCC_TJ_EXT		15:38:10:13	15:39:40:21	00:01:30:08
03_BMCC2_B1_2015-11-22_0947_C...	09:47:37:21	09:47:43:14	00:00:05:17
03_BMCC_TJ_EXT		15:35:47:16	15:37:07:17	00:01:20:01
02_BMCC1_A1_2015-11-23_0931_C...	09:31:36:11	09:31:43:23	00:00:07:12
02_BMCC_TJ_EXT		15:33:42:20	15:35:25:16	00:01:42:20
02 Audio Clips				
01_BMCC1_A1_2015-11-23_0922_C...	09:22:26:10	09:22:43:15	00:00:17:05
01_BMCC_TJ_EXT		15:30:47:12	15:31:00:17	00:00:13:05

Select all four interview clips in the Master bin.

2. From the File menu choose Import Metadata to > Selected Clips.

3. In the open dialog that appears navigate to the R12_5 Training Project folder, select the interview metadata.csv file and click Open.

    The Metadata Import dialog allows you to select the import options for how the metadata is merged with the selected clips. The default settings use the file name and timecode to match the clips, which works fine in most cases.

4. Click OK in the Metadata Import dialog.

04_BMCC2_B1_2015-11-22_0955_C...	09:55:14:23	09:55:28:11	00:00:13:12			
04_BMCC_TJ_EXT	15:38:10:13	15:39:40:21	00:01:30:08	Heat Managers	51	1
03_BMCC2_B1_2015-11-22_0947_C...	09:47:37:21	09:47:43:14	00:00:05:17			
03_BMCC_TJ_EXT	15:35:47:16	15:37:07:17	00:01:20:01	Sketching	51	3
02_BMCC1_A1_2015-11-23_0931_C...	09:31:36:11	09:31:43:23	00:00:07:12			
02_BMCC_TJ_EXT	15:33:42:20	15:35:25:16	00:01:42:20	It's Special	51	4
02 Audio Clips						
01_BMCC1_A1_2015-11-23_0922_C...	09:22:26:10	09:22:43:15	00:00:17:05			
01_BMCC_TJ_EXT	15:30:47:12	15:31:00:17	00:00:13:05	Color Glass	51	2

Metadata like description, shot and take can be manually entered or imported using a csv file.

A description, scene # and take # are added to each of the four selected clips. We'll use this metadata later in this chapter to name our interview clips.

Adding a New Bin

Although we are only dealing with a few clips in this project, most projects contain a hundred clips or more. Leaving them all in the Master bin will slow you down, so it is always better to organize clips into custom bins that you create.

1. Choose File > New Bin, or press Command-Shift-N (OS X) or Ctrl-Shift-N (Windows).

    The bin is added to the bin list, nested under the Master bin and it is ready to rename.

2. Type B-Roll as the name of the bin.

The Media Pool side bar shows a list of bins.

Bins in the Media Pool are similar to folders on your computer. You can move clips into the them to categorize clips in a better way.

Moving Clips Between Bins

In our project, all of the video clips are located in the Master bin, but it would be easier to work with them if we divide them up based on their content. For instance, we can place all the action shots of glass blowing into one bin and all the talking interview clips into another.

To move clips into a new bin, you drag them directly onto the bin name in the Media Pool.

1. Select the Master bin, and click the icon view button to view the clips as thumbnails.

The icon button in the upper left corner of the Media Pool displays the clips as thumbnails.

TIP: You can change the thumbnail image by moving the mouse pointer back and forth over it until the frame you want appears, then right-click and choose Set Poster Frame from the menu.

2. Select the first clip in the bin, then choose Edit > Select All or press Command-A (OS X) or Ctrl-A (Windows).

   Some of the selected items in the bin are other bins, like the 02 Audio Clips and B-Roll bin, while others are the interview clips which we want to keep separate. You'll need to deselect these six items.

3. Command-click (OS X) or Ctrl-click (Windows) to deselect the 02 Audio Clips bin, the B-Roll bin and the four interview shots.

Select all the clips except the four interview clips and the two bins.

NOTE: Due to differences in display and window size, the order of clips in your bin may appear different than the pictures in this book.

The remaining selected clips are supplemental footage, related to the interview. These are called B-Roll clips. You can place these selected clips into the B-Roll bin.

4. Drag the selected clips onto the B-Roll bin name in the Media Pool sidebar. When the B-Roll bin name highlights, release the mouse button.

To move clips, drag clips from one bin onto the name of a bin in the side bar.

5. Click the B-Roll bin to view its contents.

TIP: To delete a bin, select it and press the Delete key. All the clips in the bin will be removed from Resolve but will remain on your hard drive.

You've now successfully moved clips from one bin to another. Although the process is simple, it is also labor intensive. Let's look at a more efficient way to organize clips using the metadata we entered in the previous exercise.

Adding a Smart Bin

The interview keyword you added to the four interview clips can be used to automatically populate a bin. Smart bins search a project for clips based on criteria you define. Smart bins can save you the time of collecting the clips yourself but best of all, the contents of Smart bins automatically update when new clips matching the criteria, are added to a project.

1. At the bottom of the bin list, right-click in the empty area below the words Smart Bins.

2. From the contextual menu, choose Add Smart Bin.

The Create Smart Bin dialogue defines the rules used to populate a Smart Bin with clips.

Selecting Add Smart Bin opens the Create Smart Bin dialog. This dialog defines the criteria used to collect the clips, which are added to the Smart Bin. The criteria you define can use specific camera types, file types, timecode ranges, as well as custom metadata you add, such as keywords.

3. In the Create Smart Bin dialog, enter interview in the Name field.

4. In the dialog's Media Pool properties menu, choose Metadata- Shot & Scene because this is the original metadata group that contains the keyword field.

5. Change Description to "Keywords" and leave the final menu at "contains."

6. In the text entry field, type interview, then click Create Smart Bin.

    The Smart Bin collects any clips that contain the keyword "interview" and displays them. So now all four clips with the keyword interview are located in the Interview Smart Bin. When new clips are added to this project and you tag them with the Keyword interview, they will automatically be added to the Interview Smart Bin.

7. Choose File > Save Project or press Command-S (OS X) or Ctrl-S (Windows).

TIP: *Double clicking a Smart Bin will open it so you can change the name or criteria.*

Changing Clip Names

As we mentioned earlier, you cannot change a clip's name using the Filename column. That column shows the file's name in the operating system. However, the Display Name column can be changed to something more descriptive.

1. Select the B-roll bin and click the list view button to view the clips as thumbnails.

2. In the B-Roll bin, click the heading for Display Name so the small arrow points up.

    This will sort the bin in ascending order.

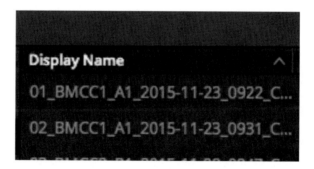

The Display Name column is used to rename clips inside Resolve.

3. Click the first clip in the list to see it in the source viewer.

Double-click the first clip to load it into the source viewer.

TIP: *If you do not see the same image for the first clip as the picture above, make sure the column heading for Display Name is sorted, with the arrow pointing up.*

4. Click the clip's Display Name and in the Display Name field, type 01 glashaus sign.

5. Click the second clip in the list view. This clip is of a door opening.

6. Click the second clip's Display Name, then type 02 opening door.

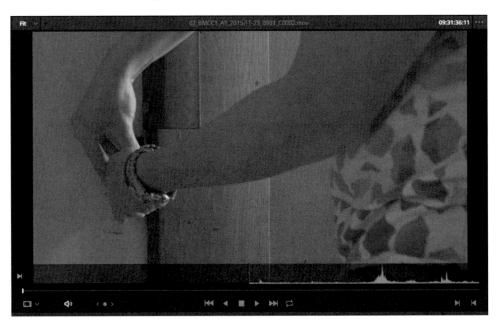

Double-click the second clip to load it into the source viewer.

7. For the next six clips, enter the following names, starting with the third clip in the list:

03 gas knob

04 furnace start

05 WS pipe warmer

06 CU pipe warmer

07 pulling out of furnace

08 Color

You may have notice that above the viewer the file name is currently used even though you have entered a new Display Name. To use the Display Name every where names are shown, you must enable it, otherwise Resolve will use the File Name.

8. Choose View > Show Display Names.

9. Choose File > Save Project or press Command-S (OS X) or Ctrl-S (Windows).

Most times clip names will be a combination of reel ID, data and time generated by the camera that captured the clip. These are not always the most descriptive names and often need to be changed. Entering the clip names manually is one way to do that but in the next exercise we'll look at an alternative method.

Using Variables as Clip Names

Typing the display name for a clip is not the only way to name it. Variables are references to other metadata that exist on the clip like Scene, Take and Shot. These are called variables since they are not the same for each clip, they vary. You can enter a variable into the Display Name and Resolve will reference the correct information for each clip. For instance, we'll use a combination of Description, Scene and Take for the four interview clips.

1. Select the Interview smart bin and then select all four clips.

Display Name		Start TC	End TC	Duration	Description	Scene	Take
01_BMCC_TJ_EXT		15:30:47:12	15:31:00:17	00:00:13:05	Color Glass	51	2
02_BMCC_TJ_EXT		15:33:42:20	15:35:25:16	00:01:42:20	It's Special	51	4
03_BMCC_TJ_EXT		15:35:47:16	15:37:07:17	00:01:20:01	Sketching	51	3
04_BMCC_TJ_EXT		15:38:10:13	15:39:40:21	00:01:30:08	Heat Managers	51	1

Select the four interview clips displayed in the interview smart bin.

2. Right-click over the clips and choose Clip Attributes from the menu.

3. In the Clip Attributes window, click the Name tab to show the Display Name field.

4. In the Display Name field, type a % sign.

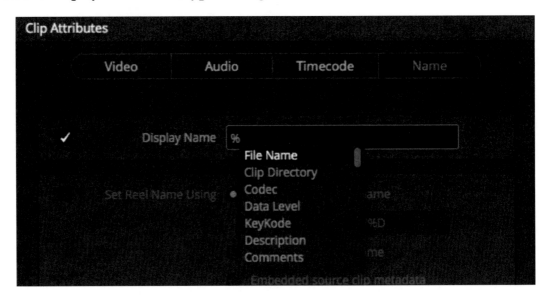

Enter a % sign to bring up a list of variables.

Entering a % sign signals to Resolve that you are about to enter a variable. Once you enter the % sign, a list of variables pops up.

5. Scroll through the list to locate Description or press D to see all the variables with a D.

6. Click Description from the pop up menu to add it into the Display Name field.

Select Description from the list to add it to the Display Name.

You can mix text that you type with variables to create a clearer name. For instance, we'll type in an _ (underscore) to separate each variable, making them easier to read.

7. Type an underscore _ after the Description variable, then press %S to see all the variables with an S.

Add underscores to make each variable easier to read.

8. Click Scene from the pop up menu to add it into the Display Name field.

9. Type an underscore _ after the Scene variable, then press %T and click Take from the pop up menu to add it into the Display Name field.

10. At the bottom of the Clip Attributes window click OK to close the window and apply the Display Name variables.

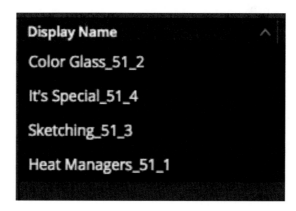

Each clip is now named using its description, scene and take field.

11. Choose File > Save Project.

If you have the metadata for your clips, then you should use it. Naming clips with variables can save hours of manual typing and give you clear descriptive names that match other documents in a production like camera logs and script notes.

You have now set up all the bins and are ready to begin editing your interview. In the next chapter, you'll use the bins and clips you've organized in this project to create a short interview scene using the Edit page and its functionality.

Chapter 2 Test Questions

Q1: How can you organize your clips?

    A) By placing clips in bins

    B) By adding metadata, like keywords

    C) By sorting clips in a list view

    D) All of the above.

Q2: The Media Pool and bin are located: (choose one)

    A) On the Media page

    B) On the Project Manager window

    C) On both pages

Q3: True or False: To move clips to a new bin, you drag them onto the bin name in the Media Pool sidebar.

Q4: What does this button do  ?

Q5: In the list view of a bin, what column is used to type a name for a clip?

Ch. 3: The Basics of Editing
Insert, Overwrite and the Edit Page

To make a program, you assemble clips together in a timeline. The first pass at creating this timeline is called the *rough cut*. The goal is to place clips, more or less in the order you want for your final production. It is the equivalent of sketching a picture rather than precisely illustrating one. In this chapter, we'll look at the initial steps to create a rough cut.

The Edit Page

The previous chapter covered many of the tasks you perform in the Media page. This chapter acts as an introduction to the editing features of the Edit page.

1. If necessary, open Resolve, then from the Project Manager open the R12_5 Starting Project that you have been working on.

2. Click the Edit page button at the bottom of the Resolve window.

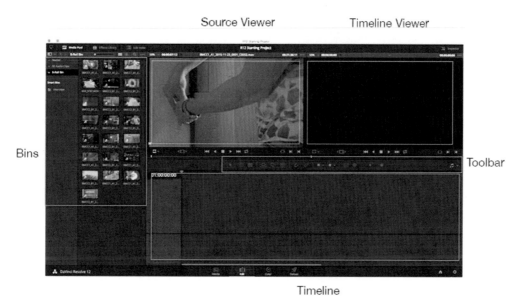

The Edit page layout includes five main areas.

The Edit page is divided into five sections:

*   The Media Pool and all the clips you imported are now displayed along the left side.

- The source viewer on the left is used to see and play the clips from your bin.

- The timeline viewer on the right is for viewing the program you are creating.

- The timeline runs along the bottom of the screen. The timeline is a graphical representation of the program you see in the timeline viewer.

- The toolbar runs above the timeline and is used to select the most common editing tools during the creation of your program.

Marking In and Out Points

To create a rough cut, you first choose a range within the clips that you plan on using. You select a range by loading a clip in the source viewer, and then marking a starting frame and an ending frame using In and Out points.

TIP: *If at any time you feel you have made a mistake; Resolve allows you to undo your most recent step. You can continue to choose Edit >Undo to undo multiple steps.*

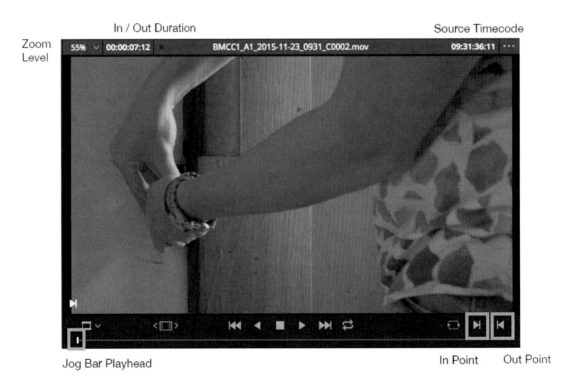

The source viewer is used to view clips and mark In and Out points.

1. Select the Interview Smart Bin.

2. Click the icon view button to display the interview clips' thumbnails.

3. Double-click the Heat Managers_51_1 clip to load the clip into the source viewer.

Load the Heat Managers_51_1 clip into the source viewer.

4. Press the spacebar to play the clip.

5. When you hear the interview subject say, "They call us glass blowers but we're actually heat managers…" press the spacebar to stop.

    To make it easier to locate the spot before she speaks, you can choose to display the audio waveform overlay.

6. Click the Options menu in the upper right corner of the viewer and choose Show Full Clip Audio Waveform.

The three dot button in the upper right corner of any panel indicates an Options menu.

    A graphical overlay of the audio waveform is displayed over the viewer. This can help you navigate to different parts of the clip that may have unusually loud or quiet areas.

7. Press the left arrow key to nudge the playhead, just before the word "They." You can use the audio waveform to locate the silence just before the word.

8. Under the source viewer, click the Mark In button ▮◀▶▮, or press the I key to mark an In point.

9. Play the clip for roughly 10 more seconds until the woman says, "... and remove it in others", then press the spacebar to stop playback.

10. Position the playhead directly after the word "others", again using the audio waveform to find the silence between here sentences.

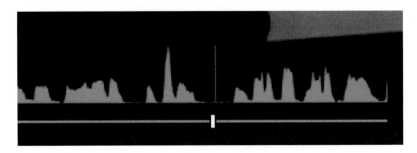

The audio waveform overlay can help locate loud sounds or silence in the audio.

11. Click the Mark Out button under the source viewer ![], or press the O key to create an Out point.

TIP: *Option-I (OS X) or Alt-I (Windows) clears an In point, Option-O or Alt-O clears an Out point, and Option-X or Alt-X clears both marks.*

12. Click the Options menu in the upper right corner of the viewer and choose Show Full Clip Audio Waveform to hide the audio waveform overlay.

With an In and Out point marked on a clip, you are ready to make your first edit.

Creating a New Timeline

Before you can edit a clip into a timeline, you need to create a timeline. On most projects you end up creating multiple timelines to save different versions of your edit. That being the case, it is always best to create a custom bin that will hold just your timelines. When you are ready to create a timeline, which ever bin is selected in the Media Pool is where the timeline will be saved.

1. Select the Master bin in the Media Pool sidebar, then choose File > New Bin.

2. Name the new bin Rough Cuts, and press Return or Enter.

3. With the Rough Cuts bin selected, choose File > New Timeline, or press Command-N (OS X) or Ctrl-N (Windows).

4. Name the timeline First Rough Cut, then click Create New Timeline.

The New Timeline Properties dialog allows you to name the timeline.

After you create a timeline, it is added to the timeline panel and a thumbnail for that timeline is added to the selected bin. The name of the loaded timeline is displayed above the timeline viewer, just as the name of the loaded clip is displayed above the source viewer.

If the name above either viewer is red, that is the active viewer. Pressing spacebar or marking In and Out points using the keyboard, will operate on the active viewer.

The active viewer shows the name of the clip or timeline in red.

You are now ready to edit clips into the First Rough Cut timeline.

Assembling the First Edits

When you are ready to add your first few clips to the timeline, the easiest way to see all of your editing functions is to use the edit overlay.

1. Make sure the Heat Managers_51_1 interview clip still visible in the source viewer with your mark in and out points.

2. Drag from the source viewer into the timeline viewer to display the edit overlay, but do not release the mouse button.

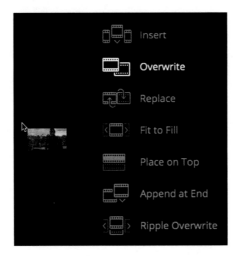

The Edit Overlay is displayed when dragging a clip from the source viewer to the timeline viewer.

The edit overlay shows all of the edit types you can use when assembling clips. You make a selection by dropping the clip on top of the edit function you want to use.

3. Release the mouse button when you are over Append to End

When you release the mouse button, the source clip's video and audio tracks are added to the timeline using the In and Out points you mark. The portions of clips displayed in a timeline are often called *segments*.

The first clip added to the timeline shows the video segment in blue and audio segment in green.

The timeline has an orange vertical bar called the *playhead*, to represent the location of the current frame displayed in the timeline viewer. After you make an edit, the playhead is placed at the end of the newly added segment.

Dragging or clicking in the timeline ruler causes the playhead to move or jump to a specific frame.

Drag the playhead in the timeline ruler area to view a new frame.

4. Drag the playhead to the beginning of the timeline.

5. Press the spacebar to play the timeline until it ends.

    When the timeline viewer is active, pressing spacebar will play the timeline. Pressing spacebar again or reaching the end of the last clip in the timeline stops playback. Let's add the second edit to your timeline.

    Append to End is a useful function when assembling your first few clips since it always places the new clips at the end of the last clip in the timeline.

6. From the Interview Smart bin, double-click the Color Glass_51_2 clip to load it into the source viewer.

Load the Color Glass_51_2 clip into the source viewer.

7. Play the clip until you hear her say, "So, most glass blowing studios…"

8. Press the left and right Arrow keys to move the playhead just before the words "So".

9. Below the source viewer, click the Mark In button ![Mark In button], or press I to mark an In point.

10. Play the clip for roughly 15 more seconds until the woman says, "You're going to add the color glass to it." Then press spacebar to stop playback.

11. Below the source viewer, click the Mark Out button ⏮ after the word "it", or press O to place an Out point.

    When using the edit overlay to append the clip to the end again.

12. Drag from the source viewer into the timeline viewer and release the mouse button when you are over Append to End.

    Once you have a couple of edits made, you will want to move the playhead back to the start so you can review them. The quickest way to do that is to use the Home and End keyboard shortcuts to jump to the start or end of the timeline.

13. Press the Home key on the keyboard.

14. Press spacebar to play the timeline until it ends.

TIP: *Some Apple Mac keyboards do not have Home and End keys. In their place, press Fn-left Arrow to move to the start of the timeline and Fn-right Arrow to move to the end.*

Yes, I know that looks pretty bad. It created a jarring cut between two very similar looking clips. This jarring cut is called a jump cut because it appears as if the person abruptly jumps from one position to another. Jump cuts are perfectly fine when you are first creating a rough cut. The audio sounds good and we'll fix the jump cut later, for now, we'll add one more piece of this interview to our timeline

15. With Color Glass_51_2 clip still in the source viewer, play the clip until the woman says "The color glass comes in three different forms".

16. Mark your In point at the beginning of the sentence, just before the word "the".

17. Play the clip again until the woman says "...very uniform, color application". Then mark your Out point when she finishes the word "application".

18. Drag from the source viewer into the timeline viewer and release the mouse button when you are over Append to End.

TIP: *The Project Settings > Editing section includes a check box to retain the last Edit Overlay used when you drag a new clip into the timeline viewer. This way you do not have to drop the clip directly over the Edit Overlay selection if it is the same choice as the previous edit you have made.*

19. Play the timeline to review your edit from the beginning.

Success! You have assembled your first edits into a timeline. This is the first step towards creating a complete program. You'll find that creating the rest of your program is often repeating similar steps in various ways, using different editing functions.

Making a Three-Point Edit

Assembling clips to the end of a timeline can only take you so far. The more tried and true method is to use a three-point editing style. Typically, you use an In point and an Out point on the source clip, as we did earlier and a third point is usually placed in the timeline to determine where the clip gets added into your program. However, an explicit timeline In point is not necessary. The location of the playhead acts as an In point. Where you position the playhead now becomes critical because it determines where the new clip is added. Let's go over the two most common three-point editing types.

> Insert Edit: When you choose insert from the edit overlay (or the button in the toolbar) the source clip is added to the timeline by pushing the other clips in the timeline down, to make room. The overall duration of the timeline is extended by the duration of the added clip.

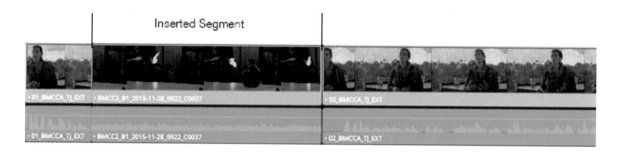

Insert edit makes room for the new clip by pushing other clips in the timeline further down.

> Overwrite Edit: When you choose Overwrite from the Edit overlay (or the button in the toolbar) the source clip is added to the timeline by covering up clips that are already in the timeline. The overall duration of the timeline remains the same.

43

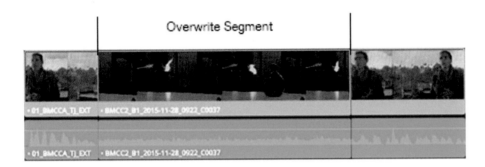

Overwrite edit adds the new clip by covering up existing clips in the timeline.

We'll use this three-point editing style to add a clip to the start of the timeline. We'll use an Insert edit so we don't cover up the first interview clip.

1. In the B-Roll bin, click the list view button to display the clips in list view.

2. Right-click over any column heading in the list view and choose the Basic View layout you created in the previous chapter.

3. Click the Display Name heading to sort the bin in ascending order (arrow up).

4. Double-click the 05 WS pipe warmer to load it into the source viewer.

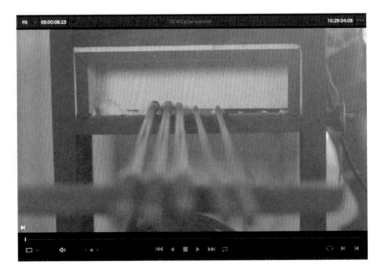

Load the 05 WS pipe warmer clip into the source viewer.

5. Play the clip until you see the blow torch come into frame, then use the left Arrow key to back up the clip until the blow torch is out of the frame.

6. Press I to mark an In point just before the blow torch enters the frame.

7. Play the clip until the torch leaves the frames, stop and press O to mark an Out point.

8. Position the timeline playhead at the start of the timeline by dragging it in the Time ruler or pressing the Home key on your keyboard.

TIP: *When using the keyboard short cuts, make sure the correct viewer is active, using the Q key to toggle between them.*

You can use the edit overlay to select insert but there is a quicker way. The toolbar contains a button for Insert as well as a keyboard short cut.

9. In the toolbar, click the insert button or press F9 on the keyboard.

The Insert and Overwrite button are located in the toolbar for faster access.

The source clip is inserted at the start of the timeline.

10. Play the timeline to review your inserted clip.

Using the Insert edit, all the other clips in the timeline are pushed further down the timeline to make room for the new clip. Your overall timeline duration is now longer.

Overwriting Video

During a rough cut, there are times when you want to show other images while a person is speaking. You do this to refocus the audience's attention or hide problems with the existing video. This is called a *cut-away* because it temporarily cuts away from the main action. You can perform a cutaway using an overwrite edit.

1. After the previous exercise, the timeline playhead should be at the start of the first interview clip, if it isn't click the Previous ⏮ or Next Edit ⏭ button under the timeline viewer, or press the up or down Arrow keys, to move to the start of the first interview clip.

Position the playhead at the start of the first interview clip in the timeline.

Let's listen to this clip to hear what the woman says.

2. Press spacebar to play the timeline, then stop after the woman says "heat managers."

    Instead of seeing her right away, it might be better to see a shot of glass blowing tools and some heat or fire while she says that sentence.

3. Use the Previous Edit  button, or press the up Arrow key, to return to the start of the first interview clip of the woman speaking.

    We'll start the edit here to cover up this first clip. Using the three-point edit technique, the playhead will act as our timeline In point.

    Now we will find a shot to add over her speaking.

4. From the B-Roll bin, double-click the 06 CU pipe warmer clip.

Load the 06 CU pipe warmer clip into the source viewer.

5. Play about two seconds in to the clip, then stop and mark an In point.

46

Above the timeline viewer the timecode number on the right should display somewhere around 10:32:04:00. We need about 3 and 1/2 seconds to cover up the clip in the timeline.

6. Drag the jog playhead under the source viewer until the timecode displays around 10:32:07:12.

7. Press O to mark and out point.

The timecode display above the source viewer on the left, shows the duration from the in point to the out point. it should read around 03:12.

For this pipe warmer clip, we only want the video. You can decide which tracks of a clip get edited into the timeline using the Destination controls located in the timeline header.

The Destination controls outlined in orange, determine which source tracks are edited into the timeline.

The reddish rectangle around a destination control indicates that the track is enabled and the track from the source clip will be added to the timeline.

8. Click the A1 Destination control to disable it.

Click the Destination control to deselect it. Deselected controls have no outline and a gray background.

9. In the toolbar, click the Overwrite button or press F10.

The Overwrite button is located to the right of the Insert button in the toolbar.

The source clip covers up the first interview clip, but only on the video track.

10. Press the Home key to position the playhead prior to the newly added edit.

11. Press the spacebar to play the timeline and review your cut away.

As you play over the timeline, you can hear the woman's voice but you see the pipe warmers. Learning to make cut-aways by enabling and disabling the Destination controls, is one of the essential editing techniques that every editor relies on.

Using Timecode to Move the Playhead

You can set In and Out points by playing the clip or dragging the playhead to locate the range you want, but you can also type an exact timecode number.

For instance, if you want to go to the timecode number 01:02:03:00 then you would type 01020300 and press Return or Enter. To make it easier, you can use a period to quickly add frames 00. That is, typing 010203. (period) will place the playhead at timecode 01:02:03.00.

1. In the B-Roll bin, double-click the first clip in the bin, 01 glashaus sign.

2. Play the clip from the beginning.

   We only need the last portion of this clip as she walks by, which lasts about 5 seconds. So, we will mark In and Out points for that section.

3. Type 092236. (period), then press Return or Enter to move the playhead to 09:22:36:00.

4. Press I to mark an In point.

   You can also type an offset number to move the playhead forward or backwards by a specific number of seconds and frames. You first give the direction you want to move. To move forwards you press the + (plus) key on the keypad. To move backwards you press the - (minus) key on the keypad. With the direction entered, then type the number of seconds (or frames). For instance, typing +5 will move the playhead forward 5 frames. Typing +5. (period) will move the playhead forward 5 seconds.

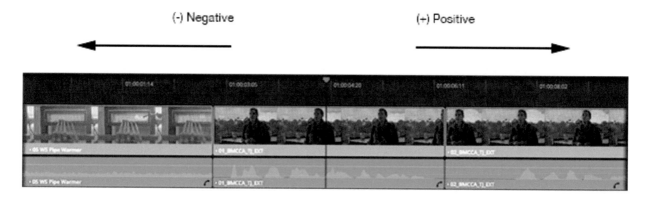

A negative (-) number moves the playhead left, a positive (+) number moves it right.

5. Type +5 . (period), then press Return or Enter.

TIP: *For keyboards without number pads, press Shift-= (equals) to enter a + (plus).*

6. Press O to mark an Out point.

   Before we make that edit, let's mark another clip as well. This will be a 4 second clip of the door opening to the shop.

7. Double-click the second clip in the bin, (02 opening door clip) to load it into the source viewer.

8. Type 093138 . (period) and press Return or Enter to mark your In point.

   Timecode is displayed above the source and timeline viewers. The timecode on the right side of the source and timeline viewers displays the current playhead position.

   The timecode in the upper left of the source and timeline viewers shows the total duration. Once you add an In or Out point, it shows the duration of the marked range.

The timecode numbers above the viewers show duration and current position

9. Then type +4 . (period), and press Return or Enter to mark your Out point.

10. Double-click the 03 gas knob clip to load it into the source viewer.

11. Play the 03 gas knob clip to view its contents.

   On this clip, it is more important that you end the clip before her arm raises into the frame and blocks the knob. So we'll set the Out point and then move the playhead backward using a negative value.

12. Using the jog bar under the source viewer, position the clip just before her arm raises and blocks the knob (right around 09:47:41:00)

13. Mark your Out point.

14. Type -3 . (period), then press Return or Enter.

15. Mark your In point.

16. Double click the 04 furnace start clip to load it in the source viewer.

17. Using the jog bar under the source viewer, position the clip just before the flames come on in the furnace (right around 09:55:18:00)

18. Type -1 . (period), then press Return or Enter. Mark your In point.

19. Type +3 . (period), then press Return or Enter.

20. Mark your Out point.

Now that you have a few clips with In and Out points, let's learn how to quickly add the entire group to your timeline at once.

Editing Multiple Clips at Once

You can drag clips from a bin directly to the timeline, but this method limits you to an Overwrite edit only. A more flexible way is to drag to the edit overlay in the timeline viewer.

1. Position the playhead at the start of the timeline.

2. Click the A1 Destination control to enable it, to edit audio with the video.

3. Select the 01 glashaus sign, then hold the Shift key and click the 04 furnace start clip.

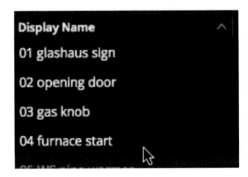

Select the four clips your marked in the B-Roll bin.

The four clips are highlighted to indicate they are selected.

4. Drag the clips directly into the timeline viewer and when the edit overlay appears, move the pointer over Insert, then release the mouse button.

The clips are inserted into the start of the timeline based on the order they are displayed in the bin.

5. Go to the start of the timeline and press spacebar to review the entire program you have created so far.

6. Choose File > Save Project to save the project.

The steps in this lesson are the fundamentals of editing. Using the three points (In and Out on source clip, In point on the timeline) then Overwrite and Insert can get you pretty far. In the next lesson, we are going to push you a bit further into more advanced editing functions beyond Overwrite and Insert. You'll use the timeline you created in this chapter to carry over into the next chapter.

Chapter 3 Test Questions

Q1: True or False: The timeline is used to assemble clips together?

Q2: The viewer on the left is called _____, while the viewer on the right is called_____?

Q3: What are the keyboard short cuts for marking an In and Out point?

Q4: If you wanted to place a clip in between two segments in the timeline, which editing functions would you use?

A) Insert

B) Overwrite

C) Over Easy

Q5: What is this button called ?

Ch. 4: Advanced Editing
Replace, Fit-to-Fill and Multicam

In this chapter, we'll use the rough cut you started in Chapter 3 and take it a bit further. Although Overwrite and Insert editing can handle the bulk of the assembling tasks, you'll find there are some situations where more specific editing functions are required. This chapter will cover the more advanced editing functions found in Resolve.

Backtiming a Cut Away

As we talked about before, the common style of editing is to use three points. Typically, it is an In and Out point in the source viewer and an In point (or the playhead) in the timeline. However, there are cases where the end of a clip is more important than the start. In these cases, you can use an Out point as the third mark.

NOTE: *The steps in this chapter use the timeline you created in Chapter 3. If you have not completed Chapter 3, return to it and complete it before continuing.*

1. Open the R12_5 Starting Project and click the Edit page button, if necessary.

    Whenever you sit down to continue editing a project, it is always a good idea to review what you have created so far.

2. Position the playhead at the start of the timeline, then press spacebar to play.

3. In the Media Pool bin list sidebar, select the B-Roll bin.

4. Double-click the clip labeled 08 Color to load it into the source viewer.

5. Play the 08 Color clip in the source viewer.

    The clip shows three different types of colored glass being placed on the table. We want to match the video of these glass types to what she says in your timeline. We'll first use the portion of the clip of the color bars being placed on the table. To make sure you don't run into the powder being added to the table, you'll mark an Out point just after the bars are placed and the hand goes away.

6. Drag the jog bar under the source viewer, to locate the frame just after the bars are placed and the reflection of some background movement stops.

7. Press the O key to mark an Out point.

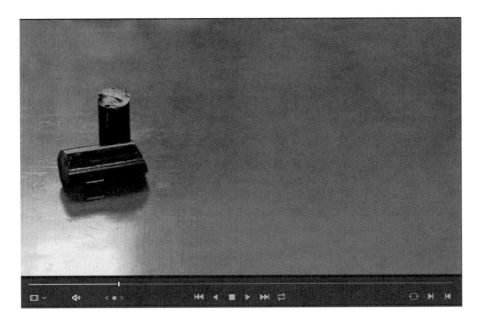

Mark an Out point in the source viewer after the hand leaves the frame.

Next, we'll locate the region in the timeline where we want the bars to be added.

8. In the timeline, mark an In point at the start of the second Color Glass_51_2 segment, where the woman says "The colored glass comes in three different forms".

9. Mark an Out point when she finishes the sentence "...concentrated color glass."

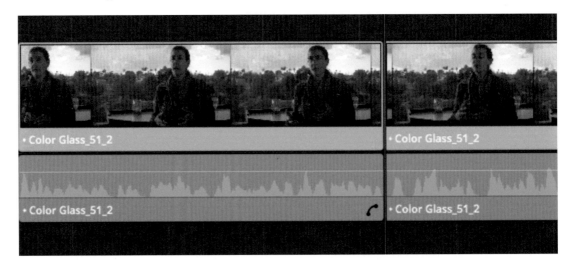

Mark an In at the start of the second Color Glass_51_2 clip.

The in point on the source clip will automatically be calculated based on the duration of the area you marked in the timeline. If you are curious about the In point, Resolve let's you see a preview of the source clip's In point without having to mark one.

10. Choose View > Show Preview Marks to view the calculated In point in the viewer.

Preview Marks show the calculated In/Out point, sometimes called a phantom mark.

11. Drag the source viewer playhead to the calculated preview mark.

    Being able to preview the marks lets you make sure it begins on an acceptable frame.

12. Choose View > Show Preview Marks to hide the source viewer's calculated In point.

13. Click the A1 Destination control in the timeline to disable audio from the edit.

The destination control enables and disables which timeline track gets edited onto.

We want to hear the interview audio but have the video cut-away to the glass.

14. In the toolbar, click the Overwrite button , or press F10.

15. Drag the timeline playhead before the colored bars clip, and press the spacebar to review your three-point edit, which in this context is also called a back-timed edit.

The three points you decide to use are flexible. In and Out points can be on the source or time timeline and your third point can be an In point or an Out point. How you decide where your points will go, all depends on the content and edit you are making.

Making a Cut Away on Video 2

You can create a cut away using another method as well. Instead of Overwriting a clip into the timeline, you can layer it on a new video track above the existing video track. Any video clip that appears above another clip in the timeline obscures the lower clips in the viewer.

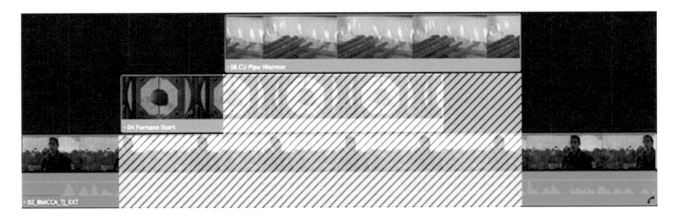

The viewer always displays the video clip on the higher track.

Resolve includes a special editing function that makes it easier to add a second video track and place a clip on it. This is called the Place On Top edit.

1. From the B-Roll bin, double click the 07 pulling out of furnace clip.

Load the 07 pulling out of furnace clip into the source viewer.

2. Play the clip until the furnace door closes, then mark an Out point

3. Click in the timeline viewer to activate it or press Q.

4. Press the up Arrow key a few times to position the playhead at the start of the 06 CU pipe warmer clip.

Position the playhead at the start of the 06 CU pipe warmer clip in the timeline.

5. Press spacebar to play the clip. Stop playback after the woman says "working to put heat in some places".

6. Under the timeline viewer, click the In Point button or press the I key to mark an In point after she says "working to put heat in some places".

7. Press spacebar to play the clip, then stop playback after the woman says "are going to be melting a furnace."

8. Press the O key to mark an Out point.

9. Mark sure the A1 Destination control is still disabled from the previous exercise.

10. Drag 07 Pulling out of furnace clip from the source viewer to the timeline viewer and release the mouse button over the Place on Top section of the edit overlay.

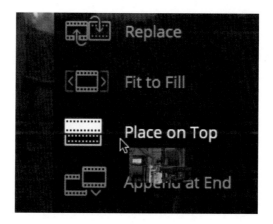

Release the mouse button over the Place on Top edit overlay.

11. Position the playhead prior to the newly added edit.

12. Press the spacebar to play the timeline and review your changes.

That's a good cutaway. It's not a perfect location for it but we will fix that in the next Chapter. For now, revel in your ability to add a clip onto another video track!

Performing a Split Edit

The edits you have made so far have audio and video starting and ending at the same time. You can make the cuts between shots smoother, by having audio extend a bit into the previous or next clip. This is called a split edit. You can do this by setting different In and Out points for video and audio.

1. Position the playhead at the end of the timeline.

2. In the Media Pool sidebar, select the Interview bin.

3. Double click Color Glass_51_2 to load it into the source viewer.

4. Play the clip to locate the woman saying, "It also comes in a powdered form." This point is located somewhere around 15:34:36:00.

5. Position the playhead just before she says "It...", then right-click on the jog bar and from the contextual menu choose Mark Split > Audio In

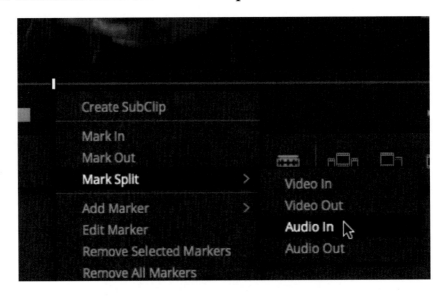

To create a split edit, right-click on the jog bar under the source viewer.

Over this audio, you probably want to show the powered form of glass. So you just need the audio here.

6. Press the spacebar to play the clip until the woman says, "...and roll it up." at around 15:34:47:00.

This is where you'd like the video to come in.

7. Under the source viewer, right-click the playhead.

8. From the contextual menu, choose Mark Split > Video In.

   When you set an In or Out point using the Mark Split pop up menu, the jog bar displays a blue line to represent the video track, and a green bar for the audio track.

The blue bar shows the video track In and Out points, while the green bar represents audio.

9. Press the spacebar to begin playback, and stop when the woman says, "...very quick, very colorful application."

TIP: *Use the left and right Arrows keys to fine tune the placement for the Out point.*

   This is where you'll want both, the audio and video to end.

10. Press O to mark an Out point for the audio and video.

11. Click the A1 Destination control to enable it.

12. In the toolbar, click the Insert edit button ![icon], or press F9.

13. Press Shift-Z to see the entire timeline.

   The insert adds the clip to the timeline leaving a large gap in the video. We'll have to fix that next.

14. Drag the playhead just before the newly added interview clip in the timeline, and press the spacebar to play through the last interview clip.

That gap is the perfect location for another of our colored glass shots.

Marking a Segment in the Timeline

Due to the audio starting before the video, the split edit has created a gap in our timeline.

The split edit has created a gap in the timeline that needs to be filled with a video clip.

To fill the gap with video, we need to set an In and Out point in the timeline to mark the gap's duration. Instead of marking an In and Out point individually, Resolve has a keyboard short cut called Mark clip, that will mark an In and Out point around a segment in the timeline. The segment that gets marked is determined using two pieces of information. The first piece of information you need to set is the placement of the playhead

1. In the timeline, drag the playhead to place it in the middle of the gap.

   The second piece of information is which track the gap on. To select the track, you use the Auto Select buttons in the timeline header.

The Auto Select buttons determine which track is used when you Mark Clip.

2. In the timeline header on Video 2 and Audio 1, click the Auto Select buttons to disable selection on those tracks.

3. Choose Mark > Mark Clip, or press X, to mark the gap.

   The gap is highlighted in the timeline, with an In point and Out point set.

4. Click the Video 2 and Audio 1 Auto Select buttons again, to enable them.

   Now, you can find a source clip to fill the gap.

5. In the Media Pool sidebar, select the B-Roll bin.

6. Double-click the clip labeled 08 Color to load it into the source viewer.

   We are back to the shot of three different colored glass types being placed on the table. This time you are interested in the second one, of the color powder being put down. Again, to make sure you don't run into the next item being added to the table, you'll mark an Out point just after the powder is placed.

7. Drag the jog bar playhead under the source viewer to locate the frame after the powder is finished being placed on the table.

Position the source viewer after the powder is placed on screen.

8. Press the O key to mark an Out point.

9. To edit only the video, click the A1 Destination control in the timeline to disable it.

10. In the toolbar, click the Overwrite button, or press F10.

11. Drag the timeline playhead a few seconds before the 08 Color powder clip, and press the spacebar to review the edit.

The Auto Select button is a tricky, but important button to understand. It helps to direct Resolve to the track you are interested in selecting for different operations. We'll use it a few more times to experience it in different situations.

Replacing an Edit

Many times you find that you want to replace a shot in the timeline with an alternate take or add a sound effect to a video clip. This sounds like it should be easy enough but sometimes knowing where to start and end the source clip is tricky.

1. In the timeline, position the playhead at the start of the timeline.

2. Play the first four clips to review them.

    The fourth clip is of the furnace starting up. It would be nice to have a more pronounced sound as the furnace lights up.

3. In the 02 Audio Clips bin, double-click the SFX Furnace Start Up clip and play it in the source viewer.

    This is a sharper, cleaner sound but you need to find a way to match up the clicking sound of the furnace with the picture of the furnace coming on. Neither of those points are at the start or end of the clip, so an In point or Out point won't do us much good. That is the job of the Replace edit.

4. In the timeline, position the playhead on the first frame when the furnace comes on.

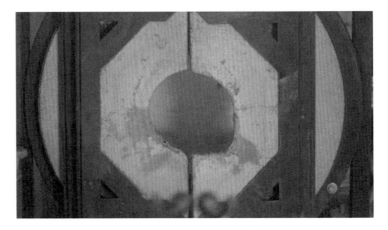

Drag the playhead where you first see light in the furnace.

TIP: *Use the left and right Arrow keys to easily position the playhead on the correct frame.*

5. In the source viewer, position the playhead on the frame where you hear the last click of the furnace flame coming on.

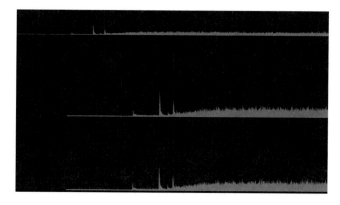

Use the audio waveform to locate the last click of the furnace lighting.

When performing a Replace edit, the In and Out points are automatically determined by the location of the timeline's playhead and the enabled Auto select button. Just position the playhead over the segment you want to replace and disable all other Auto Select button. The playheads from the source and timeline viewer are used to align the two clips. For instance, if the timeline playhead is located 10 frames in from the start of segment, the In point for the source clip will be calculated by backing up 10 frames from its playhead position.

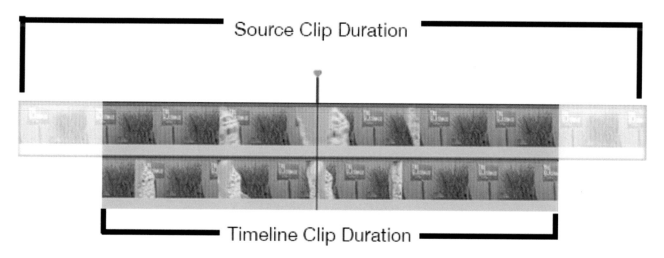

Source Clip Duration

Timeline Clip Duration

A replace edit aligns the playheads, then calculates the source duration based on the timeline clip.

6. To make sure you edit on audio only, click the V1 Destination control **V1** in the timeline header, to disable it.

7. Click the Replace edit button in the toolbar or press F11

Drag the playhead so the woman is in the middle of the frame.

8. Position the playhead at the timeline start, then press spacebar to review the edit.

Replace edits can be helpful in a number of situations. It's particularly useful when you want to align a sound effect with a picture as we have done here.

Fit-to-Fill Edit

When you have a gap in your timeline to fill but the clip you want to use is not long enough or it is too long, you can have Resolve automatically change the clip's speed so it fits the space precisely.

1. In the timeline, position the playhead at the start of the last interview clip.

Position the playhead at the start of the last interview clip.

2. Play the clip until the woman spells out "Frit F-R-I-T..."

3. When she finishes spelling the word, press the I key to mark an In point.

4. Continue playing the clip until the woman says "it's pretty granular."

5. When she finishes the word "granular", press the O key to mark an Out point.

   The Fit-to-Fill edit feature, unlike other editing features we have learned, uses four marks. You mark In and Out points on your source clip and In and Out points in your timeline. The source clip is then retimed to fit the marks you create on the timeline.

__TIP__: If you are performing a Fit to Fill edit to overwrite an entire segment in the timeline, there is no need to mark In and Out points. Similar to the Replace edit, just position the timeline playhead over the segment and enable the Auto Select control for only that track. The Fit to Fill edit will automatically calculate the In and Out points for the segment.

6. In the B-Roll bin, double-click the 08 Color clip.

7. Play the clip and mark an In point just before you see the container of teal frit.

Mark an In point just before the cup of light blue frit enters the frame.

8. Play the clip and mark an Out point just after the dark blue frit is added and the hand leaves the frame.

Mark an Out point just after the cup of dark blue frit is added and the hand leaves the frame.

9. To edit only the video, click V1 to enable it and click the A1 Destination control in the timeline to disable it.

Enable V1 and disable A1 to make sure your fit to fill edit is a video only edit.

10. Drag from the source viewer into the timeline viewer and release the mouse button when the pointer is over the Fit-to-Fill edit overlay.

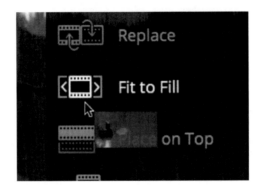

Use the Fit-to-Fill Edit overlay to retime the source clip.

11. Take a moment to review the entire timeline from the beginning, then save the project because you will be using it in the next chapter.

Whenever you have a moment while you are editing, it is always a smart idea to take a step back and watch the entire program. Sometimes we forget what the big picture is like because we spend so much time fiddling with specific clips.

Editing Multicamera Events

Certain types of productions, such as concerts or reality TV shows are shot using multiple cameras. The most efficient way to edit theses types of performances is to use the Multicam editing mode. Unlike the other advanced editing features we've covered in this chapter, Multi camera editing is a mode that synchronizes two or more source clips together and then plays all the clips simultaneously in the source viewer so you can make edits as the timeline plays.

Syncing Multicamera Angles

To begin our multicamera edit, we need to import new clips. We can use the same project but we'll bring in a folder that contains different angles of the same scene, recorded at the same time.

1. Click the Media page button at the bottom of the screen.

2. In the Media Storage browser, navigate to your Documents folder > R 12_5 Training Project folder > MediaFiles.

3. Drag the 04 Multicamera folder into the Media Pool bin list.

Add the 04 Multicamera folder to your bin list in the Media Pool.

Let's now view the clips we will be working with during this exercise.

4. In the Media Pool bin list, select the 04 Multicamera bin, then double-click the Camera Angle 01 clip to load it in the viewer.

5. Press spacebar to play the clip and review its contents. Once you have finished reviewing the clip, do the same for Camera Angle 02.

    One angle focuses on the woman speaking and the other angle is focused on her hands as she picks up tools.

    Before you can begin editing with these clips, the different camera angles need to be synced together. This will match the action from one angle with action from the other.

6. Select both clips in the bin.

7. Right-click either of the selected clips, and at the top of the contextual menu, choose Create Multicam Clip Using Selected Clips.

Choose Make Multicam Clip using Selected Clips from the contextual menu.

The Multicam Clip Properties dialog opens and you can decide which attributes of the clips you will use to synchronize them.

8. Click the Angle Sync menu to view the sync options.

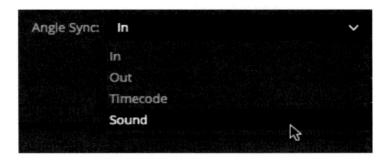

The Angle Sync menu in the Multicam Clip Properties determines how angles are synced.

There are four options for syncing the clips. The last option, labeled Sound, analyzes the sound on each clip and syncs them by aligning their audio waveforms.

9. Choose Sound to sync the clips based on aligning their audio waveforms.

10. To have the angles use clip names choose Clip Name from the Angle Name menu.

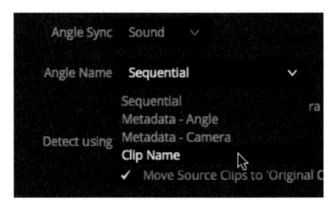

The Angle Name menu in the Multicam Clip Properties determines how angles are named.

11. Select the Move source Clips to 'Original Clips' Bin checkbox.

This option is purely for neatness. It will place our two source clips into their own folder leaving only our multicamera clip displayed in the bin.

12. Click the Create button to begin syncing the clips.

When this option is selected, Resolve takes a short time to analyze the audio. When it has finished the analysis, a new multicam clip is created that contains both of our source clips.

Viewing Multiple Angles

Once you load a Multicam clip in the source viewer, all the angles are displayed.

1. At the bottom of the Resolve window, click the Edit page button.

2. Select the Multicamera bin, and double-click the Multicam clip to load it into the source viewer.

TIP: *If you do not see any two frames in the source viewer, scrub further into the clip.*

The source viewer displays your angles.

To edit with a Multicam clip, the first step is to edit the entire clip into the timeline.

3. Choose File > New Timeline and type Multicamera timeline, then click Create New Timeline.

4. In the source viewer, mark an In point when the clapper leaves the angle on the right, then mark an Out point at the end of the clip.

5. Click the Insert or Overwrite button to edit in the clip.

   Even though it contains multiple clips, the timeline segment appears as a single "compound" clip with only one camera angle visible in the timeline viewer.

The multicam timeline shows as a single compound clip but contains both angles.

The next step before you can begin multicam editing, is to link the source viewer playhead and the timeline's playhead so they move together. To do that, you switch the source viewer to Multicam mode using the source viewer's mode pop-up menu.

6. Drag the playhead to the start of the timeline.

7. To enter Multicam mode, from the source viewer mode pop-up, choose Multicam.

Switch the source viewer to Multicam from the mode pop-up menu.

7. Press spacebar to play the timeline and both the angles as well.

Although we only have two clips, the source viewer can display up to nine angles at one time. You choose how many angles are displayed in the source viewer using the Multicam Display pop-up. We won't have to do this, but on your 29 camera, reality TV series you might.

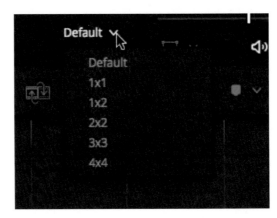

The Multicam display pop-up selects how many angles are displayed in the source viewer.

Editing with Multicam clips

When set to Multicam, the source viewer displays controls for multicam editing. The Audio/Video selection buttons determine whether you are going to cut video only, audio only, or both.

1. Under the source viewer, click the Video button.

Set to Multicam, the source viewer includes buttons for editing V, A/V or A.

When the video button is highlighted, edits you make while in Multicam mode will only be performed on the video track. This is suitable for projects where the audio has a single master audio track like a concert performance or in our case, the audio on both clips is identical.

Each angle displayed in the source viewer acts as a button to add a cut in the timeline and switch to that angle.

TIP: *If Angle 1 is not highlighted before you perform step 2 below, option-click (OS X) Alt-click (Windows) on the Camera Angle 1 in the source viewer.*

2. In the timeline, position the timeline playhead about 30 seconds in, just after the woman says "...keeps cool pretty far down the pipe."

3. In the source viewer, click Camera Angle 02, which shows the tools.

   A cut is made in the timeline and Camera Angle 02 becomes the current camera angle.

   Let's try a few more.

4. Press spacebar to begin playing and stop after she says "and these are kind of the basic four tools".

5. Click Camera Angle 01 in the viewer to switch to that angle.

6. Press spacebar to begin playing and stop after she says "This here, this is called the jacks."

7. Click Camera Angle 02 in the viewer to make the cut at this point.

   You can also switch angles to make a cut by pressing the 1 and 2 keys at the top of your keyboard or on the number pad. The numbers correspond to the quadrants within the source viewer.

TIP: *If you have multiple angles then you can use the 3 thru 9 keys to switch angles.*

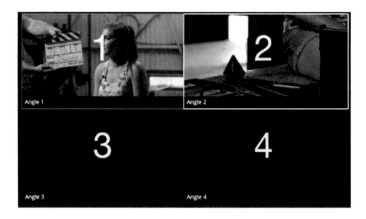

Use the number pad on your keyboard to switch to the corresponding angles.

OK, lets add some pressure to this exercise. For the next 4 edits, you'll use the keyboard to switch angles as you play the timeline.

8. Press spacebar to begin playing and make the following edits:

    - Press the 1 key after she says "it's really the most versatile tool that we have"

    - Press the 2 key after she says "really one of the most important that a glass blower is going to use."

    - Press the 1 key after she says "the tweezers and the shears."

    - Press the 2 key after she says "to pull and to cut the glass."

9. Press spacebar to stop playing,

10. Position the playhead at the start of the timeline to review your edit.

TIP: *Depending on the number of clips you have synced, and their format you may need multiple high speed drives or smaller compressed clips to achieve reliable playback.*

Modifying a Multicamera Clip

You can rearrange the angles so that the source viewer displays them in an order that makes the most sense to you. In our two camera shoot it isn't that big of a deal, but on multicamera productions with 8, 10 or more cameras it can be critical. To do so, you need to see the timeline tracks contained within the multicamera compound clip.

1. In the timeline, right-click over any clip, and at the top of the contextual menu, choose Open in Timeline.

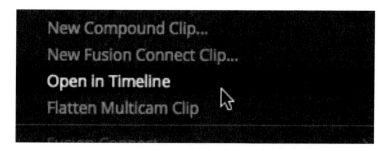

Right-click over a multicamera segment in the timeline to choose Open in Timeline.

The multicamera timeline compound clip opens to display each source clip on a track.

An opened compound clip shows all the tracks contained within it.

This view can be used to fix sync issues and to rearrange the clips' layout order.

Each video track is linked to a quadrant in the viewer when showing 4 angles. The bottom-most video track in the timeline is displayed in the upper left quadrant and the 4th track (which we do not have in our clip) would be displayed in the lower right.

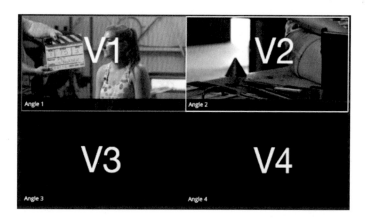

Bottom most track video 1, is upper right quadrant, while video 2 is placed to the right.

To swap the position of angles in the viewer, you must swap the tracks in the timeline.

2. Right-click Camera Angle 02 in the timeline header, and from the contextual menu, choose Move Track Down.

Right-click over the track header to move a track and change the angles position in the viewer.

Video 2 track swaps position with the Video 1 track.

To see the results in the source viewer, we need to step back out and view the timeline.

3. Double-click Multicamera timeline on the path control, in the lower-left corner of the timeline to return to the Multicam main timeline.

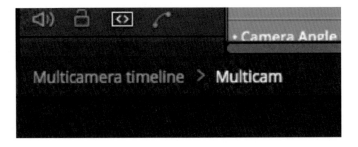

Click over the path control to return to the Multicam timeline.

Although you may have the nimblest fingers in the land, the precise location of where your edits happen, when switching from different camera angles may not be perfect. In Chapter 6, we'll learn about trimming as a way to refine the location of each cut point.

Chapter 4 Test Questions

Q1: The timeline viewer's Edit overlay includes:

A) The Replace edit.

B) The Fit-to-Fill edit.

C) All of the Above.

D) None of the Above.

Q2: Which button must be disabled if you want to make a video-only edit?

A)

B)

C)

Q3: True or False: A Replace Edit does not require any In or Out points?

Q4: What does a Fit-to-Fill edit do?

Q5: Name two ways to switch from angle 1 to angle 2 in a multi-camera clip?

Ch. 5: Timeline Editing
Moving, Deleting and Splitting Clips

The timeline is much more than just a view of the edits you make. It is also a place where you can move segments around, split clips in half, and delete segments altogether. Knowing how to operate in the timeline will improve your editing skills. In this chapter, you'll move, delete and split the clips that you edited into the timeline in the previous chapters.

Navigating in the Timeline

Before you can move clips around the timeline, you need to know how to navigate yourself around the timeline. There are a number of ways to zoom in and out, move the playhead and select clips, all of which make it easier and more accurate to edit in the timeline.

Zooming In and Out

Depending if you like using keyboard short cuts or clicking with the mouse, there are a couple of ways to zoom in and out on the timeline. The most obvious way is to use the Zoom slider in the toolbar above the timeline.

1. Open the R12_5 Starting Project and click the Edit page, if necessary.

2. In the Rough Cuts bin, double click First Rough Cut.

   Since we went off on that multicamera tangent, take a moment to review what you had been working on previously.

3. Position the playhead at the start of the timeline, then press the spacebar to play.

   OK, let's learn a bit more about moving around the timeline.

4. From the toolbar, drag the zoom slider right to zoom in, then drag left to zoom out.

Use the Zoom slider to zoom in and out of the timeline.

5. If you prefer to use the keyboard, press Command- +(plus) on OS X or Ctrl- +(plus) on Windows to zoom in.

You can also zoom out to show the entire timeline using a keyboard short cut.

6. Press Shift-Z zooms out to view the entire time.

Pressing the keyboard short cut again will return you to the previous zoomed in level.

Moving the Playhead

You will primarily move the playhead in the timeline by dragging in the timeline ruler area but there are a number of other ways as well.

To move the playhead, drag it in the timeline ruler area.

1. Press the down Arrow key to jump to the next edit, then press the up Arrow key to jump to the previous edit.

2. Press the right Arrow key to nudge the playhead one frame forward, then press the left Arrow key to nudge it one frame back.

If the Shift key is held while you use the left and right Arrow keys, the playhead will jump multiple frames forward and back.

To move the playhead with even more precision, you can enter either a positive or negative offset value. When you want to move the playhead by entering a value, it's important that nothing else is selected in the timeline.

3. Press Command-Shift-A (OS X) or Ctrl-Shift-A (Windows), or click in any empty gray area of the timeline, to deselect any clips.

4. Type +2 . (period) to move the playhead forward (to the right) by 2 seconds.

5. Type -1 . (period) to move the playhead backwards (to the left) by 1 second.

Now you are ready to begin moving clips around in the timeline.

NOTE: *The steps in this chapter use the timeline you created in Chapter 4. If you have not completed Chapter 4, return to it and complete it before continuing.*

Dragging Clips in the Timeline

No matter how well you initially choose the clips to use, changes are always necessary. Sometimes you find clips, which look perfect in the source viewer do not match up well with the other clips around them in the timeline. Moving clips to a new timeline location can easily solve some basic problems. You select a clip by clicking it in the timeline.

1. In the timeline, move the playhead over the 07 pulling out of furnace.

2. Click the 07 pulling out of furnace clip to select it in the timeline.

3. From the Playback menu choose > Play Around To > Play Around Current Clip or press Shift - / on the keyboard.

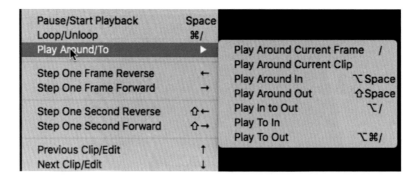

Play Around Current clip plays the selected clip as well as a few seconds before and after.

When we placed this clip on top as a cut away, we noticed it didn't appear to be in the correct location. We can drag it to a better location now.

4. Drag the 07 pulling out of furnace clip slightly to the right until it snaps into place *above* the starting point of the Color Glass_51_2 interview clip.

Drag the segment until it snaps in place over the Color Glass_51_2 interview segment.

TIP: *Pressing , (comma) moves the selected segment one frame left. Pressing . (period) moves it one frame right. Pressing Shift-, (comma) or Shift-. (period) nudges the clip multiple frames to the left or right.*

5. Shift-drag the 07 pulling out of furnace clip down in the timeline to move it onto track Video 1. By holding Shift, you restrict its movement so it can only move straight down.

6. Choose Playback > Play Around/To > Play Around Current Clip.

Play Around Current Clip backs up the playhead from the start of the selected clip and plays past the end of the clip. Doing this gives you a good idea of how clips flow together.

TIP: *The number of seconds played before and after any Play Around command, is determined by the Pre-roll and Post-roll settings in the Editing Project Settings.*

Disabling Snapping

While dragging a clip, you may notice it snaps to other segments and to the playhead. This can be helpful but snapping can also interfere with your ability to place clips near the playhead or another segment. Let's move a group of clips and learn how to disable snapping.

Let's first listen to the area we will be working on.

1. Position the playhead at the start of the 06 CU pipe warmer clip.

Position the playhead at the star of 06 CU pipe warmer clip.

2. Press spacebar to listen to the first interview clip and half way through the second interview audio clip, then press spacebar to stop.

   To make the interview sound more natural, there should be a longer pause between the first interview clip and the second.

3. Press the up or down Arrow keys until the playhead is positioned at the start of the second interview audio clip in the timeline.

Position the playhead at the start of the second interview audio clip.

4. Choose Timeline > Select Clips Forward > Select Clips Forward on All Tracks, or press Option-Y (OS X) or Alt-Y (Windows), to select all the clips from the playhead forward (to the right).

5. Try to drag the selected clips to the right 15 frames. I say try because it isn't really possible while snapping is enabled. While dragging a frame counter will appear in a tooltip next to your pointer, so you know how far you have moved the clip.

Snapping can interfere when dragging clips in the timeline.

The snapping function will not allow you to get close enough to the playhead without snapping to it. So, to make this work you need to disable snapping.

6. If you have moved the clips, choose Edit > Undo, or press Command-Z (OS X) or Ctrl-Z (Windows).

7. In the toolbar, click the Snap button to disable snapping , or press N.

8. Once again, drag the selected clips to the right, offset by +00:15.

With snapping turned off, the clips move smoothly without snapping to the playhead.

9. Enable snapping again, by clicking the Snap button or pressing N.

If you listen to the change you just made, there is a more natural pause between the sentences. We will obviously have to fix the video gap but we'll save that for later.

Moving Clips using the Keyboard

To learn another way to move clips, we will actually create another gap between the second interview clip and the third, but in this case we'll use the keyboard.

1. Position the playhead a few seconds before the third audio interview audio segment.

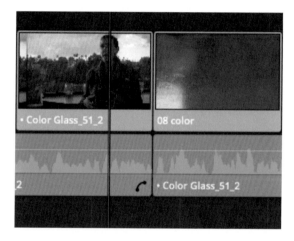

Position the playhead in the middle of second interview audio clip.

2. Press spacebar to listen to the second interview audio clip and half way through the third interview audio clip, then press spacebar to stop.

3. Press the up Arrow key to move the playhead at the start of the 00 color clip.

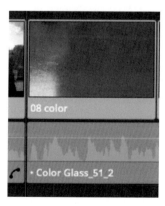

Position the playhead at the start of the third interview audio clip.

4. Choose Timeline > Select Clips Forward > Select Clips Forward on All Tracks, or press Option-Y (OS X) or Alt-Y (Windows), to select all the clips from the playhead forward (to the right).

5. To move the selected clips forward by 15 frames type +15 Return or Enter.

All the selected clips are moved to the right in the timeline creating a 15 frame gap.

Deleting Clips from the Timeline

Almost as important as moving clips around in the timeline, is knowing when clips should be deleted. To remove a selected clip from the timeline, you can press the Delete key. This seems easy enough, but as with most functions in Resolve, there are options.

There are occasions when you use delete where you want the segment lifted from the timeline, leaving a gap that you will fill later. This is useful when you want to keep the entire length of your project the same.

1. In the timeline, select the third segment, 03 gas knob.

2. Press Delete (OS X) or Backspace (Windows) to lift the segment and leave a gap.

Pressing Delete/Backspace lifts the segment, leaving a gap.

There are also occasions when you don't want to leave a gap. Instead you want the gap closed by moving the remaining clips up. This changes the total timeline duration.

3. Choose Edit > Undo, or press Command-Z (OS X) or Ctrl-Z (Windows) to undo the deletion and return the clip to the timeline.

4. Select the 03 gas knob segment again, and then press Shift-Delete (OS X) or Shift-Backspace (Windows) to extract the segment and close the gap.

***TIP:** The A1 Auto Select button should be enabled from the previous chapter. If Auto Select is not enabled, the gap is not closed up when you delete the clip.*

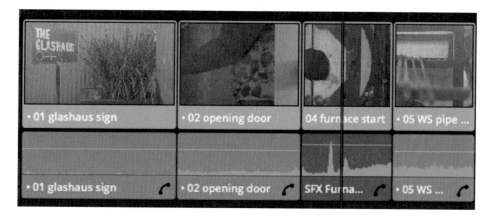

Pressing Shift-Delete/Backspace extracts the segment and closes the gap.

This time the clip is removed and the gap is closed. This type of deletion is called a ripple delete since the deletion ripples through the remaining clips causing them to move up.

Unlinking Video and Audio Segments

When you selected the segment in the timeline, the associated audio segment was selected with it. The video segment and its associated audio segment were deleted together. What if you want to delete only the audio and leave the video in place? By default, Resolve will automatically select both the video and associated audio segment, but you can change this by unlinking clips.

1. In the timeline, position the playhead over the 01 glashaus sign clip.

2. Play the timeline and listen to the audio. Yes, it is useless and should be deleted.

The Link/Unlink button can be used to remove a single track from a clip in the timeline.

The Link/Unlink button in the toolbar is enabled at the start of every project. Clicking the button will disable it, allowing you to select video or audio segments independently of each other.

3. In the toolbar, click the Link/Unlink button , or press Command-Shift-L (OS X) or Ctrl-Shift-L (Windows).

4. Select the audio track on the first clip in the timeline.

83

Only the audio segment is outlined in red.

5. Press Delete (OS X) or Backspace (Windows) to remove the audio track.

   The audio is now removed from the timeline, but the video track remains.

   That's an efficient way to unlink audio and video, but you can do it even faster using a keyboard modifier. When the Link/Unlink button is enabled, holding down the Option key (OS X) or Alt key (Windows) will temporarily disable the link between audio and video.

6. In the toolbar, click the Link/Unlink button, or press Command-Shift-L (OS X) or Ctrl-Shift-L (Windows) to enable the link behavior.

7. Locate the second clip (02 opening door) in the timeline (02 opening door), and Option-clicking (OS X) or Alt-clicking (Windows) the audio.

   Before we remove this audio, we are going to select a few more and delete them all.

8. In the timeline, Option-Shift-click (OS X) or Alt-Shift-click (Windows) the audio in 05 WS pipe warmer.

Holding Option (OS X) or Alt (Windows) temporarily Unlinks clips so you can select audio or video only.

9. With the three audio segments selected, press Delete (OS X) or Backspace (Windows).

Play the timeline with the removed the audio. In a future chapter, we'll add sound effects and music fill in the silence.

Splitting a Segment

During interviews you'll come across sentences that are superfluous or ancillary to the main topic. By splitting clips that are in your timeline, you can often surgically remove the unnecessary regions. Resolve includes a Blade tool that can split a clip into segments, allowing you to remove only a portion of a clip.

The Blade tool in the toolbar can split a clip into segments.

1. Position the playhead at the end of the second gap in the timeline.

Position the playhead at the start of the 3rd audio interview segment.

2. Press Command-+ (OS X) or Ctrl-+ (Windows) or use the Zoom slider to zoom into the timeline.

3. Press spacebar to play until the end of the interview segment when the woman says "...uniform color application".

   This section is a bit wordy. We can tighten up her interview by removing the portion of the clip where she says "These aren't pigments...at all. It's pure glass color."

   The first step is to locate the starting point for the portion you want to remove. This is somewhat easy in this case since the portion starts where the video of the color ends.

   To cut out the audio we need to create a matching cut point on the audio track.

4. Drag the playhead or press the up Arrow key until you are positioned at the end of the 08 color clip and the start of the interview clip.

Position the playhead at the cut point between the 08 color and interview segments.

5. In the toolbar, click the Blade tool , or press B.

6. Click the audio clip at the playhead location to create an audio-only cut.

Add a cut point in the audio track at the playhead location.

7. In the toolbar, click the Selection tool ⬚, or press A, to deselect the Blade tool.

We've now marked the beginning of the cut. We still need to find the exact location for the end, which will take a bit more searching. In the next exercise we'll use some special playback controls to help us.

Scrubbing with J-K-L Keys

When preparing to remove sections, it helps to slowly play backward and forward over the area you will be working on. In Resolve, you can press different combinations of the J, K, and L keys to play over the clip slowly while listening to the audio. These three keys allow you to play backward (J), pause (K), and play forward (L).

In our timeline, we are looking for the spot where she finishes saying "pure glass color".

1. Press the L key to play the timeline, then press K to stop playback when you hear her finish the sentence "pure glass color".

2. Press the J key to play backwards, then press K to stop playback when you have backed up just before she says "pure glass color". Don't worry, you don't need to be too accurate right now. We'll learn how to be more exact next.

   For narrowing in on specific words you can press J+K together to play slowly, backwards and press K+L to play slowly, forwards. These combinations of key can make it easier to find the exact locations of words or even syllables by "rocking" back and forth over the area of interest until you narrow it down to the exact location.

3. Without pressing down on the keys, use your right hand to position your index finger over the J key, your middle finger over the K key, and your ring finger over the L key.

4. Hold down the K key, then hold L at the same time to play forward at half speed until you hear her finish the sentence "pure glass color".

5. You can fine tune the exact location by holding K and tapping J or L to go one frame back or one frame forward until you are just after she finished the word "glass".

Your playhead now identifies the end of the range we want to remove. So we have to make a cut here on the audio and video tracks. While the Blade tool cuts across a single track, you can add a cut across all tracks using the Razor command.

Splitting Across Tracks

Now that you have identified the end of the area you want to remove, you need to split the clip on both the audio and video. The Blade tool is useful when you only want to split one track in the timeline. When you need to add a cut on all the tracks at the playhead location you can use the Razor function.

1. Choose Timeline > Razor or press Command-B (OS X) or Ctrl-B (Windows) to split the clip across all the tracks.

   The cut now allows us to now select the problematic region and delete it.

2. In the timeline, hold the Option key (OS X) or Alt key (Windows) and select the audio portion of the clip that you want to remove.

Option or Alt click the audio segment you want to remove from the timeline.

3. Hold the Command-Option key (OS X) or Ctrl-Alt key (Windows) and select the video portion of the clip that you want to remove.

4. Press Shift-Delete (OS X) or Shift-Backspace (Windows) to remove the region and close up the gap.

5. Since this is the end of our chapter, let's take a step back and play the entire program to get a sense of what we have done.

The result of splitting the clip may or may not be perfect. It all depends on how precisely you selected the cut points. For further practice, you can undo the last few steps and retry it, or in Chapter 6, you'll learn about *trimming* and how you can further refine the edits you've made.

Chapter 5 Test Questions

Q1: Which one of the following items can be done in the timeline?

    A) Move segments onto different tracks.

    B) Delete a segment from the timeline.

    C) Split a Segment in the timeline.

    D) All of the Above.

Q2: Pressing Delete/Backspace does what?

    A) Deletes a segment in the timeline and leaves a gap.

    B) Deletes a segment in the timeline and closes a gap.

    C) Deletes a segment in the timeline and minds the gap.

Q3: What is this button ?

Q4: True or False: Pressing the K and L keys together will play forward at half speed?

Q5: What keyboard short cut can be pressed to view the entire timeline?

Ch. 6: The Trim Tool
Ripple, Roll, Slip and Slide

Anyone can assemble clips together by dropping them in the timeline. The real artistry of editing comes from the pacing of those assembled clips. Pacing is developed through shortening or extending clips by a few seconds or even just a few frames to get the perfect timing. It adjusts where one clip ends and the next clip begins to make a perfect marriage between the two. These adjustments are achieved through trimming. In this chapter, you'll learn about different trimming methods that can help you pace your project perfectly.

Archiving and Restoring Projects

For this chapter and the following four chapters, we'll use timelines that are already assembled for you. To access the timelines, we'll need to open a different Project. Opening a project that has been created on a different computer or by a different person is a bit more involved than just opening a document.

1. If you are opening Resolve, log in to the account you created for this book and into the Project Manager window. If Resolve is open, choose File > Project Manager to open the Project Manager.

    To move a project between computers you must Archive it from one computer and Restore it on another. Both of these actions are done from the Project Manager window. The Project Manager window, as we learned back in Chapter 1, lists all the projects belonging to the logged in user account.

    When you Archive a Project, every media file, clip and timeline in the project is copied into a single folder with a .dra extension. You have already downloaded the Archive I have created for you. You now need to Restore it. The media files are used directly from the Archived folder, so you should make sure the folder is always located on a hard drive that has enough free space and is fast enough to playback the media.

2. Right-click (or Control-click on OS X) in an empty area of the Project Manager window, then from the contextual menu choose Restore.

3. In the dialog, select R12_5 Training Project.dra in your Documents folder, and click Open.

4. When Restore is complete double-click the R12_5 Training Project to open it. You do not need to save the current project.

5. To see the correct clip names, choose View > Show Display Names.

This project contains timelines associated with the next four chapters. This chapter is all about trimming, so you'll use the 06_Trim Examples timeline as a starting point.

Ripple Trimming

After you assemble clips in a timeline, you should then refine the timeline cut-by-cut. The Trim Edit tool makes this refinement process quick and precise, allowing you to shorten and lengthen the clips in a variety of ways.

1. In the Rough Cuts bin, double-click the 06_Trim Examples timeline.

2. Press Shift-Z to view the entire timeline in the window.

3. Move the playhead to the beginning of the timeline.

   If you do not have a full screen broadcast monitor, you can use Resolve's Cinema Viewer to see the project full screen on your computer monitor.

4. Choose Workspace > Viewer Mode >Cinema Viewer or press Command-F (OD X) or Ctrl-F (Windows)

5. Press spacebar to review the content we will be working on in the cinema viewer.

6. When you have finished watching the project, press press Command-F (OD X) or Ctrl-F (Windows) to exit the Cinema Viewer.

   There are a number of cuts that need to be refined. To make it easy to find the various cut points, we'll use blue markers that you'll notice along the top of the timeline.

7. Position the playhead towards the end of the timeline, at the start of the 10 rolling the shape segment. (You can also move the playhead over the 8th blue marker.)

Position the playhead at the start of the 10 rolling the shape segment.

8. In the toolbar, drag the Zoom slider to zoom in to view the clip better.

9. Press spacebar and play through half the clip.

   The start of this segment is out of focus and should be removed.

10. In the toolbar, click the Trim Edit tool button or press T.

The Trim Edit tool in the toolbar.

   The primary purpose of the Trim Edit tool pointer is to select a cut point to add or remove frames. Where the cursor is placed changes how the trimming is performed.

11. Hover the pointer on the left side of the cut, between clip 11 cutting off tip and clip 10 rolling the shape, then hover it over the right.

Position the Trim Edit pointer on the left side of the cut point.

The Trim Edit tool changes depending on which side of the cut it is over and that will affect where you are trimming.

Position the Trim Edit pointer on the right side of the cut point.

Placing the pointer on the right side of the cut will trim the beginning, or *head*.

12. Using the trim pointer, drag the beginning or head of the cut slightly to the right, until the image come into focus in the timeline viewer.

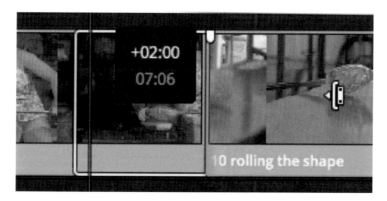

Drag right to remove frames from the head of the clip.

As you drag, the timeline viewer shows the last frame of the previous or outgoing clip on the left and the first frame of the next or incoming clip on the right. This side-by-side display allows you to evaluate how the action and framing of a cut match up.

The last frame of the outgoing clip (left) and the first frames of the incoming clip (right).

When you shorten one side of a segment using the trim tool, the remaining clips to the right in the timeline are pulled up, so as not to leave a gap. This is called a ripple trim. Ripple trimming works similarly to a word processor. When you insert words into the middle of a sentence the remaining words in that sentence are pushed down the page. If you remove words, the remaining words are pulled up.

13. Play over the clip to review your trimming.

That is a much better place to start that clip. Let's now look at trimming the end of that clip, which also goes out of focus.

Trimming to the Playhead

After reviewing the entire clip, you may have noticed the glass goes out of focus again. You can trim the end or tail of the clip similarly to how you trimmed the start. However, instead of just dragging, you can use the playhead to help you trim to an exact location.

1. Position the playhead in the middle of the 10 rolling the shape segment, where the glass is lifted off the table the first time.

Position the playhead when glass is lifted off the table.

94

After this point the clip loses focus and should be removed.

2. Position the Trim Edit tool pointer at the end of the 10 rolling the shape clip, on the left side of the cut.

Position the Trim Edit pointer on the left side of the cut point.

3. Drag the end or tail of the cut to the left until it snaps to the playhead.

4. Play over the clip to review your trimming.

Now you have a nice clean, in focus shot.

Trim by Numbers

Dragging to trim a cut point is a good visual way to trim, since you typically watch the timeline viewer until you reach the frame you want. However, when you just want to trim a few frames, using the keypad on your keyboard can be quicker.

Before you enter the number of frames you want to trim, you need to know the direction you want the cut point to move. Are you adding frames or removing them? When trimming the end or tail of a segment, a positive number adds frames and a negative number removes them. For instance, to remove 10 frames from the tail, you would type -10 Return/Enter.

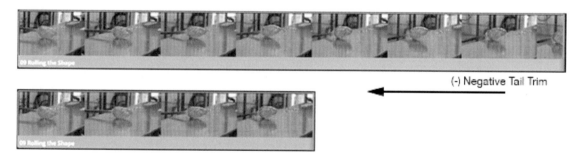

Positive numbers add frames to the tail while negative numbers remove frames.

1. In the timeline, position the playhead at the end of the 11 cutting off tip clip.

Position the playhead at the end of the 11 cutting off tip clip

2. To review the cut, choose Playback > Play Around/To > Play Around Current Frame, or press / (slash).

    We need to remove a few frames from the end of this segment. She appears as if she is getting up, but she never fully rises, so it would be better to leave her sitting.

3. Use the ripple trim pointer to select the end or tail of the 11 cutting off tip clip.

Click the tail of the 11 cutting off tip clip using the ripple trim pointer

The ripple trim pointer now points to the left and there is a green highlight on the left side indicating that you will trim the tail of the cut.

4. Type -2. (period), and then press Return (OS X) or Enter (Windows) to trim off 2 seconds from the tail.

5. To review the cut, reposition the playhead on the cut again and choose Playback > Play Around/To > Play Around Current Frame, or press / (slash).

Trimming the Head of a Clip

Trimming the head of a segment is reversed. A positive number removes frames and a negative number adds frames. For instance, to add 10 frames to the head of a segment you would type -10 Return/Enter.

(-) Negative Head Trim

Positive numbers remove frames from the head while negative numbers add frames.

1. In the timeline, position the playhead at the start of the 11 cutting off tip clip. (The 7th blue marker)

Position the playhead at the start of the 11 cutting off tip clip

2. To review the cut, choose Playback > Play Around/To > Play Around Current Frame, or press / (slash).

    We need to remove just a few frames from the head of this segment so her shears are already cutting the glass.

3. Use the ripple trim pointer to select the head or start of the 11 cutting off tip clip.

Click on the start of the 11 cutting off tip clip using the ripple trim pointer

The ripple trim pointer and the green highlight are on the right of the cut, indicating that you will trim the head.

4. Type +20, then press Return or Enter to remove 20 frames from the head.

5. Press / (slash) to play your trim results.

   Typing a positive number, removed frames from the head.

6. Once you are happy with the trim, click the Selection tool , or press the A key, to deselect Trim Edit tool.

Using a positive number to remove frames may seem a bit counterintuitive, but the positive and negative values are based on the timeline direction.

Just remember negative numbers move left and positive numbers move right.

TIP: In Trim Edit mode, you can use the "nudge" keyboard shortcuts of , (comma) and . (period) to trim the cut point left or right by a single frame. Pressing Shift-, (comma) or Shift-. (period) trims by multiple frames back or forward, respectively.

You will find that you often use a combination of dragging and the keypad to trim. There is no right or wrong way, it's just a matter of choice.

Trim using JKL Keys

Trimming with the JKL keys works similarly to the way you used them in Chapter 5 when scrubbing over the timeline. Pressing the J and K keys will trim slowly to the left while pressing K and L will trim slowly to the right. This is called Dynamic Trimming.

By default, the JKL keys only work to move the playhead so you must enable it for trimming. This is done by choosing "Dynamic Trim Mode" from the Trim menu or pressing the W key. When enabled, the words "Dynamic Trim" appear in the toolbar.

1. In the timeline, press Shift-Z to view the entire timeline.

2. Position the playhead at the 5th blue marker in the timeline.

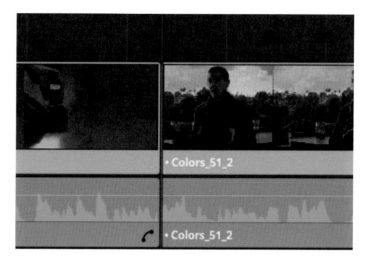

Place the playhead at the 5th blue marker in the timeline.

The interview segment includes an unnecessary sentence at the end. The clip sounds better if it ends with "color application", but it continues on to include "and that piece does need to be preheated so it is a little bit time consuming in the process."

As you play the clip, watch the audio waveform in the audio track, you'll notice there is no sound wave where she pauses. This can help you locate where she pauses after saying "color application", similar to how the waveform helped in the source viewer in an earlier chapter.

Use the audio waveform to find pauses in audio.

3. Press spacebar to listen to the Interview segment.

4. Position the playhead over the end of the interview segment after she says " bit time consuming in the process."

5. In the toolbar, drag the Zoom slider or press Command-+ (OS X) or Ctrl-+ (Windows) to zoom in to view the clip.

    You can use the JKL Dynamic Trim mode to hear the words as you trim. First, we'll play it slowly backwards to get close to the area we want. Then we'll play slowly forward to fine tune it.

6. Click the Trim Edit tool ⟨▯⟩ in the toolbar or press the T key.

7. Click over the tail of the 02 Colors_51_2 clip to get the ripple trim handle.

Use a ripple trim pointer to select the tail of Interview clip.

8. Choose Trim > Dynamic Trim Mode, or press W, to enter Dynamic Trim mode.

9. Hold down the K key, then hold J to play backwards at half speed, until you hear the woman pause.

10. To review the cut, choose Playback > Play Around/To > Play Around Current Frame, or press/ (slash) to see if you are in the ballpark.

11. If you didn't land perfectly, hold down the K key, then hold L to play forwards at half speed, until you hear the woman begin to say "and that piece..."

12. To review the cut, choose Playback > Play Around/To > Play Around Current Frame, or press/ (slash).

Trimming Clips On-The-Fly

A popular method of trimming is to Trim On-The-Fly. It is a technique used to trim using the comma and period keys while continuously looping the playback of the cut point. The comma and period keys trim by removing one frame (comma) and adding one frame (Period). It turns out to be one of the most useful styles of trimming because you are able to watch the cut play as you make adjustments. If trimming is all about pacing, then there is no better way to see the pacing of a cut than to watch it play.

1. Press Shift-Z to view the entire timeline, then position the playhead at the start of the 5th clip from the end, between the 09 rolling on color and the 11 cutting off tip.

Position the playhead at the start of clip 11 cutting off tip.

2. In the toolbar, drag the Zoom slider to zoom in.

   The outgoing clip has the glass leaving the frame at the end of the clip. We should end with the glass still in the frame. So we will remove a few frames from the end.

3. Choose Playback > Play Around/To > Play Around Current Frame, or press / (slash).

4. Click the ripple trim pointer over the end of clip 09 rolling on color.

Select the end of clip 09 rolling on color with the ripple trim pointer.

5. Click the Loop Playback ⇄ button under the timeline viewer.

6. Choose Playback > Play Around/To > Play Around Current Frame, or press / (slash).

7. Press , (comma) to remove 1 frame from the tail.

8. Watch the next loop playback to see the results.

   This will take forever to get to the right spot, so we can remove multiple frames by holding Shift.

9. Press Shift-, (comma) to remove 5 frames from the tail.

10. Watch the next loop playback to see the results.

11. Press Shift-, (comma) twice to remove 10 frames.

12. Press the spacebar to stop playback once you have seen the trim results.

13. Click the Loop Playback button under the timeline viewer to disable it.

Rolling Trims

Whereas ripple trimming adds and removes frames from a single side (start or end) of a cut, rolling trims simultaneously trim the end of the outgoing clip and the start of the incoming.

Moving the mouse pointer directly over the center of the cut point displays the rolling trim pointer. As you drag in either direction, both the head and tail are trimmed while the viewer shows both frames updating.

1. In the timeline, position the playhead at the end of the timeline between the 14 WS paddling the bottom and the 13 CU paddling the bottom. (next to last blue marker)

Position the playhead between the two paddling bottom video clips in the timeline.

2. Choose Playback > Play Around/To > Play Around Current Frame, or press / (slash).

   There is a person's sleeve in the frame in one shot and the paddle abruptly leaves the frame in the next shot. Using the rolling trim can solve both these problems by removing frames to get rid of the sleeve and adding frames to see more of the paddle.

3. Hover the pointer directly over the cut point until you see the rolling trim pointer

   . Then click to add the rolling trim handles to the cut.

   Since rolling trims remove an equal amount from one side of a cut as it takes off from the other side, the overall duration of your timeline remains the same. Maybe most importantly, if you trim just video or just audio, you won't move segments out of sync, since segments are not pushed around as they are when ripple trimming.

4. Drag the cut left to remove frames from the tail and add frames to the head.

5. Watch the timeline viewer. When the out going shot no longer has the person's sleeve in the frame and the incoming shot still has a paddle on screen, stop dragging.

Stop trimming when the person's sleeve is gone on the left and the paddle is on screen on the right.

6. Choose Playback > Play Around/To > Play Around Current Frame, or press / (slash).

TIP: *Once a cut point is selected using the ripple or roll pointer, pressing the U key will allow you to jump from side to side, faster than using the mouse.*

Trimming a Split Edit

When you select a cut that includes audio and video, if the audio and video are from the same source clip, they are selected together for trimming. To trim only the video or only the audio you must unlink the segments similar to the way you unlinked the clips earlier with the Link/Unlink button.

1. Press Shift-Z to view the entire timeline

2. Position the playhead between the 13 CU paddling the bottom and the last Interview clip. (last blue marker)

Position the playhead between the last two clips in the timeline.

3. In the toolbar, drag the Zoom slider to zoom in on these two clips.

TIP: *Press Command-+ (plus) or Command—(minus) (OS X), or Ctrl-+ (plus) or Ctrl—(minus) (Windows), to incrementally zoom in or out of the timeline.*

4. Choose Playback > Play Around/To > Play Around Current Frame, or press / (slash).

   The problem is visual here. The sound is perfectly cut but her eyes are closed when the clip begins. We can fix this by performing a rolling trim, taking away the frames where her eyes are closed and adding a few more frames to the end of the previous clip.

5. Place the trim pointer over the cut for a rolling trim, then click the cut to select it.

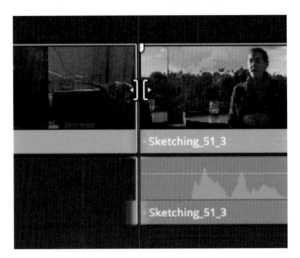

The green highlight indicates you will trim both audio and video.

   If you trim now, both the audio and the video will be trimmed. This isn't what you want since there isn't a problem with the audio. You need to unlink the audio and video so you are able to select only the video cut for trimming.

6. In the empty timeline area above the video track, click to deselect the cut point.

7. Click the Link/Unlink button to disable it.

TIP: *You can also press the Option (OS X) or Alt (Windows) key to temporarily select the video cut point without disabling the Link/Unlink button.*

8. Place the pointer over the video cut to get the rolling trim pointer, then click the cut.

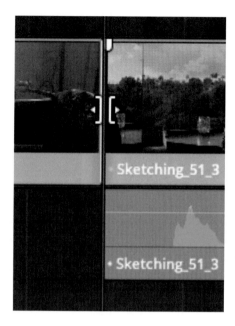

Use the rolling trim pointer to select both sides of the video cut.

9. In the timeline, drag the cut to the right until you see her eyes open (about 1:00).

10. Choose Playback > Play Around/To > Play Around Current Frame, or press / (slash).

11. Click the Link button to enable linked clips, and then click the Selection tool to deselect the Trim Edit tool.

Although the Link/Unlink function is invaluable in assisting you with keeping audio and video in sync. It's necessary to disable it in some situations to trim specific tracks.

Slip Trimming

As you go through your timeline, making a clip longer or shorter isn't always going to be the answer. Occasionally you'll want to shift frames earlier or later within a clip without changing its duration or position in the timeline. This process is called slipping a clip.

1. In the timeline, position the playhead over the 5th clip in the timeline. (The 1st blue marker in the timeline).

Position the playhead over the 5th clip in the timeline.

To view the entire clip, we cannot just play around the current frame (slash key). We have to view the entire clip, so we will use a different playback command.

2. Choose Playback > Play Around/To > Play Around Current Clip or press Shift-/.

   This clip has someone in the background and the gas torch never leaves the screen at the end. Slipping this clip so it uses a portion of the clip that is later in time may solve both these issues.

3. Use the Zoom slider to zoom into the clip.

   The placement of the Trim Edit tool pointer is important to activate the slip pointer.

   Dragging with the slip pointer will shift the contents of the clip earlier (drag right) or later (drag left). The placement and total duration of the segment will not change.

4. Click the Trim Edit tool in the toolbar, and hover the pointer over the upper, middle region of the segment.

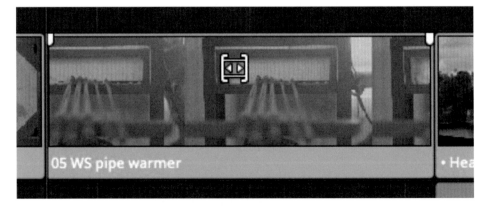

Hover the pointer over the upper, middle area of a segment to get the Slip pointer

As you drag, the viewer changes to a quad display that allows you to compare the relevant start and ending frames. The start and ending frames of the clip being slipped are displayed on the top, while the previous clip's last frame is in the lower left, and the next clip's first frame is in the lower right.

The quad split display while slipping a clip

5. Drag to the left to slip the clip until you see the person leave the background and after the blow torch leaves the frame.

6. Choose Playback > Play Around/To > Play Around Current Clip.

Slipping a clip is most often used more subtly than we have done here. You'll find that you will slip clips just a few frames to get the perfect match with clips that surround it.

Slide Trimming

Sliding a clip is the opposite of slipping. Sliding moves the clip along the timeline to change its position but keeps the contents of the clip the same. When the pointer is over the lower middle area of the segment in the timeline, it changes to a slide cursor.

1. In the timeline, position the playhead over the third 08 Color clip in the timeline (6th blue marker).

Position the playhead over the third 08 Color clip in the timeline

Like slipping, to view the entire clip, we cannot just play around the current frame (slash key). So we will use a different playback command.

2. Choose Playback > Play Around/To > Play Around Current Clip or press Shift-/.

This clip starts too late based on the voice over narration. She has already started to say "crushed up pieces of glass" before you get to see the glass. Then, at the end of the clip you are just seeing the larger gravel sized glass when she is speaking about rolling over it. Sliding this clip so it comes on screen earlier can solve these issues.

3. With Trim Edit mode selected, hover the pointer over the blue bar on the segment.

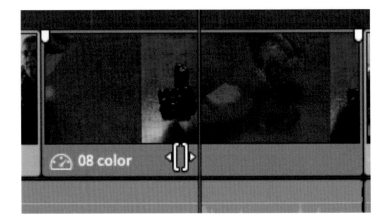

Hover the pointer over the lower, middle area of a segment to get the Slide pointer

Dragging to slide a clip displays a 4-up viewer arrangement similar to the one you used with the Slip tool. The difference is that the upper frames stay the same because they represent the first and last frames of the clip you are sliding. The lower frames change to show you the new adjacent frames as you slide.

4. Drag the clip to the left, sliding it until the tool tip says about - 5:00.

TIP: *Press the N key to disable snapping if the playhead gets in the way of sliding.*

5. Choose Playback > Play Around/To > Play Around Current Clip or press Shift-/.

6. Click the Selection tool, or press A, to disable the Trim Edit tool.

TIP: *With Trim Edit mode enabled, you can click the middle of a clip to select it, and press the , (comma) or . (period) keys to slide one frame left or right, or use them in combination with the Shift key to slide 5 frames at a time. Pressing S toggles from the Slide pointer to the Slip pointer. You can then press the , (comma) or . (period) keys to slip one frame left or right. Press S again to return to Slide mode.*

Selection Tool Trimming

For some quick, basic trimming operations, you do not have to switch to the Trim Edit tool, you can stay with the default Selection tool to shorten and lengthen clips in the timeline. This is not exactly the same as using the Trim Edit tool. Let's take a look and see the differences.

1. Press Shift-Z to view the entire timeline, and then position the playhead at the end of the gap in the timeline. (3rd blue marker)

Position the playhead at the end of the gap.

2. Press Command-+ (OS X) or Ctrl-+ (Windows) to zoom into the timeline.

3. Press / to play around the current frame and review the edit.

    If you recall, we added this gap in Chapter 5 to create a pause in the audio, making it sound more natural. It sounds fine, but we obviously can't leave the gap in video.

4. Position the Selection pointer over the start or head of the 07 pulling out of furnace (3rd blue marker) clip until it changes to a resize trim pointer.

Position the playhead at the head of the 07 pulling out of furnace clip to get a resize trim cursor.

When you hover over a cut point with the Selection tool, the resize trim cursor appears just like a ripple trim cursor. While a rolling trim works the same way as it does with the Trim Edit tool, a resize trim produces different results.

5. Drag the head of the 07 pulling out of durnace clip to the left until it closes the gap and snaps against the previous clip.

    The difference between resize trimming with the Selection tool vs ripple trimming with the Trim tool is that the Selection tool does not ripple the timeline. Notice how the Selection tool didn't push anything further down even though you added frames to the clip. The Selection tool just overwrites the adjacent clip when you add frames.

6. Position the playhead over the head of the 4th marker in the timeline.

Position the playhead at the 4th marker in the timeline.

7. Press spacebar to play through half of the clip.

    She says the word "so" at the beginning of this clip and it's unnecessary. Using the Selection tool, we can remove the word so and just open a gap in the audio, not rippling any of the other clips in the timeline.

8. Hover the pointer on the right side of the audio cut, then drag right to remove the word "so" and open up a gap. Use the audio waveforms to help find the word "so".

TIP: *It helps to zoom into the timeline when making small trims like the one above.*

Trim with the Selection tool to open a gap.

When you remove frames, the Selection tool opens up a gap. This is the fundamental difference between trimming with the Trim Edit tool and trimming with the Selection tool. Where the Trim Edit tool pushes clips around as you trim, the Selection tool overwrites or opens up gaps.

9. Play over this edit to review it without the word "so".

Now, let's sit back and see what our entire timeline looks like before we move on.

10. Choose Workspace > Viewer Mode >Cinema Viewer or press Command-F (OS X) or Ctrl-F (Windows) to view the timeline in the Cinema Viewer

11. Press spacebar to review the content we will be working on in the cinema viewer.

12. When you have finished watching the project, press press Command-F (OS X) or Ctrl-F (Windows) to exit the Cinema Viewer.

With so many options, trimming may initially seem daunting. Primarily, editors use the Trim Edit mode unless they need to open a gap in the timeline; in those situations, trimming with the Selection tool is the right choice.

Chapter 6 Test Questions

Q1: True or False: Trimming is a way to refine the pacing of a timeline, by shortening and lengthening segments in the timeline?

Q2: Which button do you select for the Trim Edit tool?

A)

B)

C)

Q3: What must be done to use J-K-L keys for trimming?

Q4: True or False: When performing a rolling trim, both the tail of the outgoing clip and the head of the incoming clip are trimmed.

Q5: What window must you be in to Restore a project?

A) The Media page.

B) The Edit page.

C) The Project Manager window.

D) None of the Above.

Ch. 7: Working with Sound
Editing and Mixing Audio

Depending on the size of your project, you as the editor, may be responsible for the basic audio edits or the entire sound design. Even if you plan on handing audio off to an audio editor, you still need to give your client a sense of what the final audio mix will sound like.

Resolve includes audio editing and mixing tools that are there to help an editor mix a soundtrack. In this chapter, you will create a soundtrack for the project by adding music and sound effects and then setting the audio levels to create a balanced mix.

Setting Up the Interface for Audio

Resolve let's you customize the user interface to make editing audio easier. The current interface has large video tracks that are unnecessary for editing audio. It also leaves very little room at the bottom of the timeline to view additional audio tracks.

The timeline has a horizontal divider that separates the audio and video tracks. You can drag up on the divider to give more room to the audio tracks. This will provide more room when we add additional audio tracks for sound effects and music.

1. Open Resolve and the R12_5 Training project, if necessary.

2. Select the Rough Cuts bin, and double-click the 07 Sound Editing Examples timeline to load it into the timeline viewer.

3. Drag up on the horizontal divider that separates the audio and video tracks until the video track is at the top of the timeline.

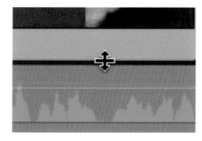

Drag the divider below the video tracks to give more room for additional audio tracks.

You can further change the timeline's appearance using the toolbar's Timeline View Options menu. In this pop-up menu, you can change the display style and height of the video and audio tracks to suit your tasks. All of these changes will help you work more efficiently with audio tracks in the timeline.

4. In the toolbar, click the Timeline View Options button to open the pop-up menu.

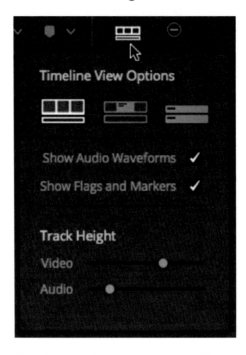

The Timeline View Options menu located in the toolbar.

The three buttons at the top change the appearance of the tracks, with the ability to display them as simple bars without thumbnails.

5. Click the last track appearance button to collapse the audio and video tracks.

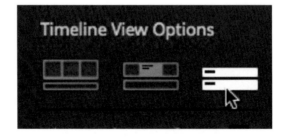

The track appearance buttons primarily hide and show the thumbnails in video tracks.

Additionally, there are options for the track height and audio waveforms.

6. Click the Show Audio Waveforms checkbox to turn it on.

7. In the pop up menu, drag the audio track height slider all the way to the right to increase the tracks' size.

8. Click the Timeline View Options button to hide the pop-up menu.

Now we can play the entire timeline from the start to see and hear the contents included in this version of our glass blowing program.

TIP: This timeline has sections with some loud audio clips. You may want to lower the volume of your sound system before playing the timeline.

9. Position the playhead at the start of the timeline.

10. Choose Workspace > Viewer Mode >Cinema Viewer or press Command-F (OS X) or Ctrl-F (Windows) to view the timeline in the Cinema Viewer

11. Press spacebar to review the content we will be working on in the cinema viewer.

12. When you have finished watching the project, press press Command-F (OS X) or Ctrl-F (Windows) to exit the Cinema Viewer.

After changing the appearance and listening to the program, you may have noticed this timeline has two audio tracks. Audio track 1 is used for the interview, while audio track 2 is used for a few sound effects. Let's explore this further and see if we can add music as well.

Assigning Color to Clips

Staying organized during the edit is always important, especially when editing audio because you can have a dozen tracks or more. Resolve can help you stay more organized by assigning colors to certain clip types. For instance, we can assign a purple color to all our sound effect clips and another color to music clips in our bin. This will make it easier to locate the different sound types when we edit them into our timeline.

1. Select the 02 Audio Clips bin, and select all the clips that start with SFX. These will be all the sound effects clips we have in our project.

Display Name	Start TC	Duration
early_morning -Instrumental versi...	00:00:00:00	00:03:03:20
04_AUDIO_TJ_EXT	15:24:16:00	00:11:09:12
SFX Furnace 01	00:00:00:00	00:00:29:07
SFX Furnace 02	00:00:00:00	00:00:21:21
SFX Furnace Start Up 01	00:00:00:00	00:01:04:04
SFX Furnace Start Up	00:00:00:00	00:00:13:12
SFX Pipe Warmer Lighting	00:00:00:00	00:00:08:23

Select the five clips in the 02 Audio bin that start with "SFX".

2. Right-click over any of the selected clips and choose Clip Color > Purple.

The existing sound effects clips in the timeline change to use the purple color. Let's change the color of a clip we haven't edited into the timeline yet.

3. Right-click over the early_morning_instrumental_version clip and choose Clip Color > Tan.

When we edit that clip into the timeline, it will carry over the tan color assigned to it. If you need to see the clip color assigned to the clips while viewing them in the bin, you can add Clip Color as a column and save it as a layout.

TIP: *You can assign color to clips in the timeline by right-clicking over the timeline segment and choosing Clip Color.*

Adding New Audio Tracks

Another method used to stay organized, is to keep similar types of sounds on the same track or neighboring tracks. This technique makes it easier to find and edit sound effects, dialogue, and music. If we want to add the early_morning music we color coded in the previous exercise, we'll need to add an additional audio track.

1. Still in the 02 Audio Clips bin, double-click early morning instrumental clip to load it into the source viewer.

2. Play a few seconds at the start of the music clip to listen to it.

3. Mark an In point at the very beginning of the music clip.

    When you add audio tracks to a timeline, you must know what type of audio you are editing into the tracks. Your choices are to add a mono, stereo, 5.1 surround, or multi-channel "adaptive" audio track. Adding a clip with more audio channels than the track allows will cause some of the clip's channels to be muted.

    This music is a stereo clip, so we should add a stereo track to the timeline.

TIP: *Using the Clip Attributes window, you can view and change audio channels of a clip.*

4. Right-click (or Control-click on OS X) the Audio 2 timeline header, and from the pop-up menu, select Add Track > Stereo.

Right-click over any audio track header and select the new track type from the menu.

Now you have the music in your source viewer and the stereo audio track in your timeline. Next, you need to figure out how to patch the music onto Audio track 3 in the timeline.

Patching Audio Tracks

By default, audio from a source clip is always edited onto Audio track 1 in the timeline. In our timeline, Audio 1 is already used for the interview and Audio 2 is used for sound effects, so we need to put the music clip onto the new Audio 3 track that we have just added.

By default, A1 from the source clip is patched to Audio 1 in the timeline.

The music will be heard from the start of the timeline to the end, so we will first set our In and Out points for the edit.

1. Press Shift-Z to view the entire timeline, if necessary.

2. Mark an In point at the start of the timeline.

3. Mark an Out point at the end of the timeline.

   Patching tracks is straight forward. Each Audio track header in the timeline includes a Destination control. The source clip's audio is outlined in red. To patch a track, you click the destination control on the track you want to edit onto. In our case we want to edit onto Audio 3.

4. Click the A3 destination control ![A3] to change it to A1.

Click the A3 Destination control to patch A1 to Audio 3.

Now you are ready for your edit.

5. In the toolbar, click the Overwrite button 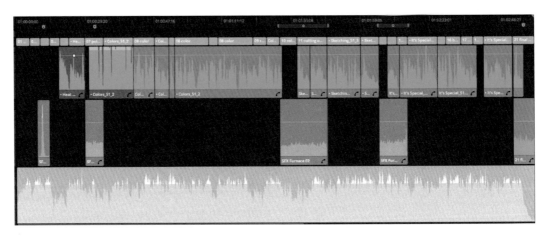, or press F10.

6. Play a few seconds from the start of the timeline to hear the music mixed with the sound effects and interview.

    After the edit is made, you have an organized track layout that places voice on Audio 1, sound effects on Audio 2, and music on Audio 3.

By patching tracks, the music is edited on the audio track 3.

It's interesting to note, at least to me, that audio clips containing multiple channel audio, for instance our stereo music (2 channels), are still represented in the timeline as a single audio segment. A clip acts as a container for the multiple audio channels within it. This makes it convenient and efficient to manage multi channels audio tracks.

Monitoring, Soloing, and Muting Audio

Although you can play the timeline while listening to all the audio tracks, to set the initial level of each track, you may want to listen to them independently.

Each audio track header includes a speaker icon that mutes or enables audio on that track.

1. Press the Home key to move the playhead to the start of the timeline.

2. Click the speaker icon on Audio 3 to mute the music audio on the track.

The speaker icon in the audio track header area mutes and unmutes the audio track.

3. Press space bar to listen to the timeline with the music muted.

4. Click the speaker icon again to enable the audio on audio track 3.

   When there are multiple audio tracks in the timeline and you only want to listen to one of them, you can solo a single track.

5. On Audio 1, Option-click (OS X) or Alt-click (Windows) the speaker icon to solo the audio on that track.

6. Play the timeline to hear the soloed track.

   When you solo an audio track, the other audio tracks are muted and will not be heard.

7. Click the speaker icon for Audio 2 and Audio 3 to enable sound on all three tracks.

Before you begin mixing, you still have a few holes in your sound effects you need to fill.

Working with Markers

A marker is a way to tag a frame on a clip in the timeline or a specific location on the timeline ruler. Since you can add notes to markers, they are often used as task reminders.

The timeline already includes a few blue markers to identify where sound effects have been added. In our project, we'll add red markers to timeline where new sound effects are needed.

1. In the timeline, position the playhead at the start of the fourth clip in the timeline.

Position the playhead in the center of the 05 WS pipe warmer clip.

119

2. Press Command-+ (OS X) or Ctrl-+ (Windows) to zoom in on the segment.

3. Move the playhead so it is centered over the 05 WS pipe warmer clip.

4. Click the down arrow to the right of the marker button, and choose the red marker.

The marker pop-up menu allows you to choose a different color.

A red marker is added to the timeline, now you can add a note to the marker to remind you what task needs to be done at this location.

5. Double-click the red marker and in the Notes area type Add pipe warmer sound.

6. Click Done.

Double clicking the marker opens the marker dialog.

Marking a Range

The next marker will cover four clips in the timeline. Instead of using a single marker to identify a single clip, you'll extend a marker to cover the range of the four clips.

1. Press Shift-Z to view the entire timeline.

2. Position the playhead at the start of the sixth clip from the end.

Position the playhead at the start of clip 15 the punty.

This is where the marker should start, so we will add a marker at this location

3. Press Command-+ (OS X) or Ctrl-+ (Windows) to zoom in on the segment.

4. Press M to apply the marker or choose Mark > Add Marker or click the Marker button in the toolbar.

5. Press Command-M (OS X) or Ctrl-M (Windows) to open the dialog, and in the Notes area type Add furnace noise to four clips. Click Done.

6. To extend the range of the marker, hold the Option key (OS X) or the Alt key (Windows) and drag the marker to the right until it covers the four clips.

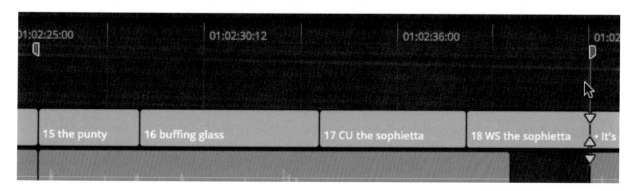

Option or Alt drag on the marker to extend it over a range.

Now, you can cut in sound effects to address the notes you have added in the markers.

Finding Markers with the Edit Index

On a longer more complex timeline than the one we have here, you'll need a way to locate a specific marker other than just visually browsing the timeline. The Edit Index is a list view of all the editing events in the current timeline, including markers.

1. At the top of the Resolve window, click the Edit Index button.

The Edit Index button in the Interface toolbar.

The Edit Index shows all the editing events and columns of metadata. There are too many events and columns of unnecessary metadata right now. All we care about is viewing the Markers and the notes. The Options menu in the upper right corner of the Edit Index allows you to choose what types of events are displayed in the Edit Index.

2. In the upper-right corner of the Edit Index, click the Options menu .

3. Choose Show Markers.

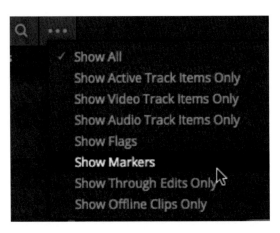

The Edit Index options menu allows you to choose to show just markers.

You can further refine the view by choosing which metadata columns to show and hide, similar to showing and hiding columns in the bins.

4. Right-click a column header to show a list of columns.

5. In this menu, turn off each column's checkbox except for Number (#), Color, and Notes.

Once you have the markers shown, and a limited subset of metadata columns, clicking on any marker event in the Edit Index list will move the Playhead to the marker.

6. Click the red marker with the note Add furnace noise to four clips.

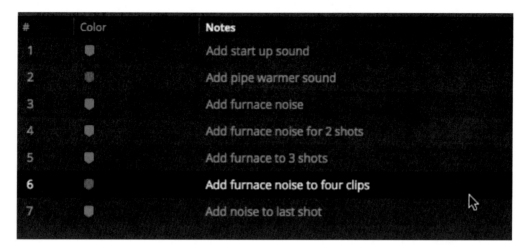

#	Color	Notes
1	■	Add start up sound
2	■	Add pipe warmer sound
3	■	Add furnace noise
4	■	Add furnace noise for 2 shots
5	■	Add furnace to 3 shots
6	■	**Add furnace noise to four clips**
7	■	Add noise to last shot

Clicking an event in the Edit Index will jump to that location in the timeline.

Clicking in the Edit Index causes the timeline playhead to jump to that location. Now it is time to do what the Marker note says and add a sound effect. The duration of the sound effect will be the length of the four video clip you want to add the sound under.

7. With the playhead at the start of the four clips, mark an In point in the timeline.

8. Move to the end of the 18 WS the sophietta clip and mark an Out point.

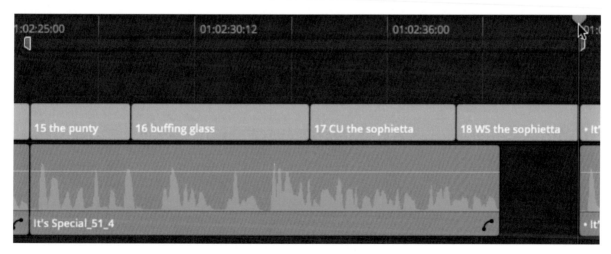

Mark an In and Out point around the four clips you identified with the markers.

While shooting this video, we knew we would need ambient sound to help fill in gaps. For that reason, we recorded the sound of the room while they were working. We'll use a part of one sound recording here.

9. In the 02 Audio Clips bin, double-click the SFX Furnace 01 clip.

10. Play a little bit of the sound effects clip to hear it.

    All of this furnace noise sounds the same so we can take any part of it.

11. Mark an In point roughly 1 second into the SFX Furnace 01 clip in the source viewer.

    Next, you need to patch the audio tracks so the sound effect is edited onto Audio 2.

12. Click A2 destination control button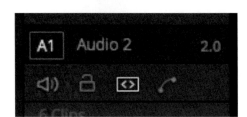

Clicking the destination control on a track will patch the source clip audio to that track.

    A1 of the source clip is now patched to Audio 2

13. Click the Overwrite button, or press F10, to edit the sound effect onto Audio 2.

    The purple SFX Furnace 01 clip is cut onto Audio 2 under the four clips.

14. Back up the playhead and play over the sound effect.

It's in the right place but it still doesn't sound right. Don't worry too much about the different sound levels right now. We'll fix that in a bit. We still have one another sound effect to add.

Using the Match Frame Feature

You still have one more sound effect to add. However, the sound for this clip is recorded with the video. You'll need to load the video back into the source viewer and just edit in the audio. Instead of searching your bins for the clip, the Match frame feature will find the clip for you.

1. In the Edit Index, click the red marker with the note Add pipe warmer sound.

2. Click the Match frame button, under the timeline viewer.

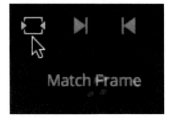

The Match Frame button under the timeline viewer finds the current clip and loads into the source viewer.

Clicking the Match Frame button searches for the current clip displayed in the timeline and loads it into the source viewer. The frame you display in the timeline is the exact frame it displays in the source viewer.

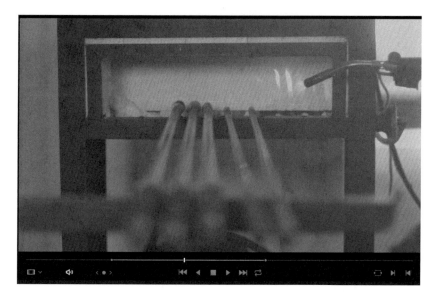

The clip is loaded into the source viewer with identical In and Out points for the segment in the timeline.

It also marks an In and Out point in the source viewer, which matches the marks used to edit the segment into the timeline originally. This makes it easy to edit the sound for the video clip, into the timeline as our sound effect.

TIP: *The Match Frame button under the source viewer is a reverse Match Frame. It finds the currently loaded source clip in the timeline.*

3. Move the timeline playhead to the start of 05 WS Pipe Warmer and mark an In point.

4. Make sure A1 is still patched to Audio 2 in the timeline header.

5. Click the Overwrite button, or press F10, to edit the sound effect onto Audio 2.

6. Back up the playhead and play over the sound effect to hear it.

7. At the top of the Resolve window, click the Edit Index button to close the panel.

You've edited all the sound effects and music, but it still doesn't sound very good because some clips are too loud and some are too quiet. The next step is to go through and set better levels for each clip so the entire sound mix is more balanced.

Modifying Volume Levels

When you want to start putting an audio mix together, you begin by setting the audio levels of the primary audio clips—in our case those are the interview segments on Audio 1.

1. Press Shift-Z to view the entire timeline.

2. Position the playhead over the first interview audio clip on Audio 1.

Select the first audio segment on Audio track 1.

3. Click the audio clip to select it.

4. Click the speaker icons on tracks Audio 2 and Audio 3 to mute those tracks.

Mute Audio tracks 2 and 3.

With an audio clip selected in the timeline, audio controls can be found in the Inspector.

5. In the upper-right corner of the Resolve window, click the Inspector button , or press Command-9 (OS X) or Ctrl-9 (Windows).

6. Click the Audio tab in the Inspector.

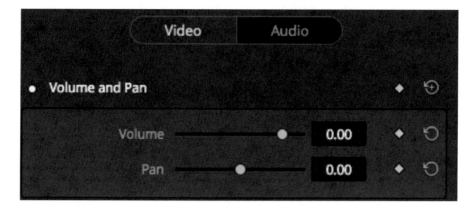

The Inspector is used to modify the properties of a clip, including audio volume and pan.

To set the optimum volume for the primary audio (the main audio you want to hear above all other tracks) your goal should be to set the loudest peaks just above the -20db level, but well below the maximum level of 0 dB. How do you find that setting?

Low audio falls in the green range, peak audio should be steady in the yellow, distortion occurs when the audio reaches red.

TIP: *Resolve uses a reference level of –20 dB by default. Use the Project Settings to change the reference level to match your preferred value.*

You can use the timeline audio waveforms as a rough guide. When viewing the waveform of an audio clip, the lighter green on the peaks of the waveform indicate the audio above the –20 dB reference level setting.

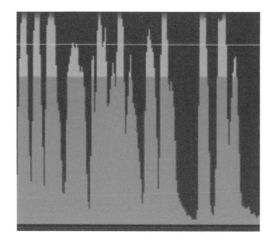

Peaks in the waveform shown in a light shade of green are above the reference level.

7. Press Shift-Z to zoom in on the timeline.

8. In the Inspector, drag the Volume slider to the right to increase the clip volume. Keep dragging until the tips of the highest peaks in the waveform have a lighter shade.

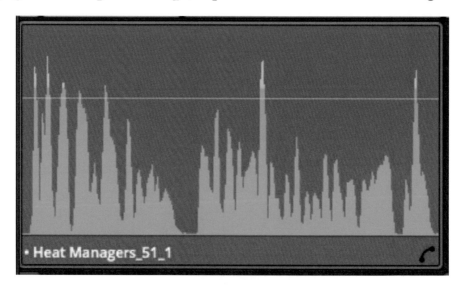

Adjust the volume until the waveform peaks are displayed in a lighter shade of green.

9. Play the clip to hear the volume setting.

TIP: *You can press Command-Option-= or Command-Option-- (OS X) or Ctrl-Alt-=, Ctrl-Alt-- (Windows) to increase and decrease the volume by 1dB*

Using the timeline waveforms are good in a pinch, but they only show you when the peaks are over the -20dB reference setting. They don't tell you how far over or if there is distortion. For that kind of information, there is no replacement for using the audio meters.

Viewing Audio Meters

The waveform display in the timeline is a nice and quick way to gauge the volume of a segment, but a more accurate way is to use the audio peak meters. The peak meters allow you to monitor the master output from the combined tracks in the timeline.

1. In the timeline, position the playhead over the second audio segment on Audio 1.

2. Click the audio segment to select it.

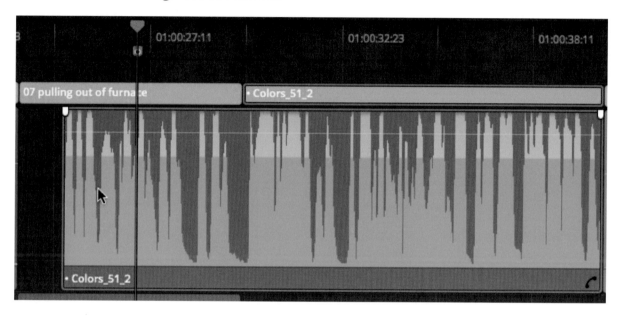

Select the second audio segment on Audio track 1.

3. In the toolbar, click the Audio Panel button.

The Audio panel button is located on the right side of the toolbar.

The Audio meters appear at the far right end of the timeline. When you play the timeline, the default audio meters show the average levels of the audio with a thin red line showing the peak audio levels. The meters appear green when the audio is below the volume reference level, yellow when the audio falls within the reference range and red when the audio is dangerously near 0dB, the point where distortion occurs.

4. Choose Playback > Play Around/To > Play Around Current Clip or press Shift-/.

   This audio is severely distorted because the volume is too loud.

5. While the clip plays, drag the Volume slider in the Inspector until you no longer see the thin red reach the top of the meters and the average stays firmly in the yellow.

129

6. Choose Playback > Play Around/To > Play Around Current Clip to hear your changes.

7. Click the Inspector button to close the panel.

After you make the adjustment, make sure the red peak line does not reach the very top of the meters. If it does, play the current clip again and modify the volume slider.

Using the Audio Mixer

The Audio Mixer is another way to adjust the volume level of a clip or entire track. One benefit of the Audio mixer over the Volume slider is the ability to make adjustments to multiple segments without selecting them in the timeline.

1. Click the Audio panel pop-up menu.

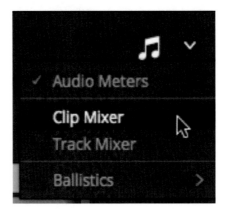

The Clip Mixer makes adjustments to segments at the playhead position.

The Clip Mixer makes adjustments on the clip(s) currently at the playhead position. The Track Mixer makes adjustments on all the clips for a given track.

2. Choose Clip Mixer.

The Clip Mixer opens to the right of the timeline, displaying a fader for each track. Next to each fader is an audio meter to display the levels for the current clip/track. The fader can be adjusted as you play the timeline.

The Clip Mixer includes a fader for each track with the name of the clip displayed.

We'll use the Clip Mixer to set the level for one of the sounds effects on Audio 2. To do this, it will be easier if we can loop the playback while we make the adjustment.

3. Click the speaker icon on track Audio 2 to unmute the track.

Unmute Audio 2 by clicking the speaker icon.

4. Press Shift-Z to view the entire timeline.

5. Position the playhead over the second blue marker.

6. Press Shift-Z again, to zoom in on the timeline.

7. Enable Auto Select on Audio 2 and disable it on Video 1 and Audio 1.

Enable the Auto Select on Audio 2 only.

8. Choose Mark > Mark Clip or press X to mark an In point and Out point around the sound effect on Audio 2.

9. Click the Loop button ⟳ under the timeline viewer.

10. Press Option-/ (OS X) or Alt-/ (Windows) to play from the In point to the Out point.

    The studio sound effect is very loud, so let's decrease the volume using the fader for Audio 2 as it plays.

11. In the Audio Mixer, drag the fader for Audio 2 down, between -10 to -15.

Drag the Audio 2 fader down to lower the sound effects volume.

TIP: *Double-clicking the Volume or Pan controls in the Audio Mixer resets them to their default settings.*

12. Press spacebar to stop playback and click the Loop button to turn it off.

13. Choose Mark > Clear In to Out or press Option-X (OS X) or Alt-X (Windows) to clear the In and Out points in the timeline.

TIP: *The Audio Mixer can record volume changes as you adjust the faders. This allows you to set multiple levels within a single audio segment. This may appeal to some users, however, it tends to add more keyframes than necessary. A neater and more direct way is covered later in this chapter.*

Copying and Pasting Audio Levels

When you have multiple clips in the timeline that should have similar audio levels to the clips you have already set, you can copy the volume adjustment from one clip and paste it to the others.

1. Click the Audio panel icon to close the Mixer **Clip** ♫ , giving space to the timeline.

133

2. Select the sound effect clip on Audio 2 that you adjusted in the previous exercise.

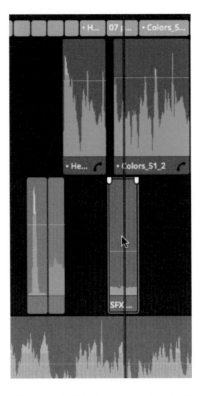

Select the SFX Furnace 01 sound effects you adjusted in the previous exercise.

3. Choose Edit > Copy or press Command-C (OS X) or Ctrl-X (Windows).

4. Press Shift-Z to view the entire timeline.

5. Command-click (OS X) or Ctrl-click (Windows) the remaining studio sound effect clips on Audio 2.

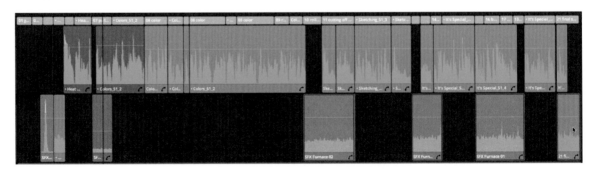

Select the remaining sound effects on Audio track 2.

6. Choose Edit > Paste Attributes, or press Option-V (OS X) or Alt-V (Windows).

   The Paste Attributes window provides options for copying and pasting the settings of one clip to another. You can use it to copy and paste the level from one sound effect onto other sound effects clips.

7. Click the Volume checkbox under the Audio Attributes, and click Apply.

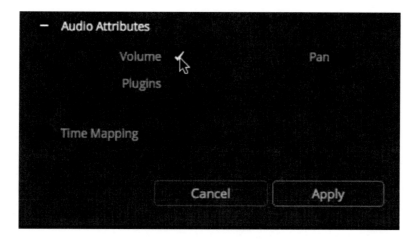

The Paste Attributes window can paste audio or video settings from one clip to another.

8. Click in an empty area of the timeline to deselect the sound effect clips.

9. Play the timeline from the beginning to listen to the mix.

If you find one of the sound effects has been set too low or too high, you can always fine tune the volume levels using the Inspector or audio mixer.

Changing Levels within a Clip

The music track is the final track to mix. Setting the level for the music is more involved because it requires two levels at different points in the timeline. During the first few shots, music should be the loudest audio. When the interview begins, the music should dip down.

Usually the fastest and most efficient way to set different audio levels within a clip is to use the Volume line. The Volume line is a thin white line running through each audio segment in the timeline. Dragging up or down on the volume line increases or decreases the volume level, just as if you are adjusting the volume in the Inspector or the Audio Mixer.

1. In the timeline header for Audio 3, click the Speaker icon to hear the music.

2. For the music clip, drag the volume line down to a slightly lower level (until the tooltip reads roughly between −2.0 dB and -3.0 dB.)

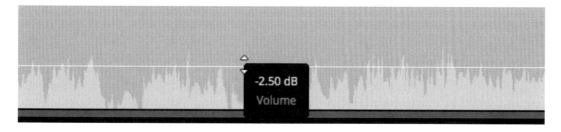

Dragging the volume line down to around -2.0 dB.

135

3. Play the timeline with the audio now mixed in, until the woman begins to speak.

    The Volume line also has the benefit of being able to set different levels within a single segment. For instance, for our music you can set the music level louder for the first few clips and then set the level lower when the woman begins speaking.

4. Position the playhead at the start of the second clip on Audio 2.

Position the playhead at the start of the 05 WS pipe warmer clip.

This is a good place to begin to lower the music level since it is just before the woman begins to speak.

Any change in audio level within a clip requires two points, called keyframes. One keyframe signifies the start of the volume change and the next keyframe signifies where the volume change should stop. This creates a gradual change in the volume.

5. To set the first keyframe on the music track, Option-click (OS X) or Alt-click (Windows) the Volume line under the playhead position.

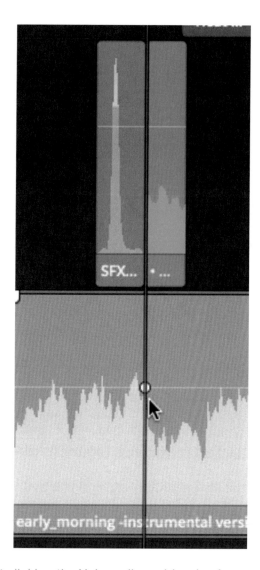

Option or Alt clicking the Volume line adds a keyframe control point.

6. Position the playhead at the start of first clip on Audio 1.

    The music level should be lowered here since we want to hear the interview clearly.

7. Option-click (OS X) or Alt-click (Windows) the volume line under the playhead.

    Dragging the second keyframe down will cause the volume to be decreased for the remaining duration of the segment.

TIP: *Repositioning the playhead is not necessary to add a keyframe. However, it does makes it easier to see the precise frame in which to place the keyframe.*

8. Position the pointer over the second keyframe on the music clip.

    The pointer changes to a move cursor to indicate it is over a keyframe.

9. Drag the keyframe down until the tooltip reads roughly −15.0 dB.

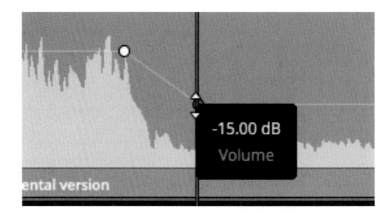

Dragging the keyframe down will decrease the volume.

10. Play back the timeline to listen to the entire mix.

Most of the mixing done while editing can be performed more easily using the level curves than in any other way. It enables great precision with limited complexity.

Adding Audio Fades

Using keyframes you can fade audio in and out. However, Resolve provides an easier way for such a common task.

1. Play over the last sound effect on Audio 2, located at the last blue marker.

   It ends abruptly while the music fades out. You can soften the sound by adding a slight fade to the start and end of this clip.

2. In the timeline, place the pointer over the sound effect segment.

   When you hover the mouse pointer over any audio segment in the timeline, two white fade handles appear in the top corners.

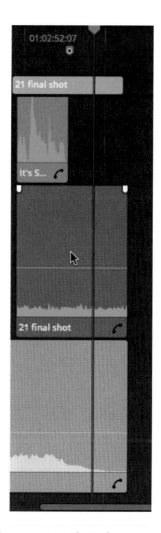

Fade handles appear when the mouse pointer hovers over a segment in the timeline.

Dragging either handle in towards the center of the segment will create a fade. The handle on the left creates the fade In and the handle on the right creates the fade out.

3. Drag the left handle in toward the center of the clip until the tooltip reads 0:15, and drag the right handle in until the tooltip reads −02:00.

4. Play over the sound effect to hear the change. Feel free to adjust the length of each fade until they suit you.

You have now mastered the majority of Resolve's audio functionality.

Chapter 7 Test Questions

Q1: Why would you add audio tracks to a timeline?

Q2: What does this button do ?

Q3: How do you open the Inspector to adjust the Volume slider?

Q4: True or False: Clicking the A2 Destination control will patch the audio from the source clip to the Audio 2 track in the timeline.

Q5: True or False: If the Audio Peak Meters display yellow, the audio is clipping and will be distorted.

Ch. 8: Applying Transitions
Dissolves, Wipes and Smooth Transition

Transition effects like dissolves and wipes can be used to convey a passage of time, draw parallels between shots or just ease an audience through a tricky cut.

In this chapter, you'll apply and modify different visual transitions that can help ease the passage from one shot to another. We'll also look at one special transition that can seamlessly repair jump cuts in an interview.

Adding and Modifying Cross Dissolves

A dissolve is a gradual blending from one shot to the next. It is the most common visual transition in every production, so Resolve makes it the quickest transition to add.

1. Open the R12_5 Training project and go to the Edit page, if necessary.

2. In the Rough Cuts bin, double-click 08_Transitions Examples timeline to load it into the timeline viewer.

    This timeline is slightly modified from the versions you have been working with so far. It has a few areas set up for you to add transition effects. Otherwise, it is fairly similar.

3. In the timeline, position the playhead over the first blue marker, at the cut between the 05 WS pipe warmer and the first interview clip.

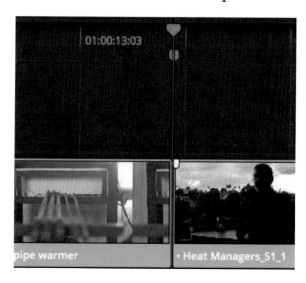

Position the playhead between the 05 WS pipe warmer clip and the first interview.

141

4. Press Command-+ (OS X) or Ctrl-+ (Windows) three times to zoom in timeline.

5. Press / or choose Playback > Play Around/To > Play Around Current Frame.

    Since this cuts from a studio shot to her first interview, we'll add a cross dissolve to signify a change of location.

6. Select the cut as if you will perform a rolling trim.

Select the cut with a rolling trim pointer.

7. Choose Timeline > Add Transition, or press Command-T (OS X) or Ctrl-T (Windows).

    A cross dissolve is added to the cut point using a one-second duration. The audio that is linked to the video also got a transition added to it.

TIP: *You can choose to add an Audio or Video Transition separately using Timeline menu commands or press Option-T (OS X) Alt-T (Windows) for a video transition and Shift-T for an audio transition.*

8. Play back over the cut to view the cross dissolve.

TIP: *The default transition duration can be set in the Project Settings > Edit category.*

When adding any transition effect, frames from the two clips equally extend to overlap for the duration of the transition. These extended frames, called handles, are taken from the unused portions of the two clips that create the cut.

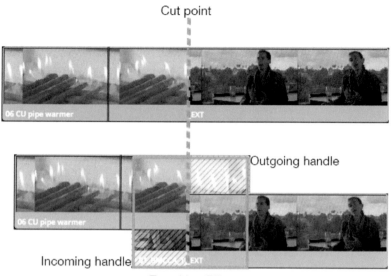

Transitions require handles from both clips to create the overlapping section.

Shortening and Lengthening Transitions

A one-second dissolve is fairly standard but no matter what duration is added, at some point you will want to change the length. One way to change the length of a transition is by dragging in the timeline. Dragging from either edge of the dissolve icon in the timeline allows you to lengthen or shorten the duration.

1. To shorten the cross dissolve, hover the mouse pointer over the right edge of the highlighted area of the cross dissolve in the timeline.

Hover the mouse over the edge of a transition to get the resize cursor

2. Drag in toward the cut until the tooltip reads -00:06 to shorten the transition.

Dragging on an edge of a transition allows you to change the duration.

3. Press / or choose Playback > Play Around/To > Play Around Current Frame to review the shorter dissolve.

The default transition is aligned to the center of the cut, so the transition will shorten or extend from both sides of the cut no matter how short or long you make it.

Changing Alignment

The problem you often run into when adding dissolves, is that they can end up obscuring import parts of an image. Depending on how the two clips blend and how long the dissolve is, you may find that you need to shift the start and end of the dissolve earlier or later.

1. Position the playhead over the first cut in the timeline, between 01 glashaus sign and 02 opening door

2. Using the Selection tool, click the cut as if you would perform a rolling trim.

Select the cut with a rolling trim pointer.

3. Press / or choose Playback > Play Around/To > Play Around Current Frame

Adding a dissolve here can create the impression of a passage of time, as she moves from outside the studio to inside.

4. Choose Timeline > Add Transition, or press Command-T (OS X) or Ctrl-T (Windows).

A dissolve is added to the cut point using a one-second duration.

5. Press / or choose Playback > Play Around/To > Play Around Current Frame.

   This is a nice transition, but you may have noticed that it is difficult to see her taking the lock off the door because the two images overlap. Watch the transition again to get another look. You could try to shorten the dissolve, but that can make it too quick. Instead, you can shift the dissolve to happen earlier by changing the alignment.

6. Right-click the transition and from the contextual menu, choose End On Edit.

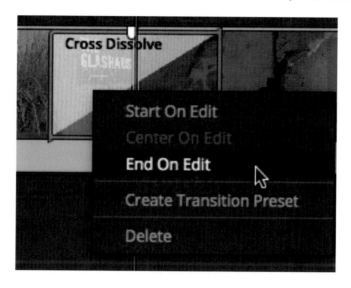

Use the right-click menu to change the alignment after a transition is applied.

   As a result, the transition now begins earlier than it did when centered on the cut and we are now able to clearly see the lock coming off the door.

7. Press / or choose Playback > Play Around/To > Play Around Current Frame.

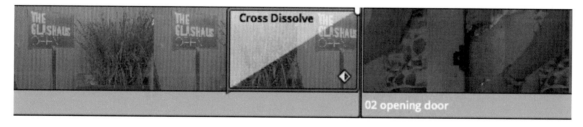

A transition ending at the cut.

TIP: *If you want to set the alignment before you apply a transition, select one side of the cut point as if you were going to ripple trim and then add the transition.*

Adding Other Effects

Resolve includes many different types of transitions, each with a unique visual style. While other transitions may not be used as often as a dissolve, they can still be handy in specific situations. Because they are not as commonly used, you add them from the Effects Library.

All transition effects and 3rd party plug-in transitions are found in the Effects Library. Clicking the Effects Library button from the Interface toolbar above the Media Pool, opens the Library where the Edit Index was previously displayed.

1. Click the Effects Library button to display the Effects Library.

To open and close the Effects Library, click the button above the Media Pool.

The Effects Library is divided into three panels. The Toolbox panel contains the transitions, titles, and generators that are installed with Resolve. The OpenFX panel contains third-party transition plug-ins that can be added to Resolve. The Audio FX panel contains third-party audio plug-ins.

The Effects Library has three panels for Resolve's effects, 3rd part visual plug-ins and audio plug-ins.

TIP: *To remove an effect that you have added, zoom in to the effect in the timeline. Using the Selection pointer to select the transition effect and press the Delete or Backspace key.*

2. Position the playhead at the second blue marker in the timeline.

3. Press / or choose Playback > Play Around/To > Play Around Current Frame.

4. From the Effects Library, drag the Dip To Color Dissolve over the cut point at the playhead position.

5. Release the mouse button when the Transition cursor is centered over the cut.

Drag the Dip to Color Dissolve centered over the cut.

6. Play over the transition to see the Dip to Color you just added.

This is a modified dissolve that dips to a color as it blends from one shot to another. The color in the Dip to Color can be changed to better fit into your program's style.

Customizing Transitions

Each transition has a number of adjustments to customize its appearance. You can use the Inspector to make adjustments and view the results instantly in the viewer.

1. Double-click the Dip To Color you added to the timeline in the previous exercise.

TIP: *You should be zoomed into the timeline in order to double click the Transition icon with the Selection pointer, otherwise you will only see the Trim pointer.*

The Inspector opens similar to when you adjusted the audio. With transition effects. the Video tab is selected and displays controls to modify the video effect.

The Video tab of the Inspector displays parameters to modify transitions.

The upper half of the Inspector has parameters that are common to all transitions. These include Duration, Alignment, and Transition Style. The lower half has parameters specific to the current transition.

2. Click the Color swatch to open the color picker.

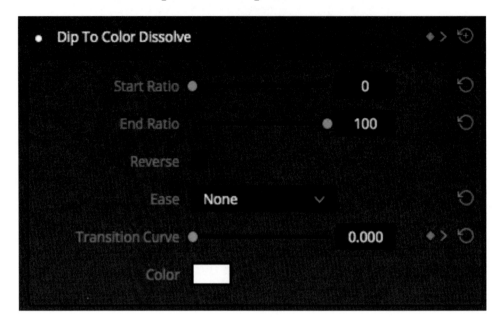

The color swatch allows you to select a different color for the Dip To Color.

3. Select your color of choice, and click OK to close the window. The dip color will update with the newly selected color.

4. Play the modified transition to view your changes.

   You can try out different colors and see how it changes the feel of the transition.

5. Click the Inspector button above the inspector to close the panel.

Marking Favorites

When you find yourself using the same transitions over and over within a project, it can be helpful to mark them as favorites. This places them on a shortlist for quicker access.

1. In the Effects Library, right-click the Additive Dissolve transition, and from the pop-up menu, choose Add to Favorites.

2. Add the Dip To Color Dissolve and Smooth Cut to your favorites as well.

3. From the Effects Library Options menu, choose Favorites to show the transitions you have marked as favorites.

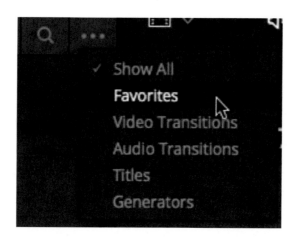

Choose Favorites from the Effects Library Options menu to view different subsets of Effects.

Now you have a subset of the Effects Library always available, so you no longer have to wade through the entire library.

Using Third-Party Video and Audio Plug-ins

Resolve uses a visual effects plug-in standard called Open FX. Open FX allows you to purchase additional effects from companies like GenArts, RE:Vision Effects and Boris FX.

Resolve also uses audio plug-in standards. The VST plug-in standard is used on Windows, while the VST and Audio Units standard are used on OS X.

The custom interfaces used by many of these plug-ins are accessed from the Inspector.

Using the Smooth Cut Effect

It's very common for people on camera to trip over words or have oddly long pauses, which can be distracting for the viewer. Although in some cases you can use a different clip, in other cases you have to deal with the issue by cutting out pauses and stuttering. This often leaves you with great audio but jarring video. We've solved jump cuts throughout this project using B-Roll. Resolve, however, offers another way. The Smooth Cut is a sophisticated transition that warps the two sides of a cut, so they seamlessly blend together. If the jump cut is subtle, the results of the Smooth Cut can make it seem like one continuous shot.

1. Position the playhead on the third blue marker in the timeline.

2. Play over this cut in the timeline to view the jump cut.

    Once again, the audio sounds good. The video however, suffers with the jump cut. Instead of adding B-Roll, we can make it appear like a single shot using Smooth Cut.

3. From the Effects Library, drag the Smooth Cut so it is centered on the jump cut.

4. Zoom into the timeline until you are able to see the name Smooth Cut clearly.

5. Place the mouse pointer over the right edge of the highlighted Smooth cut box.

6. Drag in toward the cut until the tooltip reads -00:10 on the top and 00:04.

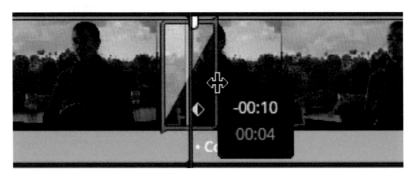

Drag in to shorten the Smooth Cut.

TIP: The Smooth Cut works best when the duration is kept under 5 frames.

7. Play the timeline to view the repaired jump cut.

TIP: If the Smooth Cut appears to stutter during playback, wait 10 seconds and then try playing it again. At the end of this chapter, we'll go over how you can improve performance when playing back transition effects.

Are there ethical questions about making it appear as one continuous shot? I don't think in this glass blowing piece there is a moral dilemma, but I'll let you decide for your projects.

Fading Video In and Out

Typically, fading the picture happens at the start (fade in) and end (fade out) of a program or scene. As with a dissolve, when you fade, you are mixing two elements. In a dissolve, both elements are video clips. In a fade, one element is a completely black frame. So, similar to fading audio, fading video clips in Resolve is performed on a single clip and not by using the Effects Library.

1. Position the playhead at the start of the timeline.

   To begin this scene, you'll add a very quick fade in for the first clip.

2. In the timeline, place the pointer over the 01 glashaus sign clip.

Hover the pointer over the first clip in the timeline to see the fade handles.

Video fade handles appear in the upper-left and upper-right corners of the clip.

3. At the start of the clip, drag the handle on the left, toward the center of the clip until the tooltip reads +01:00.

Drag the fade handle in towards the center of the clip to add a fade up.

You've added a 1 second fade to the start of the scene.

4. Play the start of the timeline to watch the fade.

5. Place the pointer over the last clip, at the end of the timeline.

6. Drag the handle toward the center of the clip until the tooltip reads −02:00.

7. Play the end of the timeline to watch the fade out.

Fade handles are a fast, easily accessed method for placing fades. In the next exercise, you'll learn how you can optimize the playback of fades, dissolve and any other transition effect you add to your project.

Rendering Timeline Effects

Effects in Resolve rely heavily on your graphics card for playback. The speed of your disk drives, the resolution of your media and the file types, also play a part.

When you are playing the timeline, each viewer has an fps indicator that shows the actual playback frame rate that your computer is achieving. If the number has a red dot next to it, you are running slower than the project frame rate.

151

A red dot indicates the clip is playing back slower than the project frame rate.

To better your chances for real-time playback of complex effects, Resolve automatically renders effects to your hard disk using a caching system. The Smart caching works with transitions and other effects in the timeline. Regions of the timeline that require caching have a red bar over them, whereas regions that are already cached have a blue bar over them.

A red line over a timeline region indicates frames that need to be cached for reliable playback.

TIP: *What's a Cache? A cache is a computer engineering term that refers to a process where data, in our case blended frames of clips, are temporarily stored in order to access them faster at a later time. In other editing systems this is often called "rendering".*

Although caching in the timeline happens automatically, there are a few Project Settings located in the General Options category that you should be aware of before starting a project.

1. Choose File > Project Settings, and click General Options.

2. Make sure the "Enable background caching" checkbox is turned on.

The Cache options in Project Settings > General Options.

3. In the "Enable background caching" numeric box, enter 3.

    Caching will begin to render effects after the computer is idle for 3 seconds.

152

You can also choose the compression format used to save the cache files. The choices common to OS X and Windows include uncompressed 10-bit and 8-bit formats and Avid's DNxHR formats. OS X also includes Apple's ProRes compression format.

4. Click the Cache Frames In pop-up menu to view it.

NOTE: *OS X and Windows use different compression formats. The screen shot below may appear different depending on your platform.*

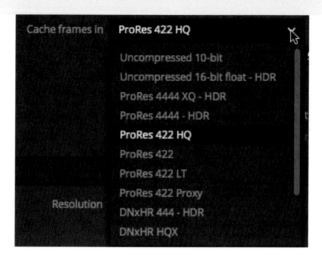

The Cache format options allow you to choose the compression for cached files.

For those not up on their codec bits and bytes, these menu options can look daunting and you might decide to stay with the default settings. In most cases, you wouldn't be wrong to do so. The default setting uses a high-quality 10-bit file that will look good in your final output. If you are temporarily working on a portable or a laptop with a slow disk drive, you may want to opt for a lower bandwidth format such as Avid DNxHR LB or ProRes 422 LT for faster processing. For now, you'll leave this setting at the default and move on to background processing.

5. Click Save to close the Project Settings dialog and save the new settings.

The last step in setting up the cache system is to turn it on.

6. Choose Playback > Render Cache > Smart, if it isn't already set.

TIP: *To delete all the rendered cache files for the current project, choose Playback > Delete Render Cache > All.*

Caching for timeline transitions and effects use the Smart render cache option. When set to Smart, Resolve automatically renders everything necessary to optimize playback. When you reopen a project, cached clips are still cached. Later, in Chapter 14, we'll learn a bit more about other forms of caching in the Color page.

Chapter 8 Test Questions

Q1: Name one way to add a transition.

Q3: Where can you find the parameters to customize transitions?

Q2: What do you do to change the duration of a transition in the timeline?

Q4: True or False: The Smooth Cut can help repair a jump cut.

Q5: Where do you set the idle time for background caching?

Ch. 9: Graphics & Animation
Titles, Alpha Channels and Animation

Good graphics, whether they are the main title, still images, or even captions throughout a program, are meant to convey important information while still being consistent with the look of the program. They also have to hold the audience's attention. In this chapter, you'll learn how to composite imported graphics, as well as use Resolve's internal titling and animation tools to attract and hold the viewer's attention.

Using Graphics with Alpha Channels

On most production main titles and animated graphics are created in another application like Adobe After Effects or Blackmagic Fusion. When you import the content generated from those applications and you want to composite them over video in Resolve, the media files need to include an alpha channel.

1. Open the R12_5 Training project, if necessary, and from the Edit page, load 09 Animation Examples into the timeline.

2. From the 05 Graphics bin, drag the Main Title 1 clip into the source viewer.

   This clip is a fancy ten second main title, created in a different application.

3. Play the clip in the source viewer.

   This clip, like all video content is made up of red, green and blue channels that determine the colors in an image, but this graphic also includes an alpha channel.

RGB pixels determine color while alpha channels determine transparency.

An alpha channel is used to determine transparency. All animation applications can create files that include alpha channels, making it incredibly easy to composite animation over video. Usually Resolve can identify files that contain or do not contain alpha channels and interpret those files accordingly when you import them.

155

4. Position the source viewer's jog bar playhead at the start of the Main Title clip.

5. Position the timeline playhead at the start of the second clip in the timeline

Position the playhead at the start of the second clip in the timeline.

6. Drag the Main Title clip from the source viewer to the timeline viewer and choose Place on Top in the edit overlay.

Edit the main title clip to V2 on the timeline.

7. Play over the Main Title clip in the timeline to view the results.

   The alpha channel is not interpreted correctly since in the viewer, we do not see the video under the title. In cases where alpha channels are not interpreted correctly, you correct interpretation using the Change Alpha Mode submenu.

8. Right-Click over the Main Title 1 clip in the bin, then choose Change Alpha Mode.

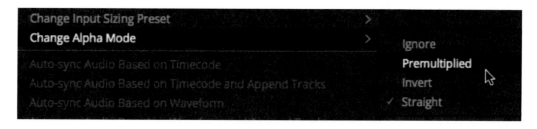

The Change Alpha Mode submenu is used to change Alpha channel interpretation.

When alpha channels are created in applications they are usually created in a form called premultiplied. Some applications generate files using an alternate method called Straight or Unmatted Alpha. You should know what method was used to generate the alpha in the file you are importing, although you can try either setting to see which is correct.

9. From the Change Alpha Mode submenu choose Premultiplied.

10. Play over the transition clip in the timeline to view the results. If it doesn't play through the first time, wait until the title caches, then play it again.

The result of correcting the alpha channel setting is that the title is now composited over the video. Next, in this chapter we'll create a lower third title using Resolve's title templates.

Choosing a Template

A main title is sometimes the only title that is required in a project. In our timeline, we also need to create a title caption that includes the name of the person we are interviewing and her job title. After all, she is the subject of the entire program. Typically, you see these captions in documentaries, news, or any interview program. The type of title is called a lower third because it is positioned in the lower third of the frame.

1. Open the Effects Library, if it is not still open from the previous chapter.

2. From the Effects Library Options menu, choose Titles.

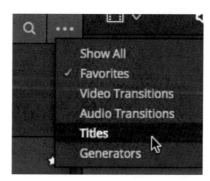

Show the title templates using the Options menu in the Effects Library.

Resolve includes five template layouts for common title styles. All of the titles are found in the Effects Library. Before you can use any of them, you must edit the title template into the timeline.

3. Position the playhead on the first blue marker in the timeline.

4. Press Shift-/ or choose Playback > Play Around/To > Play Around Current Clip.

    This clip is really the first long clip of her speaking, so it's a good place to introduce her with a title.

5. Disable the Audio Select buttons  for all the tracks except Video 1.

6. Press the X key to mark an In and Out for the entire clip.

    The title will be viewed over the entire duration of this clip.

7. From the Effects Library, drag the "L Lower 3rd" title generator into the timeline viewer. In the edit overlay, highlight Place on Top, then release the mouse button.

Drag the title into the timeline viewer to display the edit overlay.

A lower third title is cut onto Video 2 track of the timeline. Since you marked the video clip, the title lasts for the same duration as the interview it is over.

8. Position the playhead on the first blue marker again to see the title template.

9. Press Option-X (OS X) or Alt-X (Windows) to clear the mark In and Out you set in the timeline or choose Mark > Clear In and Out.

This is just a template waiting to be customized by you, to fit this program. Now that it's in the timeline, you can begin to decide how you want it to look.

Modifying Text Parameters

Once the title is added the first step is to enter the text to replace the placeholder text provided with the template. In this template there is the upper line of text and the lower line. Different templates provide a different number of lines.

1. Select the L Lower 3rd title clip in the timeline.

2. In the viewer click four times on the large Title text to select it.

Click four times on the large title text to select it.

3. Type Taryn Jayne to replace the placeholder text.

    Now, you'll do the same for the lower line of text, entering her job title

4. In the viewer click four times on the smaller Title text, then type Glass Blower.

Enter her job title in the lower text field.

When designing any title or graphic you must decide what mood will complement the video. You start by choosing a typeface. This is done in the Inspector.

5. Click the Inspector button in the upper right of the Resolve window.

    When the Inspector opens, it shows the controls for the selected title clip. There are more controls than what you see in the limited space. You can scroll the inspector window or expand it so it runs from the top of the screen to the bottom.

6. Click the Expand button  above the Inspector to view more controls.

Click the expand button to view more parameters in the inspector.

You can now move on to selecting size, style, case, and width.

When selecting a typeface for a title the main goal should be readability, but the tone that is conveyed should also be a consideration. Yes, typefaces have a tone to them. For example, **Comic sans** is whimsical and childlike while **Impact** is tense and restrained. You should start by choosing the right typeface for your project.

NOTE: *Not all computers have the same typefaces installed, so you'll select a typeface from those that you have available. Look for one that represents the tone in this scene.*

This template uses two Rich Text sections to format the two lines of text. The Rich Text section at the top is used to control the upper line.

7. For the top Rich Text box, choose a typeface from the Font Family menu, then from the Font Face menu, choose a style.

Standard text formatting controls are located in the Inspector.

8. Do the same for the lower Rich Text box using the Font Family Face menus.

TIP: *A font is a style within a typeface family, such as Garamond Bold.*

You should select colors with the same scrutiny. Basic color psychology tells us that warm colors like reds and yellows are associated with energy. Cool colors like blue, green, and purple are the colors of tranquil, contemplation.

9. Click the bottom line's color swatch and select a warm color because Glass Blowing is an exciting art form. We're dealing with fire here!

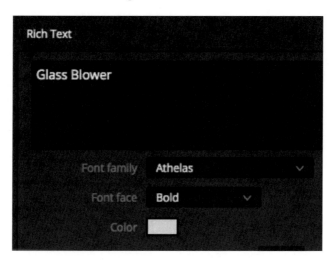

Clicking a color swatch in the Inspector brings up a Color picker window.

TIP: *You can increase or decrease the spacing between individual characters (kerning) by highlighting a character, then modifying the tracking parameter.*

The last design choice you should consider when creating a title is how well it stands out from the background. Adding background to the text that contrasts well with the video clip will help bring out the text.

10. Scroll the Inspector down until you see the Background parameter group.

Background controls can add a backdrop to help separate text from the video.

11. Drag the Height parameter to create a box tall enough to cover both lines of text.

Create Background using the height parameter.

12. Click the Background's color swatch and select a teal color.

Use the Background color swatch to set the background color to teal.

13. At the top of the Inspector click the Video tab to see the Composite parameter group.

Composite modes are mathematical operations you can use to blend overlapping colors in different ways to create unique effects. The Screen composite mode lightens layers together.

14. From the Composite Mode menu choose Add.

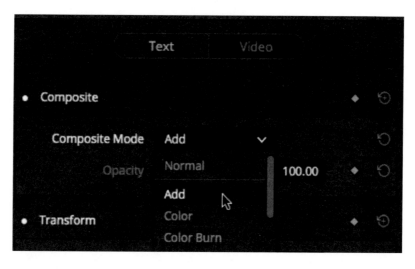

The Add Composite mode lightens the title as it blends it over the video.

15. Click the Inspector button to close the Inspector panel.

That's a great looking lower third title that hits all the marks. It is readable, well placed and interesting to look at.

Trimming Titles with Extend Edit

Although all the same trimming techniques used in Chapter 6 work for titles, a quick way to trim titles is to use the Extend Edit command. The Extend Edit command is a way to trim the start or end of a clip to where ever you position the playhead using a single keyboard stroke.

Our title comes on screen right when the interview begins. We should give the viewing audience some time to settle into the video clip before making them read something.

1. Click in an empty area of the timeline to deselect the title.

2. Position the playhead at the start of the title segment, and type +1 . (period) then press Return or Enter to move the playhead forward one second.

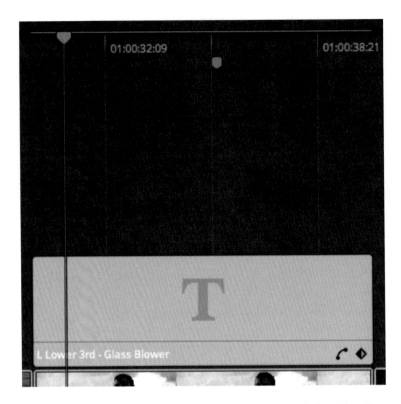

Move the playhead 1 second in from the start of the title clip.

We are going to trim off the start of the title by one second, so the title will begin where the playhead is located.

3. Select the start of the title clip, as if you were going to trim it.

Select the start of the title clip using the Rolling trim pointer.

4. Press E or choose Trim > Extend Edit.

    The start of the title now begins at the playhead location. Let's change where the end is located. To read a title like this, the audience should need only 4 or 5 seconds. So we can use the Extend feature to make it shorter.

5. Click in an empty area of the timeline to deselect the title.

6. Type +5 . (period), then press Return or Enter to move the playhead forward five seconds.

    We will now trim the end of the clip so it ends at the playhead location, making a 6 second title duration.

7. Select the end of the title clip, as if you were going to trim it.

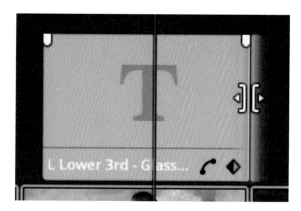

The side of the cut selected is the side of the cut that is extended.

8. Choose Trim > Extend Edit, or press E.

    The title now ends at the playhead location making a 5-second-long title

9. Press Shift-/ or choose Playback > Play Around/To > Play Around Current Clip.

The title is a more reasonable length for the amount of text on the screen. Next, you'll learn how to animate the title on and off screen.

Setting Keyframes

When you have simple graphics or titles, you can draw the audience's attention by adding a slight animation to them. Animating the parameters of an image or title over time, requires you to set keyframes. Keyframes are used to assign different parameter values on specific frames. Resolve will then interpolate between the two values to create a smooth animation.

1. In the timeline, make sure the title clip is still selected, then position the playhead at the start of the lower third title.

Select the title clip and position the playhead at the start of the clip.

2. In the Inspector, place the cursor over the Position X numeric box and drag to the left until the title is off the screen

    This is a good starting point for our animation, so we will set a keyframe here.

3. In the Inspector, click the Position keyframe button ◆ to the right of the Position X and Y value fields.

To set a keyframe, click the keyframe button on the right side of the inspector.

Animating a parameter requires that you set at least two values for it, on different frames. The first value at the start of the clip is now set. We'll set the second value where we want the title to end up on screen.

TIP: *To reset parameters to their default settings, click the gray circular reset button to the right of the keyframe button.*

4. In the timeline, position the playhead 1 second into the title clip.

    Resolve uses an Auto-keyframe model. When a parameter already has one keyframe set, changing the position of the playhead and then modifying the parameter adds a second keyframe automatically.

5. Place the cursor over the Position X numeric box and drag to the right until the value is close to 0.000.

166

TIP: *To delete a keyframe, press the] or [(right or left bracket) key to move to the keyframe you want to delete, and then click its keyframe button in the Inspector to remove it.*

6. Wait for the Caching to complete (the red line will turn blue above the clip in the timeline), then play over the title to preview your animation.

Moving your playhead, clicking the keyframe button, and changing the parameter is the basis for animating any control in Resolve.

Modifying Keyframes in the Timeline

Knowing how to modify keyframes is just as important as setting their value, since you very rarely get the timing right on your first attempt.

Changing the Timing of Keyframes

You can make adjustments to the timing of keyframes, changing where on the timeline they are placed. The timing adjustments are made directly in the timeline.

1. Zoom into the timeline to see the title clip clearly.

2. With the title still selected, in the lower-right corner of the timeline segment, click the

diamond shape keyframe button.

This exposes the keyframes on a keyframe track beneath the clip. The white dots on the keyframe tracks represent the keyframes. You can drag a keyframe to change where it happens in time.

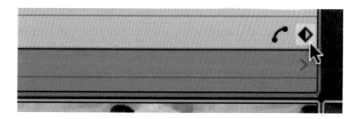

Click the keyframe button to expose keyframe tracks.

TIP: *If you do not see the keyframe button on the clip, zoom in to the timeline.*

Instead of having the slide-on animate over one second, we'll change the position of the last keyframe so the animation is done in a half second.

3. In the timeline, drag the second small white keyframe to the left, then stop dragging when the tooltip reads 00:12

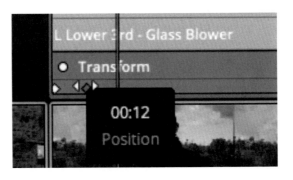

Drag the last keyframe to change its timing.

TIP: *It can sometimes be difficult to see keyframes located on the first and last frames of a clip. The pointer will change to a reposition pointer when you are over a keyframe.*

4. Wait for the Caching to complete (the red line will turn blue) then play over the title to preview your animation.

5. Click the keyframe button on the timeline segment to hide the keyframe.

    Now the title animation happens in a half second. The problem with this zoom is that it doesn't seem very natural. It comes to a stop very abruptly. As a general rule of thumb, you don't want hard stops to your animation. You would prefer animations to come to a stop smoothly. So now, let's figure out how to do that.

Easing Position Acceleration

You can further control the smoothness of position keyframes using the transform wireframe in the viewer. The transform wireframe not only allows you to change the motion path the clip animates along, but it also allows you to adjust the acceleration from one keyframe to another.

TIP: *The Curve editor button next to the keyframe button is used to control acceleration for all parameters other than position.*

1. Click the transform button ⬚ under the timeline viewer to display the transform wireframe and motion path.

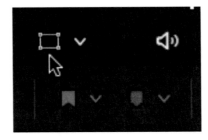

Clicking the transform button displays the transform wireframe and motion path.

You can use the transform wireframe to smooth the motion path and change the acceleration of the motion.

2. Right-click over the last position keyframe in the viewer, and choose Smooth from the pop-up menu.

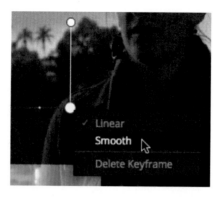

Right-click over the position keyframe to access the smoothing controls.

Enabling Smooth from the menu adds two handles you can adjust. The first large white dot handle adjusts the curvature of the motion path while the smaller white dot handle located between the keyframe and the curvature handle, adjusts the acceleration of the motion.

3. To slow down the acceleration of the animation as it reaches the last keyframe, drag the acceleration handle all the way to the right. .

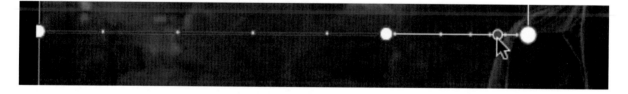

Drag the acceleration handle towards to keyframe to create an ease in.

4. Wait for the Caching to complete, then play the photo clip to preview your animation.

5. Click the transform wireframe button under the viewer to hide the wireframe preview.

Animating with Dynamic Zoom

Dynamic Zoom is another, some might say easier way to animate pan and zoom or "Ken Burns" style effects. It doesn't require any keyframing. You set up the start frame and the end frame in the viewer and the Dynamic Zoom feature does the rest.

1. Click the 03 DSLR bin and double-click the IMG_A.

By default, no matter what size the photo (or clip) is, Resolve automatically resizes it to fit the timeline resolution. This can be changed if you have a lot of clips that you want set a specific way, however, for the purpose of one large photo we can leave it at the default setting.

TIP: *The Input Scaling Preset section located in the Project Setting, determines how clips of different resolutions are automatically resized to fit the timeline.*

2. Mark an In point at the start the clip and 4 seconds later mark an Out point.

3. Go to the second blue marker in the timeline, just before the interview segment.

Position the playhead just before the segment with the second blue marker.

4. Drag from the source viewer into the timeline viewer and choose Place on Top.

5. Back up the playhead just before the photo, then play the timeline to view it.

Even though the photo is much larger than the 1080 HD resolution of the timeline, Resolve resizes it to fit the timeline viewer. However, you can zoom in to create pan and scan animations using keyframes or the Dynamic Zoom feature.

6. Select the photo clip in the timeline.

Photos have the same Inspector parameters as clips, including Size, Position, Rotation, Cropping, Composite Mode and others.

It also includes Dynamic Zoom which is perfect for creating pan and scan or "Ken Burns" style animations.

7. In the the inspector, scroll down until you see the Dynamic Zoom parameters, then click the Enable button to the left the of the feature's name.

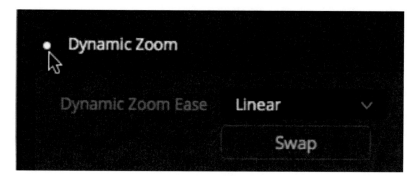

Click the Enable button to turn on Dynamic Zoom.

8. To show the Dynamic Zoom controls in the viewer, click on screen controls button under the timeline viewer and choose Dynamic Zoom from the pop up menu.

Choose Dynamic Zoom from the viewer pop up menu.

Two wireframe outlines appear in the viewer. The green outline is the starting frame and the red outline is the ending frame. By resizing and positioning each wireframe you can decide what area of the frame is shown at the start and what is shown by the end. Resolve will automatically interpolate between the starting and ending frames.

9. Click the white corner handles of the green wireframe to activate it.

10. Resize and drag the green wireframe so it roughly covers 80% of the image but positioned in the lower left corner.

Drag the green starting wireframe to the lower left corner and resize it to cover most of the image.

11. Click the white corner handles of the red wireframe to activate it.

12. Resize and drag the red wireframe so it is slightly smaller than the green starting wireframe and centered over the tip of the pencil.

Create a smaller red ending wireframe centered over the pencil.

TIP: *Resolve always uses the original, higher quality image when resizing a clip.*

13. Press Shift-/ or choose Playback > Play Around/To > Play Around Current Clip.

14. Click the Dynamic Zoom button under the viewer to hide the on screen wireframes.

Dynamic zoom creates a nice smooth pan and zoom over the photo. If you aren't happy with the results you can go back and change the position of either wireframe.

Chapter 9 Test Questions

Q1: Where are Title templates located?

Q2: True or False: Titles must be edited into the timeline before you can change any parameters.

Q3: To perform an Extend Edit you must first:

A) Select a side of the segment to extend using a trim pointer.

B) Select a side of the segment to extend using the Blade tool.

C) Select a side of the segment to extend using the playhead.

Q4: In Dynamic Zoom, what do the red and green wireframes represent?

Q5: Where do you change the interpretation of an Alpha Channel?

Ch. 10: Changing Clip Speed
Slow Motion, Retiming and Processing

Changing the speed of a clip is done for a variety of reasons. Sometimes it's used to accentuate dramatic action and sometimes it's used so the timing of a clip fits into a scene. In almost every production genre you'll have a need to speed clips up, slow them down and even stop and hold on a frame for a few seconds.

This chapter will introduce you to the two ways to perform speed changes in order to solve different problems and achieve different effects.

Constant Speed

Changing a clip's speed to play faster or slower at a constant frame rate is probably the most common type of speed change you'll make. You've already learned how to do this in chapter 4 using the Fit-to-Fill edit, but how do you do it if the clip is already edited into the timeline?

1. Open the R12_5 Training project, if necessary, then from the Rough cuts bin, load 10 Retiming Examples into the timeline.

2. In the timeline, position the playhead on the first blue marker.

Go to the first blue marker in the timeline.

3. Play over the clip (always a good idea before you make any change).

    During the last third of this clip, the camera has some unwanted movement. You could trim it out, but that can often have rippling effects through out your timeline causing music, sound effects and dialogue to go out of sync. Applying a small slow

174

motion effect will extend the good portion of the clip while not calling too much attention to the slow down in speed. These types of "hidden" slow motion effects are used more often than the hyper dramatic slow downs.

4. Select the 07 pulling out of furnace clip in the timeline, right-click (Control-click on OS X), over the clip and from the contextual menu, choose Change Clip Speed.

The Change Clip Speed dialog can be used to create constant speed changes.

The Change Clip Speed dialog operates on a clip that already exists in the timeline. You can enter the change in speed as either % of the normal speed or as a frame rate.

5. In the "% of frame rate" numeric box, enter 50, and click Change to close the dialog.

6. Play the clip to see the speed change results.

TIP: *If audio is selected, changing clip speed will also change the audio playback speed.*

A unique aspect of using the Change Clip Speed dialog is that you retain the clip's duration in the timeline. If the clip is 4 seconds long to begin with, after you change the speed it is still 4 seconds long. The only thing that changes is which frames are played in the clip.

Retiming Clips in the Timeline

An alternative to the Change Clip Speed dialog is the Retime control. Unlike the Change Clip Speed dialog, applying the Retime control does not initially change anything. You modify the clip speed by dragging the clip, similar to trimming it.

1. In the timeline, go to the second blue marker.

2. Zoom into the timeline until you see the 16 buffing glass clip and the two clips after it.

Go to the second blue marker in the timeline and zoom in on the clips.

3. Play over the marked clip and the two clips that comes directly after it.

   The narration under these three clips seems a bit early. If the Shaping clip lasted a few seconds longer until she said "a variety of tools" it would make the remaining clips fit the narration better.

4. Position the playhead just before the narration says "a variety of different tools".

   This is how far we want the 16 buffing glass clip to extend. If we were to look at the full source clip, you would see the camera shakes a little before and after this section so trimming it to extend the clip isn't an option, but retiming is!

5. Right-click over the 16 buffing glass clip and choose Retime Controls from the contextual menu, or press Command-R (OS X) Ctrl-R (Windows).

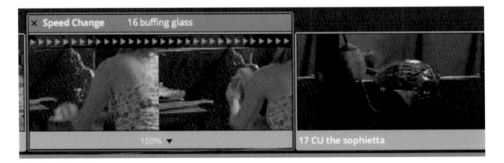

The Retime controls appear as a blue bar over the selected clip.

The Retime controls are displayed as a control bar over the clip in the timeline.

When your pointer hovers over the right edge of the Retime control bar it switches to a retime cursor.

6. Move the pointer to the upper right edge of the Retime control bar.

Placing the pointer over the right edge of the Retime control bar, switches it to a retime cursor.

Dragging the clip right will extend the clip by changing the speed to a slow rate. Dragging the clip left will shorten the clip by playing it back faster. The actual frame rate is displayed at the bottom of the segment. The pop-up menu below the clip provides access to other speed change controls.

7. Drag to the right to lengthen the clip, continuing until you reach the playhead

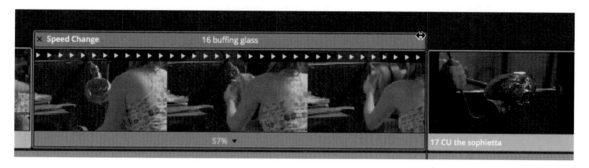

Dragging right lengthens the clip by slowing the frame rate down.

8. Play the retimed clip to see the results.

TIP: *Switching to the Trim tool and then dragging the Retime control bar will ripple the timeline instead of overwriting the next clip.*

When you change the length of a clip using the Retime controls, the timeline is overwritten, so your timeline duration remains the same.

Variable Speed Change

Once you get past the constant rate speed changes, the next step is to learn how to create variable speed clips. Variable speed clips set two or more speeds within a single clip. This technique is common in commercials or as opening shots in TV shows. Usually, the first half of the clip is sped up and the remaining half is either normal or half speed. To perform variable speed changes, you use the Retiming effect you used in the previous exercise.

1. Place the playhead in the middle of the retimed clip you just created.

   Once you apply a Retime to a clip, you then add Speed Points. Speed Points divide the clip into sections, based on the position of the playhead. You can then control the speeds in each part.

2. At the bottom of the clip, click the Retime pop-up menu and choose Add Speed Point.

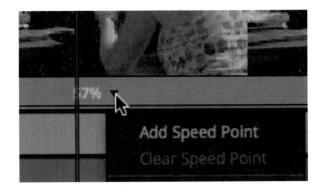

From the Retime pop-up menu choose Add Speed Point.

3. On the left half of the clip, click the Retime pop-up at the bottom of the segment.

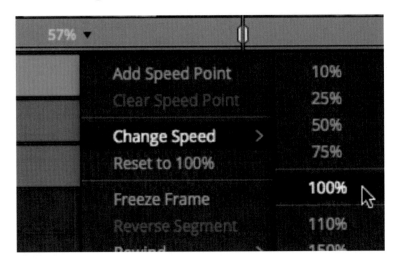

Use the Retime pop-up at the bottom of each Retimed clip to set a speed.

4. Choose Change Speed > 100%.

5. Play over the retimed clip to view the changes.

   The first half of the clip plays at normal speed. After the playhead crosses the speed point, the clip plays at a slower speed. Since the first half of the clip is sped up to play at normal speed, it leaves a gap at the end of the clip. You can also further refine the speed change using a time graph.

Using the Retime Curve

Instead of using a pop up menu to immediately change the speed of segments in the clip, you can use a graph to make a gradual change between the different speeds for each segment.

1. Right-click over the retimed clip and choose Retime Curve.

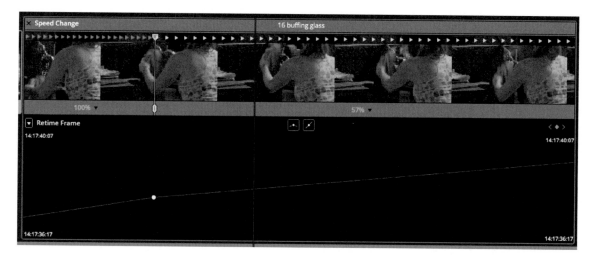

Right-click over a clip and choose Retime Curve to view the time graph.

The Retime Curve is a time graph that represents the source clip frames along the vertical axis and the timeline frames along the horizontal axis. That means normal clip speed in the timeline would be a perfect diagonal line in the retime curve, from the lower left to the upper right. A clip playing in reverse would be higher on the left and lower on the right.

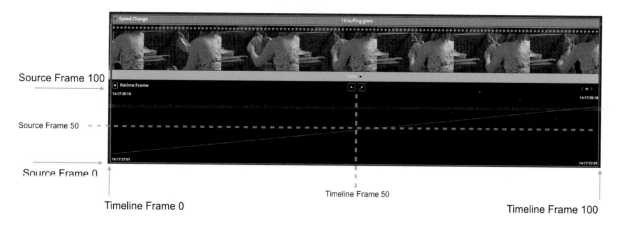

Source clip frames are along the vertical axis, while timeline frames are on along the horizontal axis.

Control points on the graph match any speed points you have added to the Retimed clip. To smooth the change in speed from one side of the Speed point to the other you can smooth the line running through the control point.

2. In the Retime Curve, select the control point, then click the smooth button at the top of the graph.

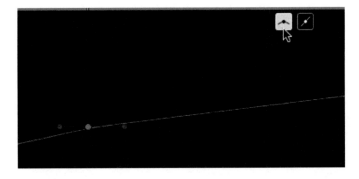

Select a control point and click smooth to create a smoother ramp between speed changes.

To increase the gradual change between speed change, you can drag the smooth handles away from the control point.

3. Drag the smooth handles away from the control point to increase the speed ramp.

Increase the ramp between speed changes by dragging the handles away from the control point.

You can add new control points to the graph, which is the equivalent of adding a speed point to the clip. You can then change the position of the new control point to increase the speed or slow it down.

4. Position the playhead at the end of the clip, then drag backwards until sparks appear on the glass.

Position the playhead roughly a half second from the end of the clip.

180

5. To add a control point on the retime curve, hold Option (OS X) or Alt (Windows) and click on the graph line directly under the playhead.

6. On the right half of the clip, click the Retime pop-up at the bottom of the segment.

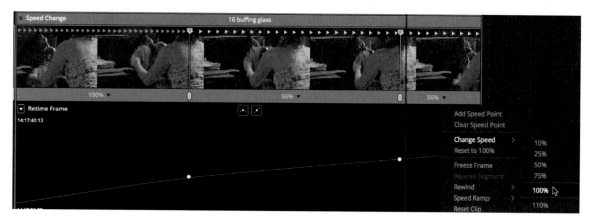

Use the Retime pop-up at the bottom of each Retimed clip to set a speed.

7. In the Retime Curve, select the control point you just added, then click the smooth button at the top of the graph.

8. Choose Change Speed > 100%.

   To close the gap, you'll trim the end of the clip as you learned in Chapter 6.

9. Select the right edge of the clip and trim it to close the gap.

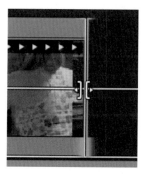

Use the selection tool to trim the clip and close the gap.

10. To hide the retime control bar, right-click over the clip and choose Retime Control or press Command-R (OS X) or Ctrl-R (Windows).

11. To close the graph click the curve editor button in the lower right corner of the segment.

The Curve editor button opens the curve editor on any clip, not just for retiming.

Now you have a segment that plays at full speed until half way through the clip. where the clip switches to half speed and then picks up again to normal speed at the end.

Processing Speed Changes

The actual method used to create a slowed down clip depends on the processing algorithm used. Resolve can use one of three algorithms: Nearest, Frame Blend, and Optical Flow. The three choices require three different levels of computing power.

1. With the 16 buffing glass clip still selected, open the Inspector.

2. Scroll to the bottom of the Inspector to the Retime and Scaling Process section, and click the Retime Process menu to view its contents.

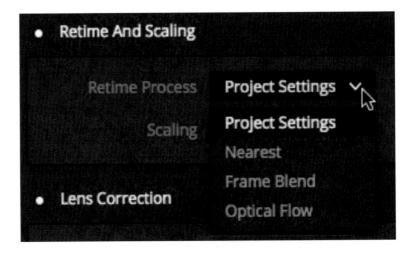

The Retime Processing in the Inspector has three options: Nearest, Frame Blending and Optical Flow.

Nearest, the default setting, is very fast to compute but delivers the lowest-quality results. The benefit is that no caching is required so your clips playback instantaneously. Frame Blend is almost as fast, but does require a very quick Caching process. The benefit is that it delivers slightly better-looking results. Optical Flow can produce the highest-quality results, but it is much more computationally intensive. It always requires caching. When using the right type of shot, the result can be very smooth even at super low frame rates. However, not every clip is a great candidate for using Optical Flow. Shots that have crossing motion in different directions (such as

182

cars going in opposite directions or legs crossing as a person walks) prove to be difficult for optical flow processing.

3. From the menu, choose Optical Flow.

4. Wait for the Caching to be completed (Caching line above the clip will turn blue).

5. Play over the retimed clip to see the results.

It's a good idea to try Optical Flow processing first to see if it produces acceptable results, and then revert to Frame Blend if necessary.

TIP: *Additional controls on the Editing page of the Project Settings for Optical Flow can some-times improve small tears or stretching artifacts.*

Chapter 10 Test Questions

Q1: Name two of the three methods you can use to change the speed of a clip?

Q2: True or False: Creating slow motion using the Change Clip Speed dialog will not change the length of the segment in the timeline.

Q3: True or False: Creating slow motion using the Retime control will change the length of the segment and the timeline.

Q4: What does adding a Speed Point allow you to do?

Q5: The Retime Curve can be used to:

A) Smooth the changes between speed point

B) Make a clip go backwards

C) Add Speed Points

D) All of the above

E) None of the above

Ch. 11: Intro to the Color Page
Conforming timelines and balancing color

No matter what kind of project you are working on, whether it is a wedding, a documentary or a sci-fi epic, there comes a time to start correcting the color imperfections that may exist in your clips. Initially, the main goal is not to create a specific look, it's just to give them all a consistent, balanced or *neutral* tone.

In this chapter, we'll import a rough cut created in another editing application. Then, we'll use Resolve to fix color and contrast on a couple of shots to get a feel for the tools. These adjustments, as well as many others, are done in the Color page. You'll use the same timeline for the remaining chapters of this book, so you should read these last five chapters in order.

Conforming a Timeline

Although Resolve includes all the tools you would need to put an entire program together, you can choose to begin editing in another application and import the timeline into Resolve for color grading and finishing. Resolve can import timelines from Avid Media Composer, Final Cut Pro and Adobe Premiere. This process is often called conforming a timeline. We'll conform a timeline in a new project.

NOTE: Although the timeline we are using comes from Adobe Premiere Pro, the steps are similar for all applications.

1. If Resolve *is not* open, launch it from the OS X Dock or Window's Start menu. If Resolve *is* open, choose File > Project Manager or press Shift-1.

2. In the lower right corner of the Project Manager window, click New Project.

3. Type Color Correction as the project name and click Create, then, double click the Color Correction thumbnail to open it.

    If you are moving from one computer to another, then the more reliable way to make sure the timeline in Resolve links to the correct media is to add all the media into the Media Pool before importing the timeline.

NOTE: For this exercise, we'll be using the same media you have been using in the previous chapters of this book. However, we'll need to import the media into our new project.

4. Click the Media button to display the Media page, if necessary.

5. From the Library browser navigate to the R12_5 Training Project folder you downloaded to your Documents folder.

6. In the R12_5 Training Project folder, drag the 01 Video Clips folder to the Media Pool.

   A warning dialog appears explaining that these clips do not match the timeline resolution. The timeline default in Resolve is 1920 x 1080 HD at 24fps. All the clips are 1280x720 at 24fps (except one DSLR clip is 23.97 fps). You can have Resolve change the timeline to match the clips or do it manually. We'll do it manually.

7. Click the Don't Change button to keep the Project Settings as they are.

8. Choose File >Project Settings or press Shift-9.

9. As you did back in chapter 1, set the Timeline Resolution to be 1280x720P.

10. From the Color Science pop-up choose DaVinci YRGB Color Managed.

Set the Color Science to DaVinci YRGB Color Managed.

11. Click the Color Management category in the Settings window, and for the Input Color Space choose Blackmagic Design 4.6K Film V3.

Choose Blackmagic Design 4.6K Film V3 as the project's Input color profile.

NOTE: *If you skipped chapter 1, go back and read the sections on What is Color Space and Setting Up Project Color Management to get a better understanding of these settings.*

12. Click Save to close and save the new project settings.

    With the project set up completed, you can now return to importing the remaining folders of media from the R12_5 Training Project folder.

13. From the Library browser, drag the 02 Audio Clips, 03 DSLR, 04 Multicamera, 05 Graphics and 06 RAW folders into the Media Pool.

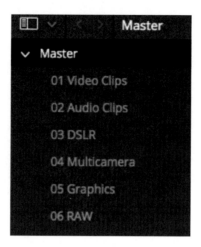

Drag the remaining five folders from the R12_5 Training Project folder into the Media Pool.

    Now you'll create a new bin and import the XML timeline into it.

14. Click the Master bin and choose File > New Bin, then name the bin 07 Timelines

15. With the new 07 Timelines bin selected, choose File > Import AAF, EDL, XML.

16. In the R12_5 Training Project folder, select the XML from Premiere.xml file and choose open.

    The Load XML dialog opens with a number of options for converting this XML file into a Resolve timeline.

NOTE: XML or EXtensible Markup Language is a text based document used to store data. In the case of film and video post production, it is often used as an intermediate file to transfer a timeline from one editing application to another.

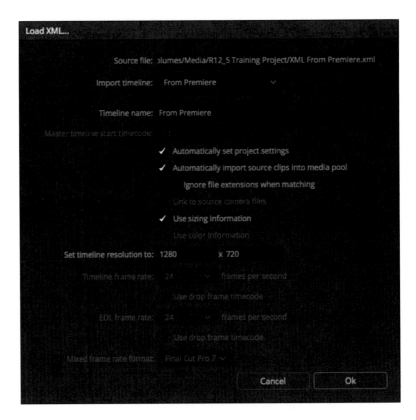

The Load XML dialog includes options for automatically importing clips required by the timeline.

For the most part these options are self explanatory (Source file path, Timeline Name etc.) and the defaults will usually go unchanged. For our purposes, we don't need Resolve to import the source media, since we have already imported it ourselves. This method is particularly useful if you edited with low resolution compressed clips in Premiere or Avid and now want to relink to the higher resolution camera originals.

17. Uncheck the setting to Automatically Import Source clips, and click OK

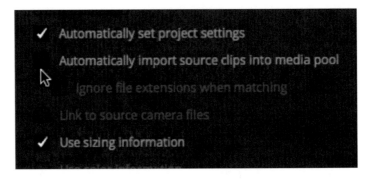

Deselect the check box to automatically import source media.

A Folders dialog appears. This is used to select the bin(s) that contain the media used in the timeline. Since all of our bins contain media used in the timeline, we do not have to deselect any of them.

18. In the Folders dialog that appears, click OK.

The Premiere Pro timeline is added to the 07 Timelines bin and loaded into the timeline panel. The timeline includes a number of cuts, four audio channels, a fade at the start of the timeline, a dissolve near the end and a fade out on the last clip. All of these elements were added in Premiere Pro.

Preparing a Timeline for Export

Let's take a quick step back to discuss how you actually get a timeline out of an application like Adobe Premiere Pro or Avid Media Composer and into a format (XML or AAF) that Resolve can read. There are a few set up and organizational steps you should perform in the editing application before you export it to Resolve.

1. **Duplicate your timeline:** You are going to be making some structural changes to your timeline, so it's a good idea to duplicate it and then make the changes.

2. **Media Manage your timeline:** If you are moving to a different computer to work on Resolve, you should media manage your duplicate "export" timeline so all of its media is on a single drive, contained in a folder.

3. **Use as few layers as needed:** If layered clips are not required for super imposing or compositing, move all straight cuts and segments with transitions between them, onto the lowest video layer you can. Sometimes editors will use a second layer for cut-aways, and while that is fine for creative editing, it is not suited for conforming.

4. **Delete empty tracks:** Delete any empty audio or video tracks in your timeline.

5. **Remove linked motion graphics or visual effects clips:** Make sure all linked After Effects, Motion or Fusion Connect clips are rendered out as standard clips and edited back into the timeline.

6. **Identify effects used:** Based on the editing application you are using, Resolve imports different transitions, and effects. The Resolve documentation provides a good list to use as a reference, so I will not bother to reproduce it here. The basics of cuts, dissolves, constant speed changes, layers, position, scale and rotation are all supported. Beyond that it depends on your application.

7. **Do not change clip names:** Do not change the clip names in the Finder or Windows file browser. Clip names are used when relinking the clips in Resolve.

8. **No nested sequences:** If you edit in Media Composer, nested sequences are not supported in Resolve. You should render out your nested sequences as a mixed down, single clip and edit them back into the timeline.

9. **Mixed frame sizes:** Set the Image Preset section in Resolve's Project Settings to configure the scaling of mixed resolution clips. Individual clips can also be scaled in the Color page.

10. **Choose Export or Output:** With the timeline selected in your bin, in Adobe Premiere Pro choose File >Export > Final Cut Pro XML, or from Media Composer choose File > Output > AAF and save the file to the same drive as your media.

About the Color Page

To begin color grading, you use the Color page. The Color page contains a number of tools for making incredibly precise color adjustments. Many of the tools do similar things, just in different ways. It can be a bit daunting at first, but it is easy when you take it in sections.

1. At the bottom of the Resolve window, click the Color button to go to the Color page.

Click the Color button to switch to the Color page.

The Color page is divided into eight main areas.

The default layout of the Color page.

190

NOTE: *If your computer display has a resolution lower than 1920 x 1080, then your screen may be different from the images in this lesson.*

When you click the Color page button, whatever timeline was loaded in the Edit page is displayed in the Color page timeline. The Color page does not change or alter any cuts or transitions, it just provides a different way of looking at your timeline. In fact, you can move back and forth between the Edit and Color pages at anytime.

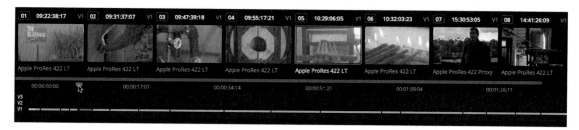

The Color page timeline uses thumbnails and a mini timeline below them.

The Color page divides the timeline in two parts. Each clip in the timeline is displayed as a thumbnail. Clicking on a thumbnail highlights it and moves the playhead to the first frame of the clip. The timeline ruler below the thumbnails, shows the entire timeline using thin bars to represent each clip.

2. Click in the center of the second thumbnail to select it.

Each thumbnail displays a number in the left corner, to make it easily identifiable.

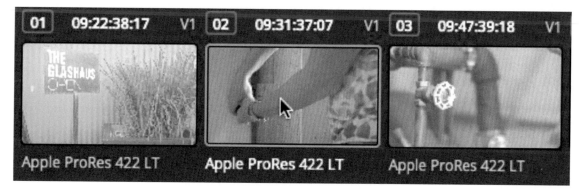

Select a thumbnail to display the first frame of the clip in the viewer.

3. Drag the timeline ruler playhead to the right until you reach the thumbnail #19. You can also click the blue segments in the mini-timeline to jump to that clip.

To scrub through the timeline, drag the playhead.

This clip, as you may recall from chapter 1, was not captured with the same camera as the other clips. That means, the Color Management profile we selected at the start of this chapter is incorrect for this clip, and we'll need to correct that.

4. Right-click over thumbnail #19 and choose Input Color Space > SRGB.

The clip updates in the viewer using the correct color profile. Now, all of our color management is correct for all the clips, and we can make some color adjustments.

TIP: *If you are creating a program for HD broadcast, then you should use an HD broadcast display connected via a Blackmagic display card to accurately evaluate color adjustments. The viewers in Resolve are not intended to give accurate color representation.*

Understanding Scopes

Because unforeseen or unavoidable situations occur during production, clips can be recorded with an incorrect color tint, or have highlights that are dull, or have shadows that are too bright. Therefore, you always start your color correction process by balancing your shots. As an objective way to evaluate what adjustments need to be made, Resolve includes four video signal scopes: The Waveform, Parade, Vectorscope and Histogram, that are used to judge the luminance, exposure, hue and saturation of a clip.

1. Click the video scope button ![scope button] on the far right of the toolbar.

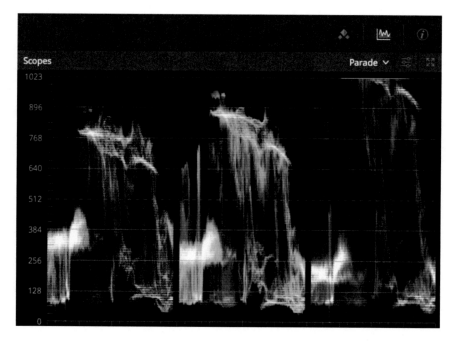

The scopes are displayed by clicking the Scopes button in the toolbar.

2. From the video scope pop-up menu, choose Waveform.

Choose Waveform from the Video Scope pop-up menu.

TIP: *You can view two or four scopes at once by choosing Workspace > Videoscopes >On.*

The waveform is a graph that is read from bottom to top, with absolute black at line 0 and absolute white at line 1023. Those numbers may seem odd, but 0-1023 is a standard scale for 10-bit video. When balancing shots, you try to ensure the image does not go below 0 or above 1023, otherwise the image will clip and lose detail.

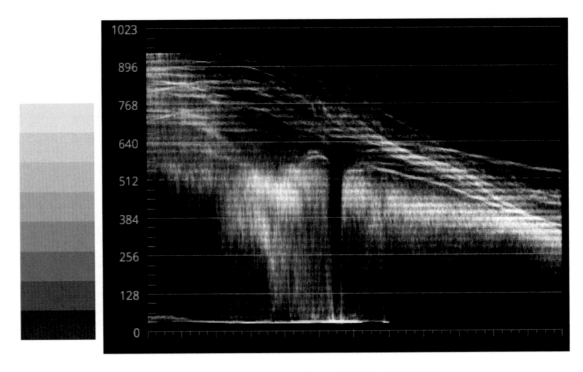

The Y axis plots luminance from 0 to 1023 for 10-bit video.

Reading the waveform horizontally corresponds to the image being displayed. For instance, the left part of the scope corresponds to the left part of the image. This makes it easy to look at the scope and know exactly the area you are evaluating.

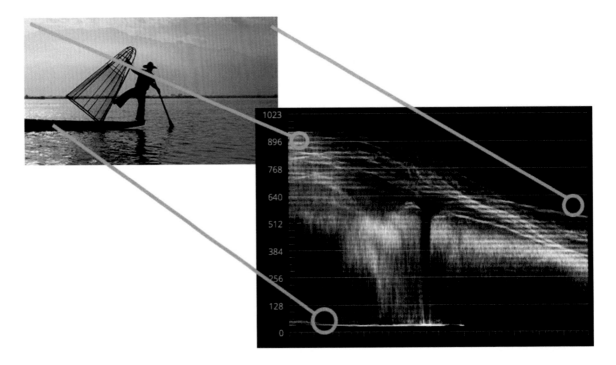

The X axis corresponds to the video frame.

194

You are now set to make some adjustments while monitoring the waveform. However, there is no reason to make the process more difficult than it already is. Why try to adjust color and luminance together, when you can divide them up. A simple approach is to tackle luminance first and save hue and saturation for later.

3. Above the waveform, click the Options button .

4. To remove color from the waveform, click the Y (luminance) button, then click the Options button again to close the window.

Click the Y button to remove color information from the waveform.

There are quite a number of ways to make luminance adjustments in Resolve, but since this exercise is more about the scopes and less about the actual tools that make the adjustments, we'll use a few of the more simplistic tools called Shared Adjustments. You may be familiar with these Shared Adjustments from other video or photo applications. These controls are located in the lower left of the window.

Shared adjustments are applied to the entire image.

TIP: *Depending on your screen resolution, the names of each Shared Adjustment control may not be visible. Hover over the icon to view a tooltip of the name.*

5. Drag the Contrast field to the right until the value reaches 1.2.

You can drag in any field to change the value.

Contrast stretches the luminance in your image by simultaneously brightening the highlights and darkening the shadows in your image. After the contrast adjustment, the waveform graph is close to the bottom but the highlights could still be brighter.

The Shared Adjustments are divided into 2 "pages" of controls. To switch to the second page, you use the 2 button on the left side of the controls.

6. Click the page 2 button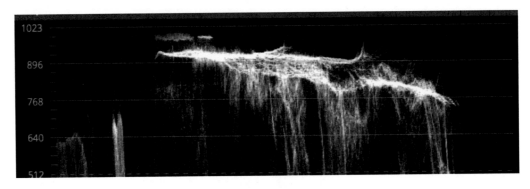

7. To increase the highlights, drag the Highlights field to the right until the graph in the waveform is almost touching the top line.

Drag the Highlights field to make brighter areas in the image, brighter.

TIP: *Double clicking on any name in the Shared Adjustment strip will reset the value.*

The goal of this exercise was to understand how to read a waveform and then use it to maximize your shadows and highlights. Now, you can learn how to evaluate and correct for an incorrect tint or *color cast* in a shot.

Correcting Color Casts with Temperature and Tint

Although adding color back to the waveform will allow you to evaluate color, color casts are easier to see on a histogram.

1. From the video scope pop-up menu, choose Histogram.

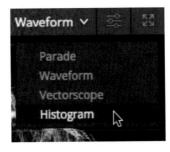

Choose histogram from the video scope pop up.

The histogram is used to measure the exposure of each channel in the image. The histogram is read from left to right, with 0, or absolute black on the left and 100, or absolute white on the right. The image gets clipped beyond those two points.

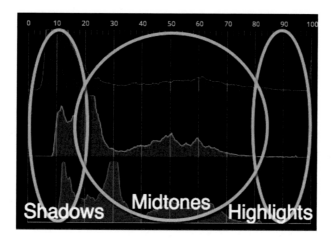

The X axis plots the tonal range from 0 to 100.

Highlights, like clouds or bright lights should not have a color cast. So your job, when balancing a shot, is to remove any irregular tint from your highlights. The histogram offers a simple way to visualize a color cast objectively. On a histogram, if any one of the red, green or blue channels is pushed further to the right, it means that color is more dominant in your highlights.

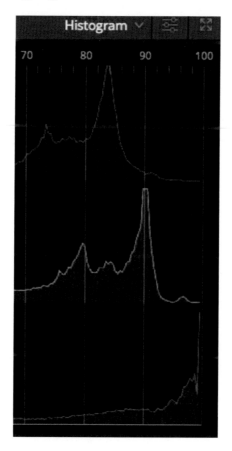

A blue color cast in highlights indicated by the blue channel being furthest to the right.

There are multiple ways to correct a color cast. A very straight forward way is to use the Temperature and Tint controls.

2. On the Shared Adjustments strip, click back to page 1

   The Temperature and Tint controls in the Shared Adjustments are designed to correct very common color casts from an incorrect camera white balance setting, or off axis light sources, like florescent lights being used in a shot.

TIP: *When using RAW files, use the Camera RAW controls to adjust Temperature and Tint.*

3. Drag the Temperature control until the blue and red channels align in the histogram.

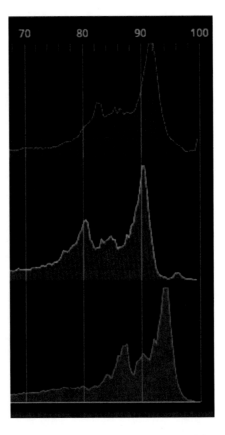

Use the temperature control to add red and remove blue from the image.

   The Temperature control adds more red to image when dragged right or adds more blue to an image when dragged left.

4. To increase the amount of green in the image, drag the tint control until the green channel aligns with the red and blue.

   The Tint control adds more green to an image when dragged left or adds more magenta to an image when dragged right.

TIP: *Switching off the video scopes when they are not in use, frees up the graphics card's processor for better playback performance.*

After making critical adjustments, it's good to compare them against the original shot.

5. Choose View > Bypass All Grades or press Shift-D to see the original image, then press Shift-D again to view your corrected clip.

The Shared Adjustment strip controls offer quick and easy ways to balance a shot, but they are not as flexible as some of the other tools in Resolve. Next, we'll use Color Wheels, which are probably the most commonly used tools for color correcting shots.

Adjusting Lift, Gamma and Gain

In this exercise we'll look at another shot that is less obvious with its problems. The corrections will require subtler adjustments. To view these issues, we can use the parade scope, and to make the adjustments, we can use the Color Wheels.

1. Select the thumbnail #25, of the woman on the bench.

Select thumbnail #25 in the timeline.

2. From the video scope pop-up menu, choose Parade.

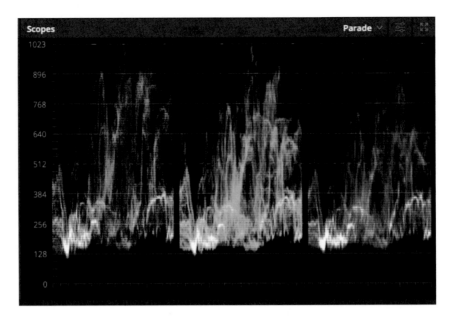

Choose Parade from the video scope pop up.

The parade is similar to the waveform, except that it shows the three color channels individually. For this shot, it shows the red, green and blue channels reaching the top line. Which means your highlights are at the maximum level. The shadows however, are raised high above the 0 line which causes the darkest parts of your image to appear muddy. Instead of using the Shared Adjustments to correct contrast, you will have more flexibility using the Master Wheels.

The Master Wheels above the Shared Adjustments strip, can adjust shadows mid tones and highlights

The Master Wheels panel, below the Color Balance controls, can adjust contrast using the Lift, Gamma, and Gain, which *roughly* equate to shadows. mid-tones and highlights respectively. The Offset adjustment is an overall luminance adjustment.

The Lift Master Wheel, located under the Lift Color Balance control, adjusts the black point for the image. When dragging it left, the darkest shadows become darker.

3. Get a feel for what the Lift Master Wheel does by dragging it left and right. Watch the viewer and the parade scope to see the results.

Our image has very few areas that should be totally black, but those areas that should be totally black, should be located near 0 in the parade scope. We'll use the Lift Master Wheel to set the darkest part of our picture just above 0 on the scope.

200

4. Drag the Lift Master Wheel to the left until the Y luminance value reads −0.05, and the bottom of the parade graph is at 0.

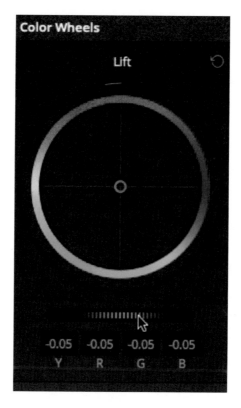

Move the black point until the parade reaches 0 on the graph.

The Gain Master Wheel adjusts the white point for the image. When dragged to the right, the brightest highlights in the image become brighter.

5. Get a feel for what the Gain Master Wheel does by dragging it left and right. Watch the viewer and the parade to see the results.

    Lowering the Gain Master Wheel will decrease the brightness in the brightest parts of our picture. Our image has bright, specular highlights on the glass but nothing else very bright so we will tone down the brightness just a bit.

6. Drag the Gain Master Wheel to the left until the Y luminance value displays 0.95 and the top of the signal reaches just below the 1023 line at the top of graph.

Move the white point until the signal in the parade just below the 1023 line on the graph.

The Gamma Master Wheel adjusts the brightness between the black point and white point. When dragging this control to the left, the mid tones becomes darker.

7. Drag the Gamma Master Wheel to the left until the Y value displays -0.03

Drag the Gamma Master Wheel to shift the image brighter or darker.

8. To compare these changes with the original, choose View > Bypass All Grades, or press Shift-D.

9. Choose View > Bypass All Grades, or press Shift-D again, to have the neutral color correction enabled.

Before (left) and after (right) black point, white point and gamma adjustments.

Balancing Color with the Color Wheels

With the luminance balanced in our shot it is time to tackle the color. Above the Master Wheels are the Color Balance controls, which are used to make hue adjustments in the lift gamma and gain regions of an image.

The Color Primaries Wheels panel for adjusting the hue of an image.

Looking at the parade scope, the top of the red channel is pushed slightly higher than green or blue. This tells us red is brighter in our highlights. Now that we know the problem, let's figure out how to fix it using the Primaries wheels.

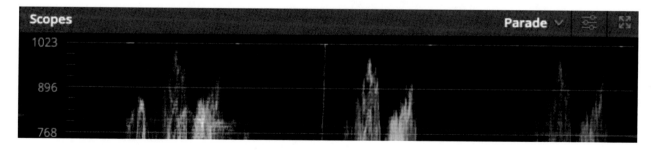

The Parade shows red as the dominant color in our highlights.

Each Color Balance control is used to adjust hue, and balance RGB levels for shadows, mid tones, and highlights. For instance, if you want to correct the red hue in the highlights, you move the Color Balance indicator in the Gain wheel.

1. Press Option-F (OS X) or Alt-F (Windows) or choose Workspace > Viewer Mode > Enhanced Viewer to display a larger viewer.

   We'll use this larger viewer to make our adjustments easier to see.

   The Color Balance indicator requires very subtle adjustments. The combined results of all the adjustments will be significant but each individual adjustment is slight.

TIP: *Adjustments made using the Color Balance controls are subtle. In most cases, the edge of the Color Balance indicator will remain very close to or even still touching the crosshair.*

2. In the Gain Color Balance control, drag the indicator slightly toward teal.

Drag the Color Balance indicator in the Color Balance control to adjust each region.

   Pushing the Color Balance indicator towards one color removes the opposite color.

3. Keep moving the Color Balance indicator until the tops of the red, green and blue channels in the parade scope are evenly aligned.

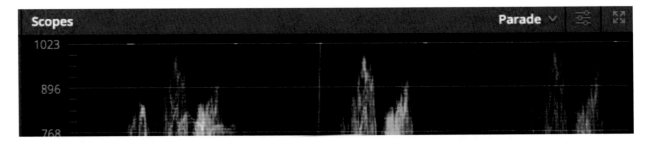

Use the parade scope to make sure the tops of each color channel evenly align.

   You can use the Offset Color Balance control to tint the entire image.

4. Drag the Offset Color Balance indicator, towards blue.

The Offset controls are use to tint or brighten the entire image.

When you make color balance and master wheel adjustments for the very first time, you can easily go too far, causing the picture to suffer. That's why there is a reset, so you can try a new. You'll probably reset these controls a few times before it is correct.

5. To reset the Offset Color Balance control, click the Reset button.

To reset a Color Balance control, click the circle to the right of the name.

Let's get a little clearer about the goal to create a balanced, sometimes called a neutral grade. These terms mean that items in the image which should be white, gray or black are indeed white, gray and black. The shot is well exposed and color accurate.

Using the Vectorscope to Evaluate Skin Tones

Skin tones are probably noticed the most by the casual viewer, so it goes to reason that they should be given special attention by you when making color adjustments. The vectorscope is used to check hue and saturation and is especially useful to evaluate skin tones.

1. From the video scope pop-up menu, choose Vectorscope.

Choose Vectorscope from the Video Scope pop-up menu.

The center of the vectorscope is the origin. The more a color is saturated, the more it extends from the center.

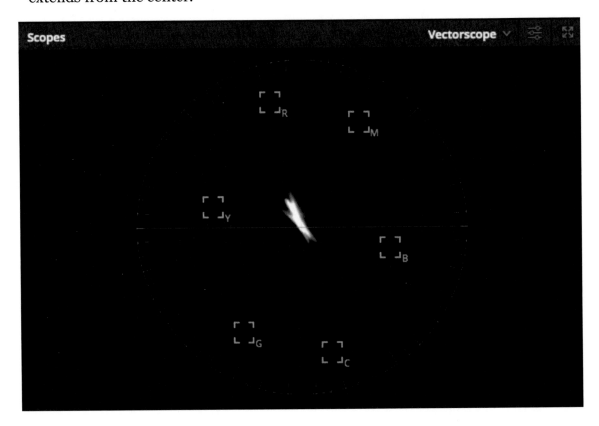

The vectorscope is used to evaluate the hue and saturation of color.

Around the circle are six boxes, three for the primary colors of red, green and blue, and three for the secondary colors of yellow, magenta and cyan. These target boxes help to understand where the colors of your image fall along the range of hues.

2. Above the vectorscope, click the Options pop-up button ⏸, then click the check boxes for Show 2x Zoom and Show Skin Tone Indicator.

The vectorscope includes options for display brightness, zoom level and skin tone line.

Each scope has an options window. The vectorscope can be incredibly helpful when judging the color accuracy of skin tones because it includes a Skin Tone Indicator line where all skin tones should align.

TIP: *No matter the race of the person in frame; all skin tones fall along the skin tone line.*

3. Click the Options pop-up menu again, to close it.

    Because the skin tones are a relatively small area in this shot, it will be difficult to evaluate them in the vectorscope but still possible.

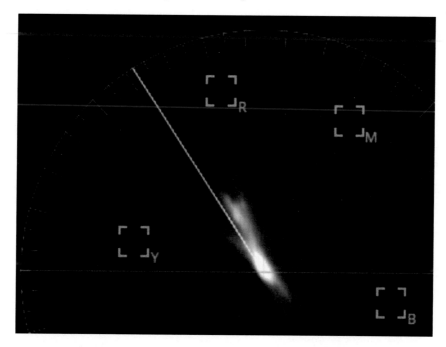

The skin tone in this clip leans towards red/magenta.

TIP: *Hold Option or Alt and scroll the middle mouse button while over the Vectorscope to increase the size of the signal greater than 2X.*

In this shot, the skin tones appear to lean a bit toward red/magenta, when they should have more orange in them. To decrease the amount of a color, you push towards the opposite color. Skin tones are adjusted in the Gamma range.

4.   To remove some red in the skin tones, drag the Gamma Color Balance indicator very slightly toward green, until the skin tones appear more natural.

When correcting for skin tones, you use gamma adjustments.

5.   To compare to the original, press Shift-D or choose View > Bypass All Grades.

6.   Press Shift-D again or choose View > Bypass All Grades to return to viewing the clip with the improved skin tone.

Before (left) and after (right) color balance adjustments.

TIP: *In the Color page, each clip has its own Undo/Redo history. That is, choosing Edit > Undo will undo different steps depending on which clip currently selected.*

Saving a Color Correction

If you want to reuse a set of adjustments on other images, you can save a group of adjustments to the Gallery as a Still. Stills save a picture of the current frame as a visual reference, in addition they save the adjustments currently applied to the clip.

1. Press Option-F (OS X) or Alt-F (Windows) or choose Workspace > Viewer Mode > Enhanced Viewer to display the thumbnails.

2. While still viewing thumbnail #23 with the neutral correction applied, right-click in the viewer and choose Grab Still from the menu.

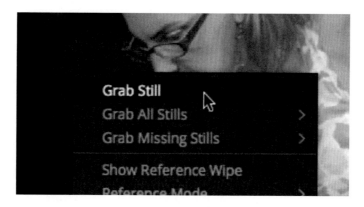

Right-click in the viewer to save a Still.

Once you save a Still to the Gallery, you'll want to give it a more descriptive name than the numbering scheme used by Resolve.

3. Right-click the Still in the Gallery, then choose Change Label.

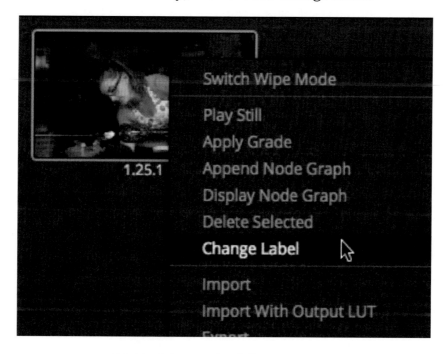

Right-click over the Still to rename it.

4. Type **neutral bench work** then press Return/Enter.

We now have a saved grade. In the next chapter we'll learn how to apply that grade to clips that require similar adjustments.

Balancing Color with Primaries Bars

So far we have been using the most common tools for color correction. A less obvious, but possibly better tool for color balancing are the Primaries Bars.

1. Select the thumbnail #10 in the timeline and play the clip to see it.

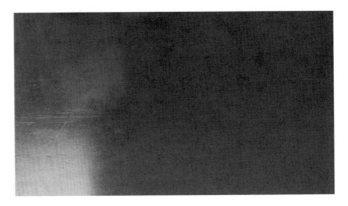

Select thumbnail # 10 to view the metal table.

2. Position the playhead at the start of the clip.

3. From the video scope pop-up menu, choose Parade.

    This clip needs a simple color balance. The highlights are too low and overall it has a bluish tint.

4. In the upper right corner of the Color Wheels panel, choose the Primaries Bars from the pop-up menu.

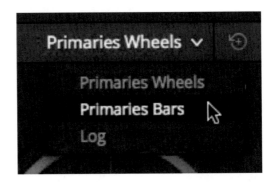

Choose Primaries Bars from the Color Wheels pop up menu.

The Primaries Bars allow you to make similar color and luminance adjustments as the Primaries Wheels, but the Bars provide independent red, green and blue sliders for lift, gamma and gain, making it a bit easier to adjust primary colors in a shot.

The Primaries Bars also include the Gain Master Wheels for adjusting luminance.

5. Drag the Gain Master Wheel to the right until the color channels in the parade almost touch the top 1023 line in the graph.

    You might be thinking the next step is to lower the Lift Master Wheel down until the color channels reach the 0 line in the Parade, but you should look at the image in the viewer first. We have a rudimentary gray card, which we can use to not only "white" balance the image, but to set the correct exposure as well.

NOTE: A gray card is typically an 8x10 gray slate used as a reference by cinematographers to determine white balance and exposure. It is designed to measure the light reflected from a subject by using a standard 18% gray color.

    To use the table as a quasi middle gray card, we align all three color channels in the mid tones (Gamma), just like we aligned all three channels in the highlights. This will eliminate any dominant color cast on the table, and balance the color in this shot. We'll balance red and blue to align with green.

6. Drag the red Gamma bar up until it aligns with the green channel in the parade scope.

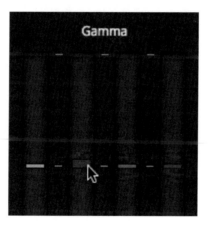

Drag the Gamma red bar up to increase red in the mid tones.

7. Drag the blue Gamma bar down until it aligns with the other channels in the scope.

    That is the balancing part, but with an actual gray card you can also set exposure as well. The correct exposure for the 18% gray in the Rec 709 color space, is located at 410 on Resolve's parade scope. Unfortunately, we don't have a true flat gray card. Our table has a wide range of grays, so we are more or less going to fudge it by setting the brightest part of our gray table at 410 in the Parade scope. To help us out, we can add a reference line to the parade scope exactly at 410.

8. Click the Options button above the parade scope.

9. In the Options dialog, click the check box to Show Reference Levels.

10. Set the Low reference level slider to 410.

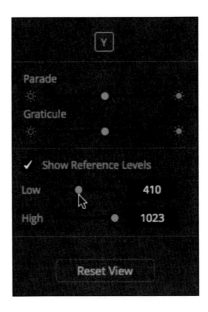

Set the Low slider to 410.

11. Drag the Graticule slider all the way to the right to brighten the lines in the scope.

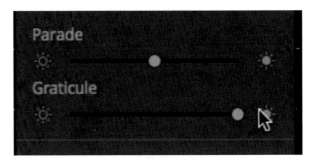

Use the Graticule slider to brighten the lines in the scope.

12. Click the Options button again to hide the Options dialog.

13. Below the Gamma Primaries Bars, drag the Master Wheel to the left until the tops of the mid tones in the parade align to the 410 reference line you added.

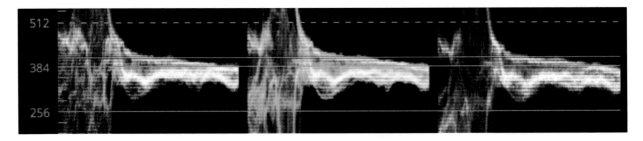

Use the Gamma Master Wheel to align the tops of the mid tone grays on the reference line.

14. Compare the original shot with the color balanced shot by pressing Shift-D to see the original and then press Shift-D again to see the corrected version.

You now have a well balanced and exposed shot. Of course, you would have a more accurate adjustment if the camera person actually used a gray card but sometimes using items in the image that you know should be neutral, middle gray is all you can do.

Using the Node Editor

After a clip in a timeline has been balanced, the next task is to correct any small areas of inconsistent lighting. This might be someone's shiny forehead or exaggerated darkness around someone's eyes. Instead of bringing the entire Gain down or bringing the Lift up to fix one small area, tasks like these are best handled by isolating the problem area.

Our newly corrected table top is well color balanced and exposed correctly for the most part, but it still has a very hot spot in the lower left, which should be toned down. You start making an isolated adjustment by adding a new node in the Node editor.

1. Place the pointer in an empty area of the Node editor, then right-click and choose Add Node > Corrector.

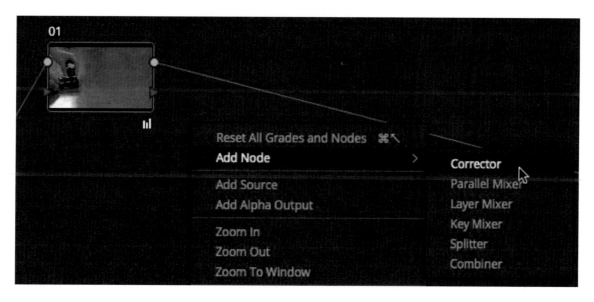

To add a node in the Node editor, right-click and choose Add Node > Corrector.

You can think of a node as a transparent layer, stacked on top of your clip. When you make any color adjustment, those adjustments are applied to the node and not directly to the clip. That makes every adjustment in Resolve, non-destructive since you can enable and disable a node at anytime.

Every adjustment we have made so far, has been saved in the default node in the Node editor. This existing node contains all of our color balance adjustments for this clip.

The second node we have just added, can take care of the hot spot. The second node needs to be connected to the first node in order to operate. The nodes flow from left to right, one to the other, carrying the adjustments contained in them, forward.

2. To connect the second node to first node, drag node 02 over the connection line. When your pointer is over the line and a green add symbol is displayed, release the mouse button.

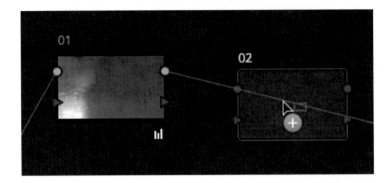

Drag the node over the connection line until you see the green Add icon.

As the number of nodes in our Node editor grow, we should keep organized by naming the nodes based on what they are doing to the image.

3. Right-click over the first node in the Node editor and choose Change Label.

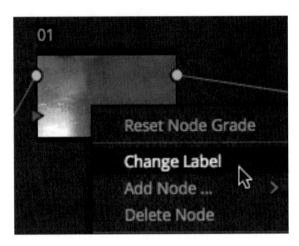

To change the name of a node, right-click over it and choose Change Label.

4. Type Neutral balance.

5. Right-click over the second node in the Node editor and choose Change Label.

6. Type Hot Spot.

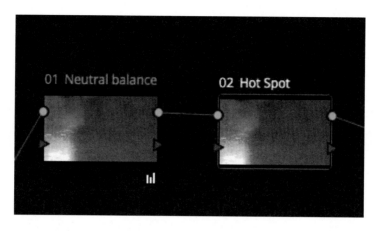

Change the name to Hot Spot.

Nodes allow you to organize your color adjustments in flexible ways. On some simple grades you may use only the default node. Other times, for complete grades you may add a dozen nodes. Using nodes allows you to quickly navigate to the exact adjustment you are looking for and combine color adjustments in different ways. As we continue using nodes over the next few chapters, we'll explore new reasons for adding nodes and how to configure them.

Fixing Specific Areas with Power Windows

Even though we've added a second node, corrections still get applied to the entire image. We only want to correct the hot spot in the image. Resolve has a number of methods to isolate areas. One of the easiest to use is called the Power Window. Power Windows are shapes like circles, rectangles or splines used to isolate an area you want to adjust.

1. Double click the Hot Spot node in the Node editor to make sure it is selected.

2. To hide the timeline thumbnails and enlarge the viewer by pressing Option- F (OS X) or Alt-F (Windows) or choosing Workspace >Viewer Mode > Enhanced Viewer.

3. Click the Power Windows button in the toolbar.

The Power windows panel displays a list of shapes used to isolate areas of an image.

4. Click the circle Power Window to add it to the image.

Click the circle shape too add a circular Power Window to the shot.

When you add a Power Window, it gets applied to the selected node and displayed in the viewer. On screen controls are used to transform the shape to fit your subject.

5. In the viewer, drag the circle to the lower left corner of the frame. Use the handles to reshape the circle so it fits around the brightest part of the highlight.

Use the handles and rotation control to fit the shape around the highlight.

216

Any adjustments made on node 02 will only apply inside the Power Window. Applying a softness to the shape will blend it in more with the image

6. In the Power Windows panel, adjust the softness parameter to around 7.0.

Increase the softness to blend adjustments in the shape, with the image outside the shape.

Now we will make some adjustments to bring down the hot spot.

7. In the Primaries Bars, drag the Gain Master Wheel down to around 0.75.

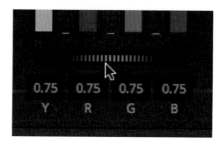

Decrease the Gain to lessen the glare of the hot spot.

8. To hide the onscreen control, click the On Screen Transform Controls button in the lower left of the viewer, and choose Off from the menu.

To hide the On Screen controls used the On Screen Transform Controls button.

Instead of bypassing the entire grade to compare it with the original, we can disable only the current node, which contains the Power Window adjustment. This will allow us to still view the neutral grade on node 01.

9. Press Command-D (OS X) or Ctrl-D (Windows), to disable node 02 with the Power Window.

10. Press Command-D (OS X) or Ctrl-D (Windows), to re-enable node 02 with the Power Window.

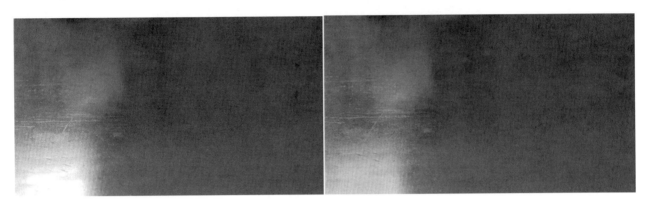

The hot spot before (left) and after (right) the Power Window adjustment.

11. Choose File > Save Project to save the entire project.

At this point you have completed this chapter but you will continue using this same project in the next chapter to create some more sophisticated grades.

Using the Viewers for Color Grading

As we mentioned earlier, Resolve's viewers are not intended to be displays used for color critical work, especially for television broadcast or digital cinema. However, not everyone has a calibrated monitor or DLP, and some people have no need for one, since the majority of their work is for web or tablets.

In those cases, all you have are the Resolve viewers. The most important thing you can do for yourself is to calibrate your Mac OS or Windows display.

OS X and ColorSync

On the OS X version of DaVinci Resolve 12.5 or later, there is a check box in the Project Settings Color Management panel labeled Use Mac Display Color Profile for Viewers. When enabled, this setting uses the current Apple ColorSync profile to color manage the Viewers.

In OS X El Capitan or later, ColorSync includes a Rec. 709 profile with gamma set to 2.22 and a P3 profile for digital cinema. These profiles are not intended to replace an external calibrated display since the standard profiles are generic to your Mac model. They only approximate the response of your display. Unless you are consciously using a Rec. 709, P3 or sRGB profile, in most cases you would disable the Mac Display Color Profile setting. However, if your color profile is attempting to match an external monitor by using a specific icc ColorSync profile, then this might be helpful. For instance, if you are on a 5K iMac, then setting ColorSync to a P3 setting and enabling this option in Resolve can give good results in the absence of a true, digital cinema projector.

If you have not calibrated you Mac monitor for REC 709 or P3, disable the Use Mac Display setting.

Chapter 11 Test Questions

Q1: What format is used to bring a timeline from Premiere Pro into Resolve?

Q2: How do you access the Color page?

Q3: What happens to the timeline you had loaded in the Edit page, when you switch to the Color page?

Q4: Lift roughly equate to:

A) Highlights

B) Midtones

C) Shadows

D) None of the Above

Q5: What are Nodes used for?

Ch. 12: Color Correcting Multiple Shots
Node editor modes and copying grades

I think we can all agree that every project you work on will have more than one shot, so learning how to quickly group and grade multiple shots that appear to be in the same location at the same time, is an important step in color grading.

The previous chapter, focused on a few of the basic tools for balancing one shot. This chapter will focus on ways to quickly copy corrections to others shots, as well as making adjustments to multiple shots simultaneously.

Applying Stills to Clips

In the previous chapter you saved a Still from a neutral balance you created for the shot of the woman working on the bench. That Still is saved in the Gallery. Looking at our timeline, there are other clips from this same scene of the woman working on the bench that need the same neutral balance correction.

1. To show the timeline thumbnails press Option- F (OS X) or Alt-F (Windows) or choose Workspace >Viewer Mode > Enhanced viewer.

2. Select the two remaining shots of the woman working on the bench by clicking thumbnail #23, holding Command (OS X) or Ctrl (Windows) click on thumbnail #35.

Select thumbnails @23 and #35 in the timeline.

3. Middle-mouse-click on the Still in the Gallery or right-click over the Still and choose Apply Grade.

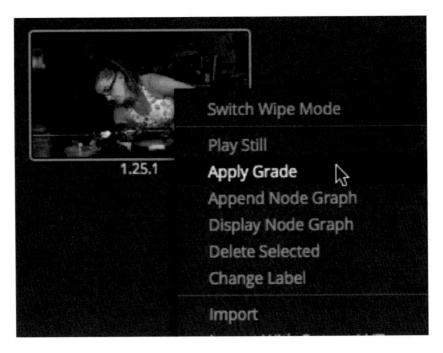

Right-click over the Still and choose Apply Grade to add the correction to the selected clips.

The correction is now added to the two clips, but how can you be sure? All the clips with some kind of color adjustment applied, have a rainbow colored outline around their thumbnail number.

A rainbow outline indicates the clip has some form of color adjustment applied.

Balancing Shots with a Color Chart

Cinematographers can help achieve a natural or *neutral* grade by recording a clip with a standardized color reference chart for each lighting set up. Then, in Resolve you can analyze the chart to calculate any correction required. All the shots taken with the same lighting set up, can use the same correction. In Resolve this process is called Color Match.

An X-Rite Color Checker chart.

1. Press Option-F (OS X) or Alt-F (Windows) or choose Workspace > Viewer Mode > Enhanced viewer to display the normal viewer.

2. In the timeline, drag the playhead right until you are on clip thumbnail # 28 and it is displayed in the viewer.

A shot with the color chart must be inserted into your timeline.

This clip has been temporarily inserted into our timeline, so we have a clip with a color chart. It can be removed after we create the analysis and copy the correction to the other clips captured under the same lighting set up.

3. On the left side of the Color page toolbar, click the Color Match button.

The Color Match button in the toolbar.

The first step is to select the correct color chart captured in your clips.

4. From the upper right area of the Color Match panel, click the X-Rite Color Checker pop-up menu.

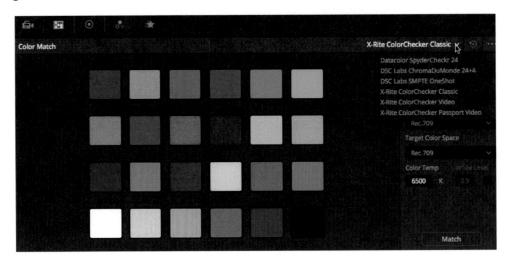

Select the correct chart from the pop up menu.

Resolve offers four choices from the pop-up menu in the Color Match panel. The color chart we used on set happens to be the default, X-Rite Color Checker Classic. Since our menu is set correctly already, we won't select anything new in the menu.

5. Click the pop-up menu again to close it, leaving it on the X-Rite Color Checker Classic.

You must also set the Gamma setting of your source clips. In our case, we already used the Project Color Management system back in Chapter 1 to set our clips and timeline color space to Rec. 709. So, these settings can be left alone.

TIP: *Color Match is a color operation that is calculated after the Camera RAW adjustments, Color Management setting or an Input LUT.*

Set the correct Source Gamma, Target Gamma and Color Space.

The last step before analyzing the chart is to align the color chart overlay in the viewer to the color chart in your clip.

6. Under the viewer, click the tool pop-up menu and choose Color Chart.

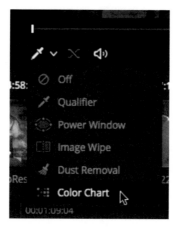

Choose Color Chart from the tool pop-up menu under the viewer.

Each sampling box should line up with the actual color patches of the chart in the clip. To make this easier, we can expand the viewer by hiding the timeline and thumbnails.

7. Press Option-F (OS X) or Alt-F (Windows) or choose Workspace > Viewer Mode > Enhanced viewer.

8. Drag the corners of the color chart overlay to align it with the chart in your clip. Be careful not to include the shadow in the lower left, on the white patch. If included, it will impact the accuracy of the analysis.

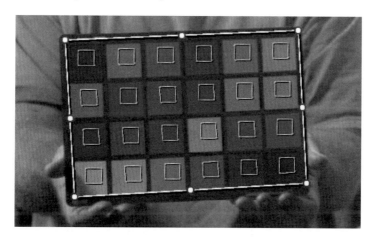

Align the overlay in the viewer with the color patches in your clip.

TIP: *When shooting the sample grid, make sure the entire chart is evenly lit. Uneven lighting can impact the match.*

9. At the bottom of the Color Match panel, click the Match button.

   The clip is adjusted to be color neutral with no color cast. You can compare what it looked like before the Color Match if you bypass the adjustment.

10. Under the viewer, click the tool pop-up menu and choose Off to hide the overlay.

11. Press Shift-D or choose Viewer > Bypass All Grades to view the original image, then press Shift-D again to view the clip with the Color Match adjustment.

Before Color Match (left), and after (right).

   You can now take the adjustment from this temporary clip, and copy it to all the clips shot with the same lighting set up.

12. Press Option-F (OS X) or Alt-F (Windows) or choose Workspace > Viewer Mode > Enhanced viewer to display the thumbnails again.

13. Press the down arrow to move to the next thumbnail (Number 29), then press the = (equal) key on your keyboard or choose Color > Apply Grade From One Clip Prior.

   The Color Match adjustment is now applied to the selected clip. The next five clips use the same lighting set up, so the adjustment will be the same. You can apply the correction to the next five clips.

14. Do the same for the next five clips. Press the down arrow, then press =.

You've now balanced seven clips in a few, quick steps. If you had used a color chart for every lighting set up, your color balancing job would be easy. Since it is not often the case, we need to learn another way to balance our shots.

Using Shot Match

Color Match is great for bringing color continuity to a group of clips recorded under the same lighting set up, but what about those clips recorded under a different lighting set up? If they are in the same scene and same location, but use a different lighting set up, you still want them to appear similar. Shot Match is an incredibly quick way to bring continuity to clips with different lighting set ups and even shot with different cameras.

1. Select thumbnail # 25 in the timeline.

Thumbnail #25 is the reference clip that others should match.

This clip has the right exposure and color balance that you would like for other glass blowing action shots.

2. Select thumbnail # 26 in the timeline.

Thumbnail #26 is the clip you want to adjust.

This clip was recorded at a different time, under a different lighting set up. Still, it is recorded in the same studio. To bring the look of the two clips closer together, we can have Shot Match adjust thumbnail #26 to be closer in tone to #25.

3. Right-click (Control-click on OS X) over thumbnail #25, your reference clip.

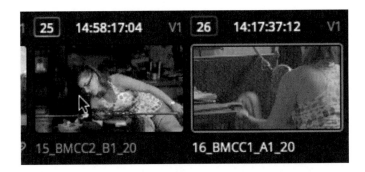

Select the target clip(s), then right-click over the reference clip.

4. From the contextual menu, choose Shot Match to This Clip.

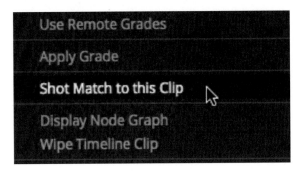

From the contextual menu, choose Shot Match to This Clip

Shot Match does some internal calculations to make the selected clip have the same color and tone as the clip you right-clicked over. Now let's compare the original clip with the new Shot Matched version.

5. Choose View > Bypass All Grades or press Shift-D, to view the original image, then press Shift-D again to view the clip with the Shot Match enabled.

Reference Clip (left), before Shot match (center) after Shot Match (right).

Shot Match is not meant for clips that already appear similar. Shot Match works best when the shots are not close to each other in terms of brightness, contrast and color.

Filtering the Color Timeline

Unlike editing, when you are making color adjustments to clips, you do not necessarily deal with them in the order they are strung out in the timeline. You often want to filter the timeline to see all the clips from the same source file, or clips from the same scene. This way you can quickly apply color adjustments to all the clips that require a common treatment. Similar to creating a Smart bin, you can filter the Color page timeline to show only the specific clips that you want to deal with.

1. In the upper right corner of the interface toolbar, click the down arrow next to the Clips button.

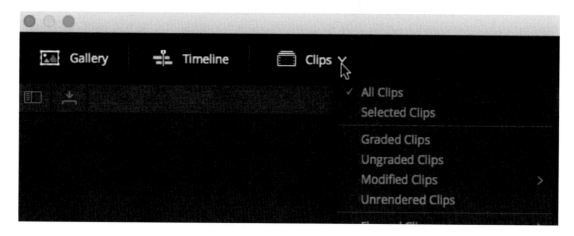

The Clips interface toolbar pop up menu displays filtering options for the timeline

The Clips menu allows you to filter the timeline based on a number of preset criteria, or you can create a Smart Filter, similar to creating a Smart bin.

2. From the Clips pop-up menu choose Create Smart Filter.

The Clips Smart Filter dialog works similarly to the Smart Bins dialog.

You can enter different criteria in the Smart Filter dialog to determine which clips are displayed in the timeline. We'll create a filter based on the clip names.

3. From the Color Timeline Properties menu choose Metadata-Clip Details.

Choose Metadata- Clip Details for the first criteria menu.

The remaining two pop-up menus in the dialog are set correctly for us to filter the timeline based on the clip's name (File name). Now we'll just enter the clip name we are looking for. All of the interview clips end with "..TJ_EXT" so we will look for that.

4. Enter TJ_EXT in the final field, then click Create Smart Filter.

Enter the file name you are looking for and then click Create Smart Filter.

The timeline now displays only the clips that contain TJ_EXT in the name. That happens to be all the external interview shots. We can now use that filtered timeline to create a group.

Creating Groups

When you have multiple clips requiring the same adjustment, like our filtered timeline, rather than copying the correction from one clip to another, you can group clips together so any correction made to one clip, gets applied to all the clips in the group.

1. Select the first thumbnail #01, then hold the Shift key and select the last thumbnail #08 in the timeline.

Select all the clips in the filtered timeline.

These are eight interview clips that should receive the same balance adjustments. Putting them in a group will allow us to correct one, but have the adjustments applied to all them.

2. Right-click over any of the selected clips and choose Add into a New Group.

3. Type Ext Interview as the Group name, then click OK.

   A small Link badge appears on each thumbnail assigned to the group.

Clips in a group have a small link badge added to their thumbnail when selected.

Using Groups to Adjust Multiple Clips

Once you create the Group, the Node editor modes pop-up menu allows you to choose if the adjustments you make are applied to all the clips in the Group or only to the selected clip.

1. Click the first thumbnail in the group.

2. From the Node editor mode pop-up menu choose Group Pre Clip.

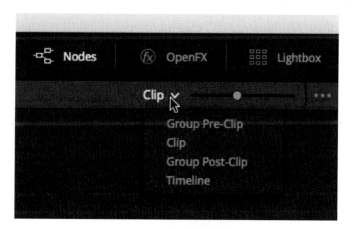

Choose Group Pre Clip from the mode pop-up.

The Node editor modes pop-up menu includes four options:

- The Clip option is the default setting. Adjustments you make are only applied to the one selected clip.

- The Group Pre Clip setting applies adjustments to all the clips in the group *prior* to applying any adjustments you created on a single clip, in the Clip mode.

- The Group Post Clip setting applies adjustments to all the clips in the group *after* applying any adjustments you created on a single clip, in the Clip mode.

- The Timeline Group applies adjustments too all the clips on your timeline regardless of which group they are in.

This may seem like no big deal, but the order of color operations has a big impact on the results. For example, applying a desaturation, then a tint has a very different look than first applying a tint, then a desaturation.

Example: Desaturated first and then tinted (left), tinted and then desaturated (right).

TIP: *Clips can only belong to one Group. Removing a Clip from a Group will remove any Pre Clip or Post Clip corrections applied.*

With the Node mode pop up set to Pre-Clip, we'll create a balanced correction for all of the clips.

3. Set the Video Scopes pop-up menu to Parade.

4. In the upper right corner of the Primaries Bars, choose Primaries Wheels from the pop-up menu.

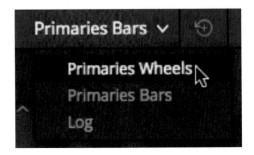

Choose Primaries Wheels from the pop up menu.

5. Adjust the Lift Master Wheel to set the black point just above 0 line in the parade.

6. Adjust the Gain Master Wheel to set the White point just below the 1023 line in the parade.

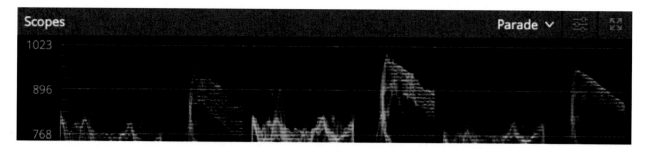

Set the brightest white to be below the 1023 line in the parade.

7. Adjust the Gamma Master Wheel until the Y value reads 0.04, this will brighten up the mid tones.

8. Adjust the Lift and Gain Color Balance control to correct for any color cast in the shadows and highlights, as you did in the previous chapter.

Drag the Color Balance Indicator to correct any color cast.

9. In the Shared Adjustment controls, click the page 2 button

    Two unique and useful controls on page 2 are the Color Boost and Midtone Detail. Color Boost is used to increase the saturation of non-saturated colors, like skin tones.

10. Drag the Color Boost field to the right until the value reaches 10.

Color boost can be used to add vibrancy to an image.

Unlike Saturation which increases all colors equally, sometimes you just need to boost skin tone color and Color Boost is the perfect adjustment.

Midtone detail is a sharpening adjustment. It can be used to add more definition to edges. It can also be used, with a small negative value, to soften the image.

11. In the Midtone detail field, drag to the right until the value reaches - 20.

Now let's compare the corrections you have made to the original image.

12. Choose View > Bypass All Grades, or press Shift-D, to disable all color adjustments.

Before (left) and after (right) adding negative Midtone detail.

13. Choose View > Bypass All Grades, or press Shift-D, to enable the color adjustments.

TIP: *To reset a Shared Adjustment control, double-click the name or icon of the parameter that you want to reset.*

14. Click each thumbnail in the timeline to view the changes made to each clip.

TIP: *You must be careful when working with groups. Anytime you click on a thumbnail not in a group, the Node editor switches to the Clip setting. If you return to a clip in a group, the Node editor will still be set to Clip.*

After clicking through the clips, you more than likely noticed the last three clips have a decidedly different lighting condition. The sunlight has come out making the last three shots considerably brighter than the first five. Switching the Node mode menu to Clip, will allow us to make corrections to any clip individually.

15. Click thumbnail #06 in the group.

16. From the Node editor mode pop-up menu choose Clip.

Switch the Node editor mode pop-up menu to Clip to adjust clips individually.

Any adjustments made now, will only be applied to the selected clip.

17. Drag the Offset Master Wheel to the left until the graph in the Parade scope reaches the bottom of the 0 line.

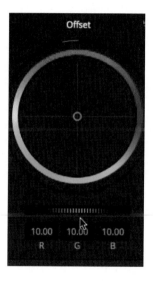

Adjust the Offset Master Wheel to shift the entire image darker.

18. In the Shared Adjustments decrease the Color Boost to -15.00.

19. Press the up arrow on the keyboard to show the previous clip, then press the down arrow to compare it with your adjusted clip. You can go back and tweak any adjustment you think needs to be fine tuned.

Each option in the Node editor mode pop-up menu is suitable for a specific task and often switching between them in necessary. The Pre Clip option is useful for balancing similar shots, while the Clip option helps to make adjustments on clips individually.

Making Adjustments to the Entire Timeline

In the previous exercise, we used the Group Pre Clip to apply a neutral grade to multiple clips at once. In cases where you want to make an adjustment to the entire timeline, you can use the timeline group from the Node editor mode pop menu.

235

1. To remove the Smart Filter and view all the timeline thumbnails, click the down arrow next to the Clips button and choose All Clips.

Choose All Clips from the Clips interface pop up menu.

2. Select thumbnail #07 in the timeline.

3. From the Node editor mode pop-up menu choose timeline.

Choose Timeline from the Node editor mode pop-up.

When you select the Timeline group from the Node editor pop-up menu, it is empty. You need to add a node, and connect it to the Source Input and the Node Tree Output.

4. Right-click in the empty Node editor and choose Add Node > Corrector.

5. To connect the node, drag from the Source Input to the node's RGB input.

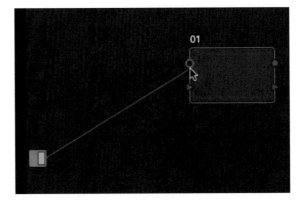

Drag from the Source Input to the RGB Input on the node.

6. Drag from the node's RGB output to the Node Tree Output.

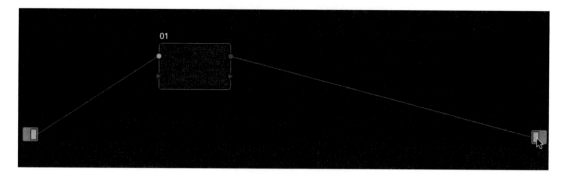

Drag from the node's RGB output to the Node Tree Output.

TIP: *To remove a connection from a node, click the connection line and press Delete (OS X) or Backspace (Windows)*

Now, with a Timeline Group Node set up and ready to go, in the next exercise you'll actually add the effect to the entire timeline.

Applying Presets from the Gallery Window

A common adjustment to apply over an entire timeline (and I admit there are not too many) is a vignette. A vignette is easy enough to create, but Resolve also provides a number of commonly used color adjustments as presets. These presets called Looks, are found in the Gallery window. No, not the Gallery you used earlier, that's the small Gallery. The Gallery window is a larger area for organizing your Stills, copying them between projects, and for accessing a dedicated collection of DaVinci Resolve Looks.

1. Choose Workspace > Gallery from the main menu bar.

   The Stills navigator in the Gallery window, is used to access saved Stills from other projects, as well as DaVinci Resolve Looks. DaVinci Resolve Looks are a collection of color correction presets provided with the application.

2. On the left side of the Gallery window, click the disclosure arrow for the DaVinci Resolve Looks, then select the Scene category.

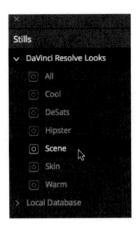

Click the Scene Category in the DaVinci Resolve Looks.

To use a Look, you drag it onto a node in the Node editor.

3. Arrange the Gallery window so you are able to see the Node editor.

4. Drag the Vignette Look onto the node in the Node editor.

Drag the Vignette Still onto the node in the Node editor.

5. Click the Close button in the upper left corner of the Gallery window.

    Now you can modify the Vignette for a softer appearance. The Lift, Gamma and Gain are all modified to make the Vignette darker. It is a bit too dark for my taste, so we will lessen it by removing the Gain and Lift adjustments.

6. In the Color Wheels panel, click the Lift and Gain color wheel reset buttons.

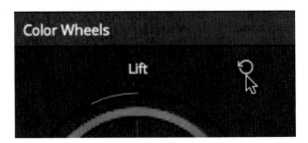

Click the Lift and Gain reset buttons to remove it from the Vignette.

7. To add blur to the Vignette, click the Blur button in the toolbar.

Click the Blur button in the toolbar to open the Blur panel.

8. Drag the Radius RGB slider up to 0.75 to increase the amount of blur.

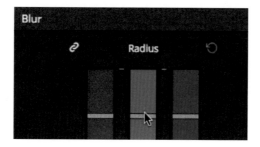

Drag the Blur Radius to increase the blur.

9. To change the size and shape of the Vignette, click the On Screen Transform Controls button and from the menu choose Power Window.

10. Drag any corner handle on the blue rectangle to slightly increase the sides of the oval.

11. Click the On Screen Transform Controls button, and from the menu choose Off.

Set the On Screen Transform Control pop-up to Off to hide the on screen controls.

12. Click on a few thumbnails to view the vignette added to every clip in the timeline.

13. We'll use this timeline in the next chapter, so choose File > Save Project

These are the basic steps to create a neutral color correction on your clips. Some projects may only require these minor adjustments, while other projects will require a larger effort. No matter how tempting it is to skip these steps and jump directly into creating unique looks, to get the best results, you need to start each clip from a corrected, neutral baseline.

Chapter 12 Test Questions

Q1: How do you apply a Still to a clip?

Q2: What are Groups used for in the Color page?

    A) Applying Grades to multiple clips.

    B) To make the timeline neater.

    C) To cut, copy and paste multiple clips

    D) All of the Above.

    E) None of the Above.

Q3: In order for Color Match to work, what is required in the frame?

Q4: True or False: Shot Match only matches clips from the same source clip?

Q5: True or False: A Smart Filter shows and hides clips in the Color page timeline based on criteria you define?

Ch. 13: Grading
Curves, Nodes and Versions

Color correction and color grading are two terms often used interchangeably. If we really want to be accurate, color correction was the process we just covered, and for many projects creating that neutral grade maybe all you need to do. Color Grading is when you create an overall look or color style for your project. When you are color grading you aren't worried about keeping things neutral. You are trying to create atmosphere to help sell the story.

In this chapter, we will recreate a few popular styles you've seen in feature films, television shows and commercials. The goal isn't really to recreate these looks perfectly, it is to use these looks as a vehicle for learning a broader range of tools.

Adding Clips to a Group

Throughout this chapter, we'll use the timeline you imported and balanced in the previous two chapters. While the Primaries Wheels tend to be the first place people gravitate towards, there are other tools that can handle similar tasks. In this exercise, we'll start to develop your grading skills by creating a unique look using Custom curves. Let's begin by making a group of all the clips we want to create the look for.

1. Open the Color Correction project and click the Color page button, if necessary.

2. Select thumbnail #30 in the timeline.

Select the in-door interview to display it in the viewer.

We are going to group the clips that will share this look. In some complex looks, Groups can add more complexity than they are worth, but on simple grades, like this first one, Groups can come in handy. First, we'll locate all the clips that belong together.

3. From the Clips pop-up in the Interface toolbar, choose Common Media Pool Source.

To display clips from the same source file as the selected clip, choose Common Media Pool Source.

All the clips that came from the same source clip as the selected clip, are displayed.

4. Select the four clips, then right-click over one and choose Add into New Group.

Add all four clips into a new Group.

5. Type **Int Multicam Interview** as the Group name and click OK.

There are other clips that were recorded at the same time as part of the second camera angle in the multicamera set up. We'll add those to the group as well.

242

6. From the Clips pop-up menu in the Interface toolbar, choose All Clips.

7. Select thumbnail #29.

Select the CU camera from the in-door interview multicamera scene.

8. From the Clips pop-up menu, choose Common Media Pool Source.

9. Select the three clips, then right-click over them and choose Add to Current Group.

Choose Add into Current Group from the pop up menu.

The Current Group is defined as the Group that contains the last clip you selected. So now, the Int interview clips along with these CU shots of the tool are all added into the same Int Multicam Interview group.

10. From the Clips pop-up menu in the Interface toolbar, choose All Clips.

11. From the Node editor mode menu, choose Group Post Clip.

Select Group Post Clip from the Node editor mode menu.

With the group created, you can set the Node editor mode pop-up to Group Post Clip. When set to Group Post Clip, any new grade you create will be applied after the neutral balance that you created earlier on these clips.

Color Grading with Curves

In this exercise, you'll create the very common Hollywood Blockbuster look using Custom curves. It's a look that has been used regularly on big budget action films and TV shows for most of the past decade. The core of the look uses complimentary colors of teal for the shadows and orange for skin tones. The goal is to make the skin tones pop out from the background, but tightly control the cross over of the colors.

1. Select thumbnail #30. Since we are using Groups, the grade we create will apply to all the clips.

2. Choose Workspace >Viewer Mode > Enhanced viewer or press Option- F (OS X) or Alt-F (Windows) to expand the viewer.

3. Click the Curves button in the toolbar to show the Curves palette.

Click the Curves button in the toolbar.

The Custom curves are displayed under the viewer in the default Color page layout. There are four curves, one for each RGB color component and one for luminance. Our look starts by adding more contrast using the luminance curve.

4. At the top of the Curve controls, click the Y button to get a curve for luminance.

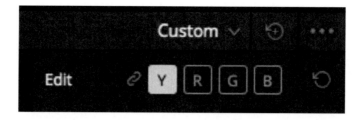

Click the luminance button to make adjustments on the luminance curve.

The Curve editor is a plot graph for making subtle, but incredibly flexible adjustments to specific tonal ranges of images. The X axis is the image's tonal values going from the darkest shadows on the left, and brightest highlights on the right. Along the Y axis are the output or offset values with darker adjustments being lower in the graph and brighter adjustments being higher.

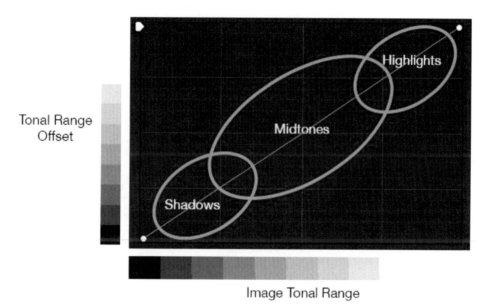

Image Tonal Range

The X axis is the original tonal value (input), the Y axis is the change to the original tonal value (output).

The benefit of color grading with curves is that they allow for great flexibility and very specific changes to narrow tonal ranges of your image. You make these adjustments by adding anchor points along the diagonal line, then dragging those points up to make the tonal area brighter, or down to make it darker. Two anchor points are already given to you. The one in the lower left represents the black point and the one in the upper right represents the white point. These work similarly to the Master Wheels for Lift and Gain.

5. To compress the black point, making your darkest point darker, drag the anchor point in the lower left, to the right about half way to the first major grid line.

Dragging the lower left anchor point is similar to adjusting the Lift Master Wheel in the Color Wheels panel.

Compressing the range with the Black point has a nice de-hazing effect on the image.

To adjust other tonal regions, you need additional anchor points. The easiest way to add an anchor point is by selecting a tonal area from the image with the eye dropper.

6. Hover the pointer over the back of her head, then click to add an Anchor point on the curve.

Use the eye dropper to select a tonal range you want to adjust.

The anchor point is added along the Curve line, where it matches the same tonal range you clicked with the eye dropper. Dragging the anchor point down will darken the image in that range. In our case, it will darken the shadows.

7. Drag the anchor point down, to darken the shadows slightly.

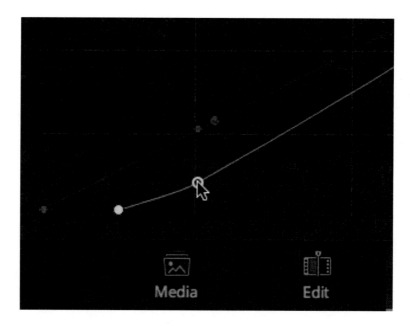

Drag the anchor point to make a tonal adjustment.

The more you offset the control point from its original location, the darker the region will become. To brighten highlights, we'll use the eye dropper again to identify an area in the image with highlights.

8. Hover the pointer over the highlight on the woman's shoulder, then click to add an Anchor point on the curve.

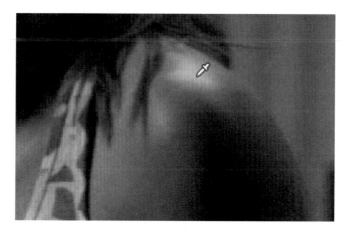

Click the shoulder highlight to add a control point in the highlights areas.

9. Drag the anchor point just above the diagonal red line, to brighten the highlights.

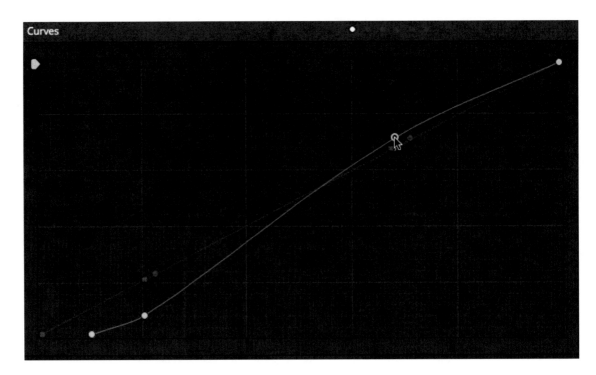

Drag the anchor point up to brighten the highlights.

Creating this S-curve is a typical way of increasing contrast in an image. You can perform similar adjustments using the three different color components of red, green and blue.

TIP: *Clicking on the line will manually add an anchor point, right-clicking the anchor point will remove it from the curve.*

Using Custom Curves to Correct Shadows

Your next goal is to shift the shadows to teal. Could you do this using the Custom curves on the node you've been using? Yes, you could, but to give yourself more control, and an easier way to evaluate different adjustments, you'll use a new node.

1. Choose Workspace >Viewer Mode > Enhanced viewer or press Option- F (OS X) or Alt-F (Windows) to show the Node editor.

2. Choose Nodes > Add Serial Node or press Option-S (OS X) or Alt-S (Windows) to add a node after the current node in the Node editor.

TIP: *You cannot have detached or isolated nodes. All nodes in the Node editor must be connected to other nodes, which eventually connect to the Output.*

3. Choose Workspace >Viewer Mode > Enhanced viewer or press Option- F (OS X) or Alt-F (Windows) to expand the viewer.

To create teal shadows, you mix blue and green. First we'll increase the blue.

4. In the Custom curves controls, click the B button to limit changes to the blue channel.

Click the Y, R, G B buttons to select a color channel or luminance channel to modify.

Instead of adding anchor points with the eye dropper, you can instantly add four Anchor points using the Options menu. The Anchor points are placed in default locations along the curve line to divide the image into shadows, low midtones, medium midtones, high midtones and highlights.

5. From the Curve Options menu choose Add Default Anchors.

You can add four default anchors to divide the image into five tonal regions.

6. Drag the shadows control point up to increase the blue in the shadow areas.

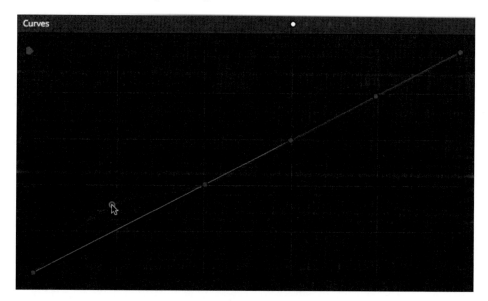

Increase the blue shadows.

Teal is created by mixing blue and green, so you need to add green to the shadows. You won't add as much green as you did for blue, only about half as much.

7. In the Custom curves controls, click the G button to enable the green channel, and then from the Curve Options menu, choose Add Default Anchors.

8. Drag the shadows anchor point up slightly to increase the green in the shadow areas. Stop dragging when the background is tinted a dark teal color.

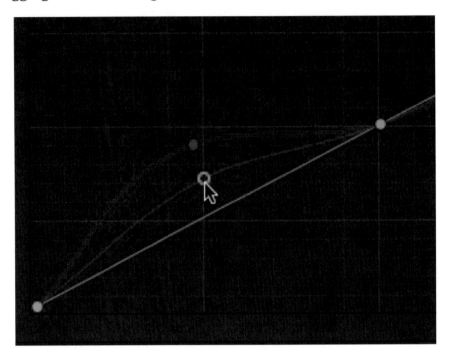

Add green to the shadows until the background is more teal than blue.

Using Custom Curves to Correct Midtones

Your next goal is to bring more orange into the skin tones. And once again we will organize our adjustments into separate nodes.

1. Choose Workspace >Viewer Mode > Enhanced viewer or press Option- F (OS X) or Alt-F (Windows) to show the Node editor.

2. Choose Nodes > Add Serial Node or press Option-S (OS X) or Alt-S (Windows) to add a node after the current node in the Node editor.

3. Choose Workspace >Viewer Mode > Enhanced viewer or press Option- F (OS X) or Alt-F (Windows) to expand the viewer.

You can start adjusting skin tones by adjusting the red color component.

4. In the Curve controls, click the Red Channel button, and from the menu, choose Add Default Anchors.

Add Default Anchors from the Options menu.

Skin tones mostly fall in the midtones, but we also want any adjustments to spread out into the highlights a bit. To do that, we will remove the highlight anchor point

5. Right-click over the second from top anchor point to delete it.

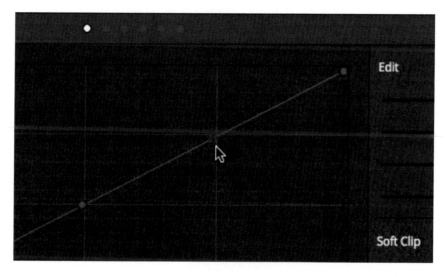

Remove an anchor point by right-clicking over it.

6. Drag the anchor point to the left, up to increase the red in the mid tones.

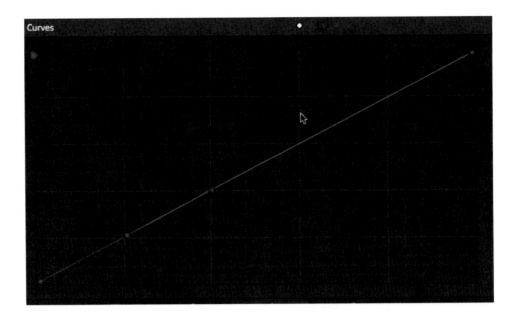

Increase the red midtones using one of the mid tone anchor points.

That adds red, but to add orange we need to include some green in there. Again, not as much as the red, but maybe half as much.

7. In the Curve controls, click the Green Channel button, and from the menu, choose Add Default Anchors.

8. Right-click over the top, highlight control point to delete it.

9. Drag the green midtone anchor point up slightly, to make the skin more orange.

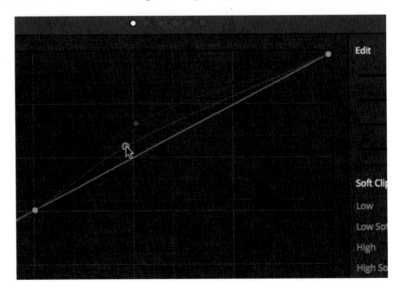

Drag the green midtone anchor point to create an orange color skin tone.

To compare the image before the Group Post Clip curve adjustments, but still with the color balanced clip adjustments, you can disable all the nodes in the current Node editor mode group.

10. Press Option-D (OS X) or Alt-D (Windows) to view the color balanced shot without the Group Post Clip curve adjustments. Press Option-D or Alt-D again to enable the curve adjustments.

Original (left) and after color balance (center) after curve adjustments (right).

Using Hue Curves to Modify Skin Tone

To move the look forward, let's see how far we can push the skin tones before we end up with an Oompa loompa. To do more skin tone work, we can add another serial node and make our adjustments in the new node.

1. Choose Workspace >Viewer Mode > Enhanced viewer or press Option- F (OS X) or Alt-F (Windows) to view the Node editor.

2. Choose Nodes > Add Serial Node or press Option-S (OS X) or Alt-S (Windows)

3. Choose Workspace >Viewer Mode > Enhanced viewer or press Option- F (OS X) or Alt-F (Windows) to expand the viewer again.

   When targeting one specific hue in an image, Resolve includes a number of useful Hue curves. Using a Hue vs Hue curve is one way to adjust skin tones. The Hue vs Hue curve is able to select a specific hue range and shift it towards another hue.

4. From the Curves mode pop-up menu, choose Hue vs Hue.

To access different Curve controls, select the curve from the Curves mode pop-up menu .

An eye dropper is used to select the hue directly from the image.

5. Move the pointer anywhere on the woman's far shoulder, then click the eyedropper pointer to sample the skin tone hue you want to change.

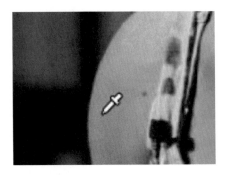

Sample the area you want to adjust using the eye dropper.

A control point is added along the Hue line precisely where the sampled hue is located. Moving the control point up or down will shift the hue.

6. Ever so slightly, drag the middle control point down, to shift the hue away from red and towards orange. Be careful not to move it too much that she turns jaundice.

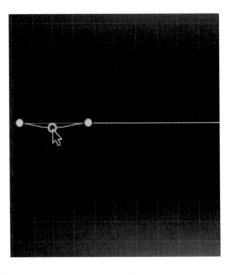

Drag the middle control point down just a hair to shift the skin hue.

Now we can use another Hue curve to control the saturation of the specific color.

7. From the Curves mode pop-up menu, choose Hue vs Sat.

8. Move your pointer in a similar area on the woman's far shoulder, then click the eyedropper pointer to select the skin tone hue.

9. Drag the middle control point up, to increase the skin tone, just below Oompa Loompa land.

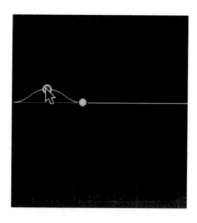

Drag the middle control point down just a hair to shift the skin hue.

10. Press the down arrow key to view the next three clips with the new grade applied.

11. Press the up arrow three times to return to the clip you have been working on.

    You've completed your Hollywood Blockbuster look. If you like, you can continue to tweak this clip individually, by switching to Clip mode in the Node editor mode menu.

Saving Stills from Groups

You already know how to save a Still using the Gallery from a previous chapter, but Stills saved from groups are a bit different. Stills saved to the Gallery only save the nodes based on the Node editor mode pop up setting. If you want to save the Nodes from the Group Post Clip, you must set the Node editor pop-up to that mode.

1. Choose Workspace >Viewer Mode > Enhanced viewer or press Option- F (OS X) or Alt-F (Windows) to view the timeline thumbnails.

2. Make sure the Node editor mode pop-up is still set to Group Post-Clip.

3. Right-Click over the Viewer and choose Grab Still.

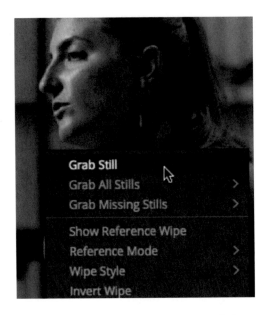

Save a Still to the Gallery using the right-click menu.

4. In the Gallery right-click over the saved Still and choose Change Label.

5. Type Hollywood Blockbuster as the Still's name.

    No, really. Go back and name the Still. You are going to need it in the next chapter.

6. From the Node editor mode pop-up, choose Clip.

    You'll now save a Still for the color balance adjustments you created.

7. Right-Click over the viewer and choose Grab Still.

8. In the Gallery right-click over the saved Still and choose Change Label.

9. Type INT Interview Color Balance as the Still's name.

Stills are saved in the Gallery with a still frame and all the adjustments you have made.

Now that these adjustments are saved, we are going to begin to work on a completely new look for a new shot.

Saving Versions

Before you begin a new grade, you can give it a name as a way to compare it to other grades you may create on the same shot. Versions are a way to name and save your color grading work and easily recall it at a later time. You can either create Versions for a single segment in the timeline or linked across timelines to all clips originating from the same source clip, called Remote versions. Since the majority of our clips do not stem from a larger master source clip, we'll use local versions.

1. Right-click over the thumbnail # 07 and from the contextual menu, choose Local Versions > Create New Version.

The versions contextual menu.

2. In the New Version dialog, type SoCal, then click OK.

With the version named, we can begin creating the look in the next exercise. Each clip can have as many versions as you want. Later in this chapter, we'll use this Version and another one we create, to compare them side by side in the viewer, and pick a winner.

Using Qualifiers

The last look was your typical, over the top Hollywood blockbuster look, aimed at introducing you to different Curves and creating a grade with multiple serial nodes together. The look we will create in this exercise will be a bit more natural, but also a tiny bit more involved. We will create a warmer, southern California sunset grade. That's probably not too far off from where and when this was shot. It will be subtle, but it will also explore a number of different tools. Let's start by setting up our workspace and applying a slightly warmer tone from the neutral one we created in the previous chapter.

1. Choose Clip from the Node editor mode menu.

Choose Clip from the Node editor mode pop up menu.

Our new look will be created for the EXT interview shot using the Node editor mode menu set to Clip. It will become clear to you towards the end of this grade, why the Group Pre Clip and Group Post Clip options will not work. For right now, just know this grade will not be automatically applied to each clip in the group.

2. Choose Workspace >Viewer Mode > Enhanced viewer or press Option- F (OS X) or Alt-F (Windows) to expand the viewer again.

3. In the Primaries Master Wheel panel, set the Lift Master Wheel to - 0.02, causing the black point to be darker.

4. Set the Gain Master Wheel to 1.03 to increase the white point.

Moving the black point down and the white point up is another way of increasing contrast in a clip.

5. Set the Gamma Master Wheel to 0.05 to increase the midtones.

Increase the contrast and brighten the mid tones by adjusting the Master Wheels.

6. On page 2 of the Shared Adjustments increase the Color Boost to 20.

Increase the Color boost to add color to less saturated colors.

7. To disable the selected Node and see the change, choose Nodes > Enable/Disable Current Node or press Command-D (OS X) or Ctrl-D (Windows).

OK, those are just a few minor adjustments to start. There are two main parts to this look. First, we create a nice warm skin tone and then we create a warmer sunset feel. In every grade you always work on skin tone and you do it in different ways. The tactic in this exercise is to isolate the skin tone using a Qualifier.

8. Choose Workspace >Viewer Mode > Enhanced viewer or press Option- F (OS X) or Alt-F (Windows) to display the Node editor.

9. Choose Nodes > Add Serial Node or press Option-S (OS X) or Alt-S (Windows).

10. Choose Workspace >Viewer Mode > Enhanced viewer or press Option- F (OS X) or Alt-F (Windows) to hide the Node editor.

11. Click the Qualifiers button [icon] in the toolbar.

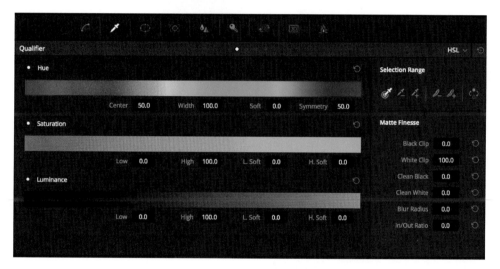

The default HSL Qualifier allows you to select a range based on Hue, Saturation and Luminance.

Qualifiers are ways to select regions of an image based on the red, green or blue channel; hue, saturation or luminance components; or using a traditional blue screen/green screen keyer. Once the sampled region is selected, you can refine the selection to the exact area you are interested in changing. The selected area can then be adjusted using any of the color adjustment tools in Resolve.

12. Move the pointer over the image in the viewer and click the right side of the woman's face to sample her skin tone.

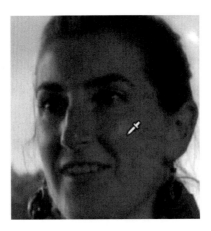

Sample the area you are interested in using the eye dropper.

The sampled area is the area you plan on adjusting, in this case the skin tone. A Highlight control is available at the top of the viewer, to better see the selected region.

13. Click the Highlight button ![icon] in the upper left corner of the viewer, or choose View >Highlight > Highlight.

The sampled region is shown in the actual color. The result of the selection is technically called the matte. A matte is used in many instances, but its basic function is to isolate and protect areas of an image. When evaluating the selected region, you can change the Highlight so the matte is displayed in black and white, sometimes making it easier to make further refinements to the selection.

14. To change the matte to black and white, click the B&W Highlight Overlay button in the upper right corner of the viewer or choose View > Highlight > Highlight BW

The Highlight control above the viewer displays the matte from your selection.

Now comes the fiddling part. There are controls in the HSL Qualifier panel used to hone the matte using hue, saturation and luminance. The goal is to make the matte that represents areas of her skin as uniformly white as possible and the rest of the image as uniformly black as possible. There is no magical formula here, each shot will be different and you will often go back and forth between some of the controls to get it just right. You hardly ever get it completely uniform so don't worry too much.

15. Under the HSL Hue bar, increase the width until her face is almost entirely white.

Use the Hue controls to encompass all the hue found in the subject's face.

16. Adjust the HSL Qualifier Saturation and Luminance controls to make her face as white as possible while keeping other areas as dark as possible.

Make adjustments to make everywhere skin is shown to be white in the matte.

Off to the right of the HSL controls are Matte Finesse controls, which can help fine tune some of the spottiness and "holes" you see in the black and white matte.

17. In the Matte Finesse controls, use the Clean Black and Clean White controls to further refine the white and black areas of the shot, then add a small amount of blur.

The Matte Finesse controls can greatly reduce holes and noise in a matte.

18. To turn off the Highlight, click the Highlight button 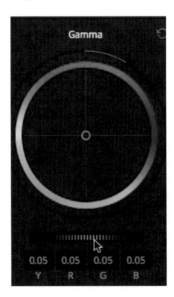 in the upper left corner of the viewer or choose View >Highlight > Highlight.

   Now, with a matte isolating her skin tones from the rest of the image, we can make adjustments to just those areas.

19. To brighten the face a bit, drag the Master Wheel for Gamma to the right, until the Y parameter reaches around 0.05

Use any of the Primaries Wheels controls to make adjustments to the sampled region.

20. Drag the Gamma Color Balance Indicator towards red to add more blush to her face.

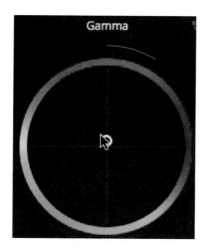

Use Gamma Color Balance Indicator to adjust the hue of skin tones.

21. Press Command-D (OS X) or Ctrl-D (Windows) to disable the selected node and compare the image with and without the skin tone node adjustments.

22. Tweak any parameters to refine the skin tone adjustment as you see fit.

Adding the Warm Sunset with Power Windows

Now, it is time to work on your background. We want to make adjustments to everything except the woman's face, which we just spent a fair amount of time getting just right. After using a Qualifier or a Power Window, Resolve gives you access to a new node. The Outside node reverses the matte selection made from the Qualifier or Power Window, allowing you to make adjustments on everything else.

1. Choose Workspace >Viewer Mode > Enhanced viewer or press Option- F (OS X) or Alt-F (Windows) to display the Node editor.

2. Right-click over the last node with the HSL Qualifier and choose Add Outside node.

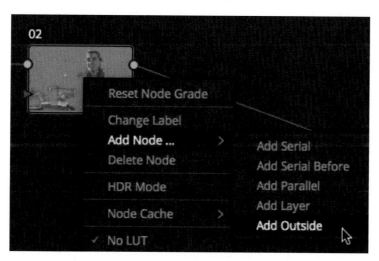

The Outside node inverts a Qualifier or Power Window selection.

The Outside node is added. It shows the RGB color adjustments connected through the connection line with green circles and the matte or alpha connected though the connection line with the teal triangles.

3. Choose Workspace >Viewer Mode > Enhanced viewer or press Option- F (OS X) or Alt-F (Windows) to hide the Node editor.

    To give this shot a brighter, southern California look, we'll boost the blue and green colors for the sky and trees in the background.

4. In the Primaries Wheels, drag the Gamma Color Balance Indicator toward blue to increase the color in the sky.

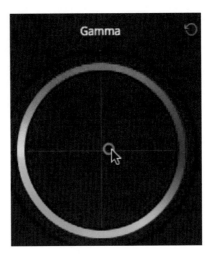

Use the Gamma Color Balance Indicator to increase the blue sky.

5. Drag the Lift Color Balance Indicator toward green to increase the color in the trees.

6. Press Command-D (OS X) or Ctrl-D (Windows) to disable the selected node and compare the image with and without the added color.

7. Choose Workspace >Viewer Mode > Enhanced viewer or press Option- F (OS X) or Alt-F (Windows) to display the Node editor.

    To create a warmer sunset, we'll add another node and use a Gradient Power Window. The Gradient Power Window uses a gradient to gradually apply an adjustment over an area of the image.

8. To create the warmth of a sunset, press Option-S (OS X) or Ctrl-S (Windows) to add another serial node.

9. Choose Workspace >Viewer Mode > Enhanced viewer or press Option- F (OS X) or Alt-F (Windows) to hide the Node editor.

10. Select the Power Windows button 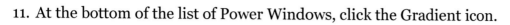 in the toolbar.

11. At the bottom of the list of Power Windows, click the Gradient icon.

The Gradient Power Window applies an adjustment gradually over an area.

Using the two-handle on screen control, you can change the center point, angle and amount of feathering for the gradient.

12. Drag the center handle to the upper left corner, where the sun should be coming from.

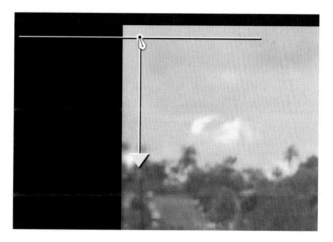

Drag the Gradient Power Window handle to the upper left.

13. Drag the arrow out towards the center of the frame to define the direction and feathering of the gradient.

Drag the arrow to the the center of the frame.

TIP: *To place the Gradient's handle slightly outside the frame, press Command- - (minus) on OS X or Ctrl - - (minus) on Windows to zoom out. Then press Command-Z (OS X) or Ctrl-Z (Windows) to fit the frame in the viewer.*

Next, we can add some color to the gradient.

14. Drag the Gain Color Balance Indicator in the Primaries Wheels towards orange.

    We can add a second Gradient so the sun shines over the entire left side.

15. To add a second Power Window on this node, click the Add Gradient button above the Power Window list.

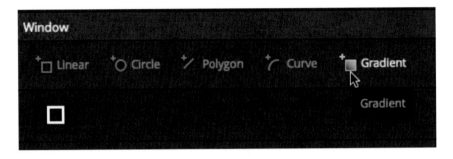

Add a second Gradient Power Window.

16. Drag the second gradient's center handle to the lower left corner of the frame.

Drag the Gradient Power Window handle to the lower left.

17. Drag the arrow out towards the center of the frame.

18. To compare the original image with the new grade, choose View > Bypass All Grades or press Shift-D.

Original image (left) and So Cal grade (right).

This is the basic look we wanted, a warm glowing sunset in southern California. Although this looks good, we still need to evaluate it over the entire length of the clip, not just a frame.

Combining Qualifiers and Power Windows

This image looks good as long we don't play it. When you play the clip there is a lot of noise coming from the matte.

1. Click the Loop Play button  under the viewer.

2. Press Command-F (OS X) or Ctrl-F (Windows), then press spacebar to play the clip full screen.

3. Stop playback after you have see the clip one or two times, then press Command-F (OS X) or Ctrl-F (Windows) to exit full screen.

4. Click the Loop Play button under the viewer to disable it.

    Since the dirt on the road behind her has a similar color and tone as her skin, the changes to her skin were applied to the dirt road as well. You can isolate the color adjustments even more, by combining a Power Window with the Qualifier. The Power Window will further limit the area where the Qualifier adjustments are applied.

5. Move the viewer playhead to the first frame of the clip.

6. Choose Workspace >Viewer Mode > Enhanced viewer or press Option- F (OS X) or Alt-F (Windows) to display the Node editor.

7. In the Node editor, double-click the node 02, the HSL Qualifier node.

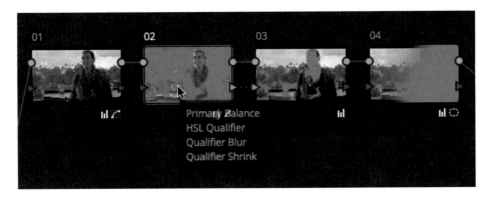

Double-click the skin tone node to select it.

8. In the Power Window list, click the Circle Power Window.

Select the circular Power Window.

9. Drag the circle over the woman's face, then use the handles to reshape it into an oval.

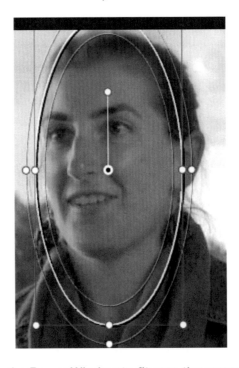

Reshape the Power Window to fit over the woman's face.

To see the area impacted by our adjustments, let's look at the matte.

10. Click the Highlight button 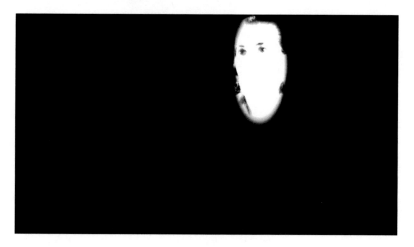, above the viewer.

View the matte to see how the Power Window has eliminated the background noise.

Now, the HSL matte is sampled only from within the Power Window.

11. Click the Highlight button above the viewer to return to the image.

12. To hide the onscreen control, click the On Screen Transform Controls button, and from the menu, choose Off.

We still have one more thing to check before we can move on.

Tracking Power Windows

The Power Window worked great to separate the face from the similarly colored background objects. However, that was only for one frame. You need to check it over the entire clip again.

1. Click the Loop Play button under the viewer.

2. Press Command-F (OS X) or Ctrl-F (Windows), then press spacebar to play the clip full screen.

3. Stop playback after you have see the clip one or two times, then press Command-F (OS X) or Ctrl-F (Windows) to exit full screen.

4. Click the Loop Play button under the viewer to disable it.

   When you play the clip, the woman's head moves, making the oval Power Window ok for some frames but not ok for others. The best way to make sure the Power Window fits over the woman's face, even as she moves, is to use a Tracker.

5. Move to the first frame of the clip, if necessary.

6. Click the Tracker button in the toolbar.

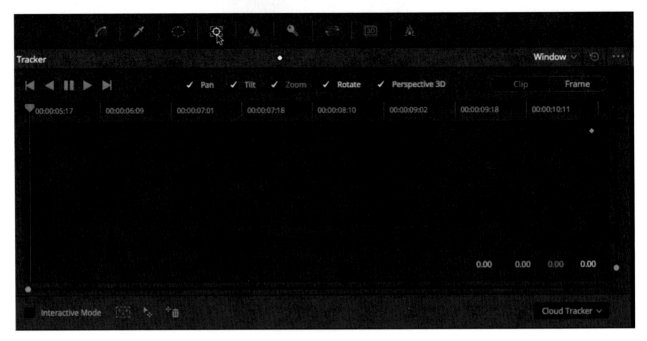

The tracker panel is used to initiate the tracking analysis for a Power Window.

The tracker allows you to have a Power Window follow any moving feature in clip. This avoids the need to manually keyframe a window's position. The tracker will modify a Power Window's position, size, rotation and tilt based on what you track.

Tracking is an analysis you must initiate. When begun, the image is analyzed using multiple tracking points that follow multiple pixels, which fall under the Power Window. After the tracking analysis is complete, the Power Window automatically moves, resizes, rotates, and skews to match the motion of the subject you tracked.

7. Click the Track forward button to begin tracking.

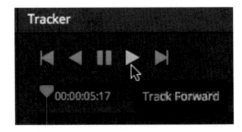

The analyze controls are where you start and stop the tracking process.

TIP: *Clips that have been tracked, include a small tracking badge, which looks like a target, on the timeline thumbnail.*

When the analysis is finished, you can go to the start of the clip to see the results.

8. Use the jog bar under the viewer to scrub back to the start of the clip.

9. Click the Loop Play button under the viewer.

10. Press Command-F (OS X) or Ctrl-F (Windows), then press spacebar to play full screen.

11. Stop playback after you have seen the clip once, then press Command-F (OS X) or Ctrl-F (Windows) to exit full screen.

12. Click the Loop Play button under the viewer to disable it.

TIP: *Tracking cannot be performed on a Clip when the Node editor mode pop-up is set to Group Pre Clip or Group Post Clip. Tracking is only available in the Clip setting.*

This is the completed SoCal look. It is a very saturated, cotton candy look but fits the shot nicely. We'll create one more grade so we have options when selecting the final look.

Layering with Blend Modes

In this exercise, you'll create a Bleach Bypass look for the same shot, then you will be able to evaluate it next to the SoCal look and choose the best one.

The Bleach Bypass process, sometimes called a Silver Retention or ENR process, basically layers a black and white copy of the image over a color copy to achieve a low saturated, high contrast look. It stems from a film development process where the bleaching stage was, well...bypassed. It has been used on many television shows and films including Reds, Saving Private Ryan and Seven. Let's set it up, first by naming and saving the Version.

1. Right-click over the thumbnail #07, which you have been working on.

2. From the contextual menu, choose Local Versions > Create New Version.

3. In the New Version dialog, type Bleach Bypass, then click OK.

   We'll need to remove all the previous nodes in the Node editor, leaving one to start our Bleach Bypass look. To remove all the nodes in the Node editor, you can draw a lasso around them and delete them all at once.

4. Draw a lasso around nodes 2, 3 and 4 to select them, then press Delete.

Delete all the nodes except for node 01.

For the last remaining node, we will reset it, so no adjustments are made on the clip.

5. Right-click over node 01 in the Node editor, then choose Reset Node Grade.

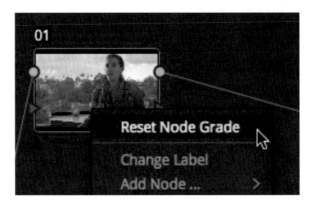

To reset a node, right-click over it or, choose Color >Reset Selected Node Grade.

The Bleach Bypass look uses a low color saturation. In this first node, we'll decrease the saturation using the Shared Controls under the Master Wheels.

6. On page 1 of the Shared Adjustments, lower the Saturation parameter to 25.

Lower the Saturation in the Shared Adjustments.

Up to this point, we have been using Serial nodes. Serial nodes are strung, one after the other. They pass along color adjustments as they progress. Now, we'll use a Layer node. The Layer node works more like Photoshop and other layer based applications. It composites images together, one on top of the other.

7. From the main menu bar, choose Nodes > Add Layer Node or press Option-L (OS X) or Alt-L (Windows)

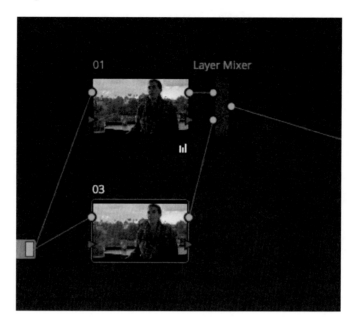

Adding a Layer node automatically connects the selected node and adds a second node.

The node with the low saturation (node 01) is automatically connected to the Layer node into the top connection. A second node (node 03) is automatically added and connected into the Layer node below node 01. Nodes connected below another node are actually composited over the top connected node.

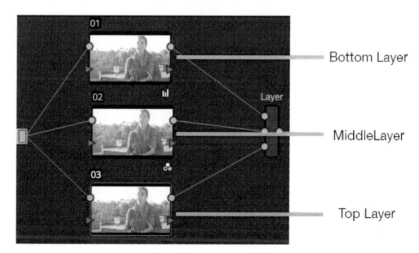

Example: Node 03 is composited on top of node 02 and 01. Node 02 is composited on top of node 01.

To create a black and white version on node 03, we can use the RGB Mixer. The RGB mixer proportionally remixes the red, green and blue color channels by adding or subtracting red, green and blue. It also has a Monochrome mode, which gives you more control over the black and white look, than just lowering the saturation.

273

8. Double-click node 03 in the Node editor

9. Click the RGB Mixer button 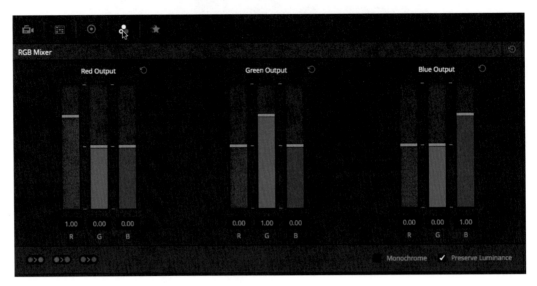 in the toolbar.

The RGB Mixer allows you to adjust the amount of red, green and blue in each color channel.

10. Click the Monochrome checkbox at the bottom of the RGB Mixer.

The RGB Mixer monochrome setting uses RGB channels to adjust contrast in a black and white image.

11. In the RGB Mixer, brighten her up by increasing red to 50, bringing green down to 50 and removing blue by dragging the slider all the way down.

TIP: *The bars can be very touchy. It is sometimes easier to use the scroll wheel on the mouse to adjust the bar you hover over.*

Drag the RGB sliders to increase red, then decrease green and blue.

These two nodes form the basic Bleach Bypass look. Now we need to blend them together. Right-clicking on the Layer node allows you to select how the nodes blend on top of one another using Composite modes. Composite modes perform mathematical operations to blend the color and luminance of the nodes. Using them is mostly an experiment because they are hard to predict. Still, we can talk at a high-level, of what they do when compositing images.

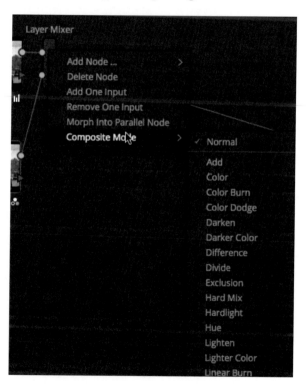

The Layer node contains ten Composite modes for blending the input nodes together.

You can categorize Composite modes based on how they impact the layers.

- Darken Colors: Darken and Multiply

- Lighten Colors: Add, Lighten and Screen

- Increase Color Contrast: Hardlight, Overlay and Softlight

- Cancel Out Colors: Subtract (Simple version of Difference)

- Invert Colors: Difference (Similar to Subtract but with negative results)

    The most commonly used Composite modes tend to be Multiply for darkening, Screen for lightening, and Overlay or Soft Light for increasing contrast.

    We'll use the Softlight Composite mode to blend the nodes, and increase the contrast.

12. Right-click over the Layer node, and choose Composite Mode > Softlight.

TIP: *You can add more inputs to connect new nodes to the Layer node, by right-clicking over the Layer node and choosing Add One Input.*

    Let's add another node to make some minor adjustments to the overall composite. You can add nodes after the Layer node, to modify the entire composite.

13. Double-click the Layer node, then press Option-S (OS X) or Alt-S (Windows) or choose Nodes > Add Serial Node from the contextual menu.

    The node is added after the Layer node, just like the Serial nodes we've added before. Since the Bleach Bypass look can typically crush shadows. We can make final corrections to the tonal range using this last node.

14. Select the Curves button in the tool bar.

15. From the Curves menu choose Custom.

Choose Custom from the Curves pop up menu.

16. Click the Y channel, if necessary.

Click the Y buttons to select the luma channel to modify.

We will add the anchor points using the Options menu.

17. From the Curve Options menu choose Add Default Anchors.

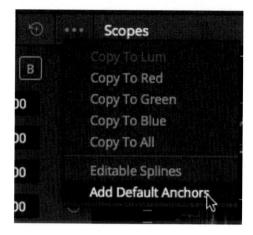

You can add three default anchors instead of adding them manually.

18. Drag the shadows anchor point up to brighten the shadow areas. Stop dragging when you have brought in more detail to her jacket.

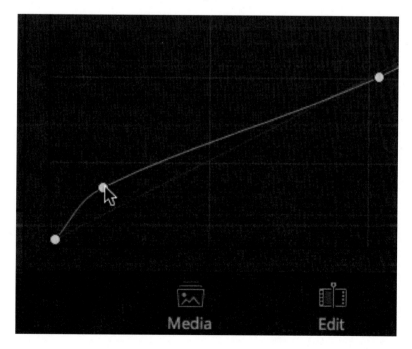

Increase the shadows until there is more detail in her jacket

277

19. Drag the highlights anchor point up to brighten the highlights areas. Stop dragging when the waveform is a bit below 1023.

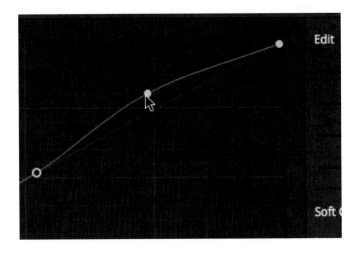

Increase the highlights until the Waveform is just below 1023.

Now you have a classic Bleach Bypass look. Once the basic look is in place, you can decide to go back to any node and adjust parameters based on the entire look.

Comparing Versions

When working with the different looks you create, you'll want to compare them side-by-side on the same clip to see which you prefer. You can create and save as many versions for a single clip as you like. In the end, you need some way to evaluate them. Resolve includes a flexible Split Screen view, so you can display multiple versions in the viewer, simultaneously.

1. Choose Workspace >Viewer Mode > Enhanced viewer or press Option- F (OS X) or Alt-F (Windows) to enlarge the viewer.

2. Click the Split screen button [image] above the viewer.

3. In the upper right of the viewer, choose Versions and Original from the pop-up menu.

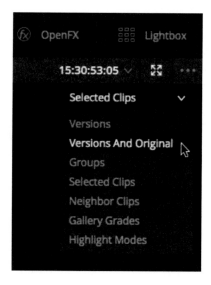

The split screen pop-up menu, choose Versions and Original to compare the original clip.

The split screen viewer will show three images, even though we've only saved two versions. The upper left quadrant is the original clip. The upper right is the first version we saved, the SoCal look. The lower left is the the Bleach Bypass grade.

The split screen viewer shows the saved Versions as well as the original clip.

TIP: *The current version displays a light outline around it.*

4. Choose Workspace >Viewer Mode > Enhanced viewer or press Option- F (OS X) or Alt-F (Windows) to show the timeline thumbnails.

Currently the label under the thumbnails show the compression format for the clip.

5. Double-click the Apple ProRes 422 LT label under thumbnail # 06.

Double-click the thumbnail label to see the currently loaded version name.

Double-clicking the thumbnail label displays the current Version name.

To my eye, the SoCal look is a better fit for this shot, so this is the look we will use.

6. Double-click the SoCal Version in the viewer to apply it to the clip.

7. Click the Split screen button above the viewer, to disable it.

The SoCal look is applied to the clip. It is such a good look we should learn how to save it, not only for other clips, but for other projects.

Saving Grades Across Projects

Some grades you put time and effort into may be worth saving so they can be reused in different projects. In the previous chapter, we saved a Still in the Gallery. In this chapter, we'll save a special kind of Still called a PowerGrade. PowerGrades are shared across all projects you create, based on your user login.

1. Click the Stills Album button above the Gallery.

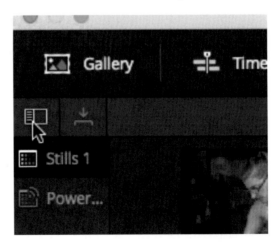

Click the Stills Album button to display the sidebar.

2. Select the PowerGrades Album from the Album list.

3. Right-click in the viewer and choose Grab Still from the menu.

TIP: *By right-clicking in the Album list, you can create additional Albums for categorizing different Stills and PowerGrades.*

4. Right-click the Still in the Power Grades Album, then choose Change Label.

5. Type SoCal into the Change Still Label dialog, then click OK.

TIP: *Stills and PowerGrades save the grade based on the currently displayed view in the Node editor mode menu. If you are displaying Clip, then only the nodes in the Clip view are saved with the Still.*

Comparing Images

In addition to comparing multiple versions on a single clip, you'll want to compare a single grade across multiple clips to achieve color continuity. In our timeline there are a few clips from this interview. It would be smart to check the two shots with the SoCal look. One way to compare a clip in the timeline with a saved Still is to use an image wipe.

1. In the timeline, select thumbnail #09. This is the next outdoor interview clip.

Select the next Ext interview clip in the timeline.

2. Right click over the SoCal Still in the Gallery, and choose Apply Grade.

    Now we can compare how the grade looks on this clip, with the previous clip.

3. Click the Image Wipe button in the toolbar above the viewer to enable it.

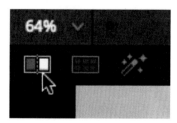

Click the Image Wipe button, in the upper left corner of the viewer.

When the Image Wipe button is selected, the viewer updates to display the current clip on the left half of the frame and the selected Gallery Still on the right.

4. Choose Workspace >Viewer Mode > Enhanced viewer or press Option- F (OS X) or Alt-F (Windows) to hide the Node editor.

    Dragging on the divider between the clip and the Still will move the wipe across the frame, allowing you to compare different areas.

5. Drag the dividing line separating the two clips in the viewer, to move the wipe.

Drag the dividing line to move the wipe.

Using the Image Wipe, you can evaluate the differences between them and determine if either clip needs to be tweaked for a better match.

6. Choose File > Save Project to save the entire project.

At this point you have completed this chapter, but you will continue using the project in the next chapter to create some effects in the Color page.

Chapter 13 Test Questions

Q1: Why would you create a Version?

Q2: Which tool is used for color grading:

    A) Custom Curves.

    B) Color Wheels.

    C) Hue Curves.

    D) All of the Above.

    E) None of the Above.

Q3: What are Qualifiers used for?

Q4: True or False: Serial Nodes pass color adjustments from one node to another, but Layer Nodes combine images.

Q5: True or False: Qualifiers and Power Windows are always used on separate nodes.

Ch. 14: Color Page Effects
Stabilization, Cloning and Resolve FX

The Color page holds more tricks up its sleeve than just an incredible range of color grading tools. It also includes different ways to fix shots, mask shots and add special effects. Some effects are subtle, and can be used on almost every project, while others help to create a fresh look. In this chapter we'll look at fixing erratic camera movement, then we'll create a more radiant furnace shot using the new ResolveFX, and finally we'll repair a small area of the final shot, using a clone effect.

Stabilization

In the previous chapter, we used the Tracking capabilities to track the Power Window onto the woman's face. Being able to track features can be helpful in other ways as well. Tracking is a way to calculate how the pixels in a shot are moving, once you have that information you can apply an inverse motion to stabilize camera movement. In Resolve, stabilization can entirely eliminate bumpy camera movement or smooth the motion out to make it less objectionable, but still retain some of the camera's original movement.

1. Make sure you are viewing the thumbnails in the timeline, then select thumbnail #26.

Select the thumbnail 26 to display it in the viewer.

2. Choose Workspace >Viewer Mode > Enhanced Viewer or press Option- F (OS X) or Alt-F (Windows) to display a larger viewer.

3. Click the Loop button under the viewer and then play the clip a few times to review it.

This clip has some abrupt camera movement that detracts from the shot. Using the tracker, we can attempt to fix this.

4. Click the Tracker button in the toolbar.

Click the Tracker button to display the tracker palette

The Tracker has a few modes you can set from a pop-up menu. The default is the Window tracker, which we used in previous chapter. Another mode is the Stabilizer.

5. From the Tracker palette's pop-up menu, choose Stabilize.

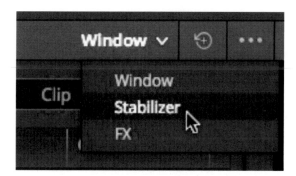

Choose Stabilizer from the Tracker mode pop up menu.

6. In the Tracking palette, drag the playhead to the start of the clip.

   There are two parts to stabilizing a clip. The first part is to analyze the clip's motion. Then, once you have it analyzed, you can stabilize it.

7. Click the Track Forward button to begin the analysis.

8. Once the analysis is complete, click the Stabilize button then play the clip again.

Click the Stabilize button to stabilize the shot after the analysis is complete.

Well, that doesn't look good for a number of reasons. The first is that it doesn't appear stable. That's because the default "cloud" tracker uses every valid pixel area to do the analysis of the movement. Her arms, the spinning glass and her shirt are all used in the analysis, though they have no relation to the bumpy camera move. Luckily Resolve allows you to eliminate portions of the frame from the analysis

Using Interactive Mode when Stabilizing

Resolve includes an Interactive mode to provide a way for you to manually intervene in an otherwise completely automatic analysis process.

1. From the Options pop-up menu, choose Clear Track Data.

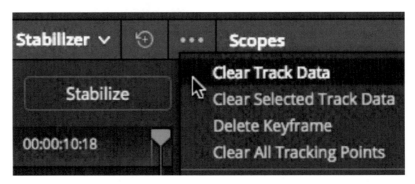

Clear the existing Track data and stabilization using the options menu.

2. In the Tracking palette, drag the playhead to the start of the clip.

3. Click the Interactive Mode check box.

Click the interactive Mode check box to manually add and remove points.

The Interactive Mode check box allows you to manually modify the points (sometimes called the *point cloud*) that Resolve automatically sets when tracking. You can decide to add new points or remove some of the automatically created ones. When you click the Interactive Mode check box, Resolve calculates the point cloud that it will use in the tracking analysis and displays it in the viewer.

4. In the viewer, draw a rectangle starting at the pipe in the upper center of the frame and going down to the lower right corner of the frame.

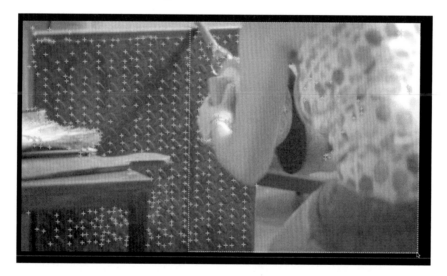

In the viewer, draw a rectangle around the area you want eliminated from the analysis.

The rectangle identifies the area of the frame you want Resolve to ignore when it performs the analysis again.

5. Click the Delete button to remove the points from the point cloud.

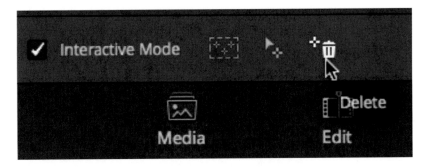

At the bottom of the Analysis graph, click the Delete button to eliminate points.

Once the points are deleted, you can perform the analysis again to get better results.

6. Click the Track Forward button to begin the new analysis.

7. Click the Stabilize button and then press spacebar to play the clip again.

TIP: *If the point cloud and rectangle still appear in the viewer, preventing you from accurately judging the stabilization quality, click off the Tracker palette to another tool in the toolbar, then click back to the Tracker palette to clear the viewer.*

Notice how much better the result is? No, it's not perfect, just better. The remaining problem is a common result of stabilization. In order to remove the camera motion, a reverse motion is added to the frame. The result is that the entire frame must move up and down and side to side in order to negate the camera movement. To correct this, you scale the image up so it fills the entire frame. How much scaling is required depends on how much camera movement exists in the shot. Resolve makes this calculation automatic, using the Zoom check box.

8. Click the Zoom check box button, and then click Stabilize button again.

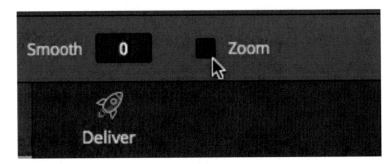

Click the Zoom check box to scale the image up and compensate for the transform adjustment.

9. Press spacebar to play the clip again.

Although the shot now completely fills the frame and is stabilized, the amount of scaling required is too much. The only real remedy for this is to split the difference. Using the Strong value field, you can add some percentage of the original camera movement back in and thereby reducing the amount of scaling required. A value of 0 returns the clip to the original camera movement and a value of 100 as we saw, is a locked down shot with no movement.

10. Lower the Strong value to 75, then click the Stabilize button and play the clip.

Enter the percentage of original motion you want to reintroduce to the clip.

The motion is acceptable but the scaling is only a bit better. Another adjustment you can make is for smoothing. The Smooth value introduces a smoothing algorithm that results in less jarring movement and less scaling. A Smooth value of 0 will add no smoothing and a value of 100 introduces maximum smoothing.

11. Increase the Smooth value to 75, then click the Stabilize button and play the clip.

Now the clip has smooth camera motion and an acceptable amount of scaling.

Disabling Stabilization

It is difficult to really gauge how much better this stabilized clip has become compared to the original. Unlike color correction, Stabilization is not a Node based effect, it is a clip based effect. It doesn't matter what node is selected. You can't disable it by disabling the node. To compare it with the original clip's motion you must disable the Sizing keyframes used in the Color page keyframe editor.

1. On the right side of the toolbar, click the Keyframe editor button.

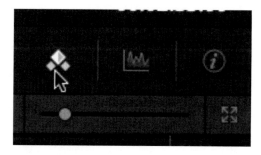

Click the Keyframe editor button in the toolbar to view the Keyframe editor.

Clicking the keyframe button hides the scopes and displays the keyframe editor. The Color page has a separate keyframe editor from the one we used in the Edit page. This keyframe editor can be used to animate color changes over time. It is also where resizing animation occurs, like the resizing we are doing with the Stabilizer.

2. In the keyframe editor, click the white Enable button to the left of the Sizing label.

Click the Enable button to enable and disable the animation on a specific track.

3. Press the spacebar to play the clip and view the original camera motion.

4. In the keyframe editor, click the white Enable button again to enable the stabilization.

5. Press the spacebar to play the clip with stabilization enabled.

Using the stabilizer in conjunction with the Strong and Smooth settings, allows you to salvage a wide range of bumpy or wobbly shots.

Collapsing Nodes Together

As you may have noticed when creating the looks from the previous chapter, the Node editor can get fairly crowded as you get more sophisticated with grading. How you manage the nodes in the Node editor can determine how quickly you can make changes. Let's take a look at one of the common ways you can manage space in the Node editor.

1. Choose Workspace >Viewer Mode > Enhanced Viewer or press Option- F (OS X) or Alt-F (Windows) to display thumbnails in the timeline.

2. Select the thumbnail #08 and play it a few times in the viewer.

Select thumbnail 08 to display it in the viewer.

This is one of the few clips we have not had a chance to grade. However, since we saved Stills in our previous chapter, we can use those to quickly add a grade.

3. In the Gallery, right-click over Hollywood Blockbuster and choose Apply Grade.

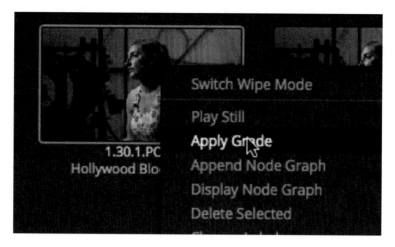

Choose Apply Grade from the contextual menu.

The four nodes required to create the Hollywood Blockbuster look are added to the Node editor for shot #08. In the next exercise, we are going to do more work on this shot that will require a number of additional nodes to be added. To give ourselves more room, we can collapse these four nodes into a *Compound node*.

4. Draw a lasso around the four nodes in the Node editor.

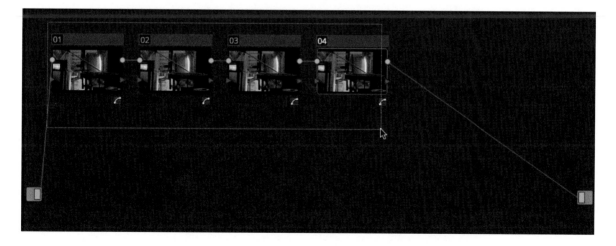

Lasso the four nodes to select them.

5. Right-click over any of the selected nodes and choose Create Compound Node from the contextual menu.

The four nodes collapse into one Compound node. The individual nodes are still available if you choose to expand or *Decompose* the compound node. In a way, you

291

can think of the Compound node as a folder containing the other nodes. For our purposes, we will treat it as a single node that creates our Blockbuster look.

TIP: *There are two ways to open a Compound node. In the contextual menu, choose Decompose Compound Node to remove the Compound node and return to individual nodes in the Node editor. Alternatively, choose Show Compound Node to open a new Node editor window with the individual clips displayed. When you return to the original Node editor, the Compound node is still in-tact.*

Adding ResolveFX

Resolve 12.5 includes more than 20 filter effects you can use to create unique looks and effects. Filter effects like blurs, glows and light rays, can open up new creative options that are not possible with the color corrections tools we've been covering.

1. With thumbnail #08 still selected, play it a few times in the viewer.

2. Position the playhead on the first frame of the clip.

   This clip would look better if a nice hot glow was created around the furnace.

3. Press Option-S (OS X) or Alt-S (Windows) to add a node after the Compound node.

4. Click the OpenFX button to open the library of Resolve FX.

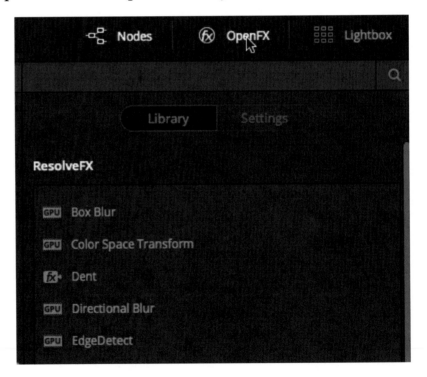

Click the OpenFX button to open the OpenFX library and the list of ResolveFX.

The OpenFX library displays ResolveFX, as well as any 3rd party OpenFX plug-ins you have installed on your system.

ResolveFX are included filter effects that extend the visual effects capabilities of Resolve. They are located in the OpenFX library, along with OpenFX plug-ins developed by 3rd party companies.

5. Drag the Glow filter onto node 02 in the Node editor.

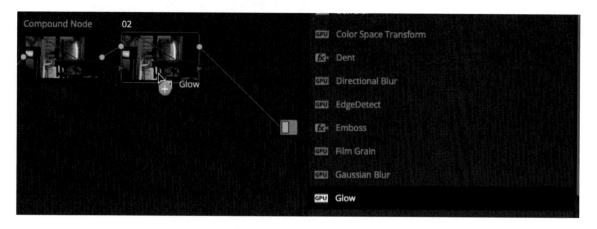

Drag the Glow effect onto to the node in the Node editor.

***TIP**: To remove a ResolveFX filter or an OpenFX plug-in, right click over the node and choose Remove OFX Plugin.*

Once you add a filter from the OpenFX library, the settings are shown so you can adjust the filter. Glow works best on bright highlights. The default threshold setting is too low for this shot, so we'll change it to have more effect on the furnace opening.

***NOTE**: The adjustments to filters in this exercise are partly experimental, so once you complete the exercise, feel free to return and experiment with the settings.*

6. In the Glow Settings, drag the Shine Threshold somewhere between 0.3 and 0.4.

The Shine Threshold determines how bright a highlight has to be in order to receive the glow effect. Setting the threshold low applies it to more of the image.

7. Drag the Brightness up to .70 to create a brighter glow.

The Glow effect added to the last clip in the timeline.

You can compare the shot with and without the glow effect to see the results clearer.

8. Press Command-D (OS X) or Ctrl-D (Windows) to temporarily disable the glow effect, then press the keyboard short cut again to show the effect.

    We've brightened the shot with a very romantic glow, but we can further enhance it with a second ResolveFX. However, you can only apply one ResolveFX per node, so we'll need to add another node. This one we'll add before the node with the glow on it.

9. Right-Click over the node 02 and choose Add Node > Add Serial Before.

    The new node (node 03) is added before node 02 with the glow on it. This gives us a clean, unaffected node to create an additional effect just for the furnace.

10. Drag the Light Rays filter onto node 03 in the Node editor.

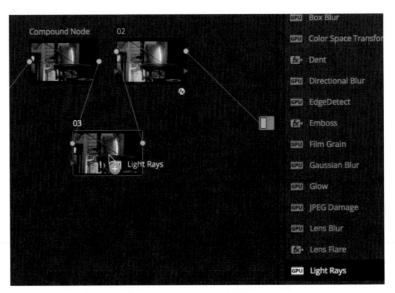

Drag the Light Rays effect onto to the node in the Node editor.

The Light Rays can be a very overpowering effect but easily customized.

11. From the Source of Rays pop up menu choose Edges to cause the rays to come from the edges in the image.

12. Drag the Source Threshold to around 0.700.

Increasing the threshold will limit the edges in the image that produce rays.

13. Drag the X and Y position sliders to locate the center of the lights rays directly over the furnace opening. (roughly X and Y =.60)

Use the X and Y position sliders to locate the center of the light rays over the furnace opening.

14. Press spacebar to play the effect and see the results.

NOTE: *Depending on the computer's graphics card, it may not achieve real time playback*

This is a nice effect but there are ways we can make it better. The center of the light rays does not move along with the camera. If we could make it follow the camera movement, the light rays would always be coming from inside the furnace, which would be more realistic.

Single Point Tracking

Certain ResolveFX including the Light Rays filter, can have their center point tracked using Resolve's tracker. Up until now, we have only used what is called the Cloud Tracker which uses a large number of points. Resolve also include a single point tracker that you can use for tracking ResolveFX onto a specific item in the clip.

1. Position the playhead on the first frame of the clip, if necessary.

The Tracker is most likely still on the Stabilize mode from the first exercise in this chapter, so we will need to switch it to track the ResolveFX.

2. From the Tracker palette's pop-up menu choose FX.

Choose FX from the Tracker mode pop up menu.

Unlike the Cloud tracker, it is up to you to position the point tracker on a high contrast object that moves exactly how you want the center of the Light Rays to move.

3. Click the Add Tracker Point button to add a cross hair to the viewer.

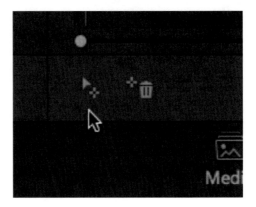

Click the Add Tracker button in the lower left corner.

4. In the viewer, position the cross hair on the third rivet from the top of the furnace

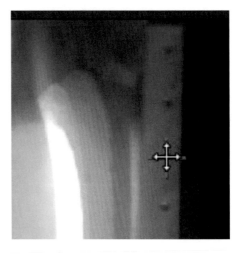

Position the cross hair over the rivet on the furnace.

When selecting a point to track, choose a clearly defined, high contrast point, that preferably remains unobscured for the duration of the clip.

5. Click the Track Forward button to begin the tracking.

6. Once the tracking is complete, press the spacebar to watch the center of the light rays remain in the furnace even as the camera moves in the shot.

   The light rays look good on the furnace but it overpowers the rest of the frame. In the next exercise you'll learn how to combine the single point tracker with Power Windows to limit where the light rays fall.

Point tracking a Power Window.

You can use the single point tracker with Power Windows to limit where the light rays emit in the frame. Using the single point tracker is handy when you have a very specific spot that you want the Power Window to follow, like the rivet on the furnace.

1. Position the playhead on the first frame of the clip, if necessary.

2. Click the Power Window button in the toolbar.

3. Place a circle Power Window over the furnace opening and reshape it so it doesn't cut out too much of the light rays.

Shape the circle Power Window so it doesn't cut off the light rays.

We can use the Softness parameter of the Power Window to create a smooth fall off of the Light Rays, instead of a harsh cut off line.

4. Increase the Power Window's Soft1 value to around 4.

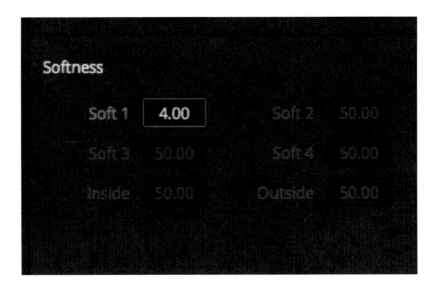

Increase the softness of the Power Window.

With the Power Window in place for the first frame, we can use the single point tracker to position it for the rest of the shot.

TIP: *You can also copy and paste tracking data from one point to another using the Copy and Paste Tracking Data selections from the Tracker Options menu.*

5. Click the Tracker button in the toolbar.

    The Tracker is likely still on the FX mode from tracking the Resolve FX, so we will need to switch it to track the Power Window.

6. From the Tracker palette's pop-up menu choose Window.

Choose Window from the Tracker mode pop up menu.

Power Windows can use the Cloud tracker, or the point tracker.

7. In the Tracker palette, from the pop-up in the lower right corner, choose Point Tracker.

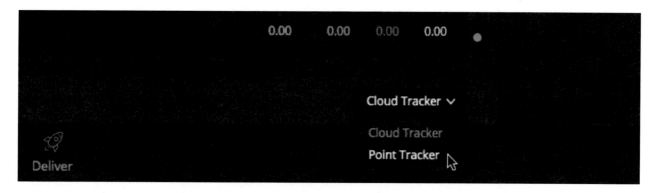

Choose Point tracker from the pop-up menu in the lower right corner.

8. Click the Add Tracker Point button to add a cross hair to the viewer.

Click the Add Tracker point button to add a tracker in the viewer.

9. In the viewer, position the cross hair on the third rivet from the top of the furnace, just as you did for the Light Rays.

10. Click the Track Forward button to begin the tracking.

11. Once the tracking is complete, press the spacebar to see how the Power Window limits the light rays, making them appear as if they are emitting from the furnace.

There are over 20 ResolveFX to choose from, but a few of them, including Lens Flare, Film Grain and Lens Blur, are reserved for DaVinci Resolve Studio version.

Using Node Resizing for Cloning

Occasionally, you will have the need to remove something objectionable or distracting from a shot. It could be a sign on a wall or a blemish on someone's skin. Resolve has a unique resize feature that works very well for removing an object by duplicating or *cloning* an area from the frame and copying it over the objectionable area.

1. Select thumbnail #37, the last clip in the timeline, then press spacebar to play it.

Select the thumbnail 37 to display it in the viewer.

The last shot in the timeline has a dissolve into it and a fade out. Those two transitions obscure the viewing of the entire clip, so we need to temporarily disable them in the Color page while we fix the shot.

2. Under the viewer, click the Unmix button to temporarily hide the transition effects.

Click the Unmix button to hide all transitions from displaying in the viewer.

To quickly grade this shot, we will use the Hollywood Blockbuster grade again.

3. In the Gallery, right-click over Hollywood Blockbuster and choose Apply Grade.

4. Press spacebar to play the clip again.

The object we want to get rid of, is the metal tool sticking into the lower right corner of the frame. We'll insert a node directly after the first node to perform the clone.

5. Right-click over the first node in the Node editor and choose Add Node > Add Serial.

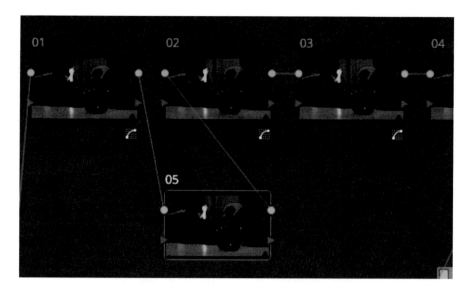

Add a new node after the first node in the Node editor.

6. Press Option-F (OS X) or Alt-F (Windows) to hide the thumbnails and Node editor, providing more room for the viewer.

7. Click the Power Window button in the toolbar.

   We'll use a Power Window to outline the area in the frame that we will use to cover up the object. The goal should be to create the smallest size window you need to cover the object and create it as near to the object as you can to limit the color and lighting differences between the source and target location.

8. Click the rectangle Power Window to add it to the viewer.

9. Resize the rectangle to be slightly larger than the object in the lower right, and position the Power Window to the left of the object.

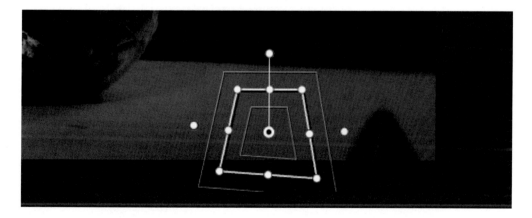

Create a small rectangle and position it next to the object you want to hide.

10. Click the Sizing button in the toolbar to display the Sizing palette.

The Sizing button in the toolbar.

The Sizing palette is commonly used to resize clips that do not match the timeline resolution. However, instead of resizing the entire clip, you can also use Node sizing to resize a specific node, like the one with the Power Window.

TIP: *When resizing, no matter what the timeline resolution is, the original clip's resolution is always used. This means you get the best possible resizing quality, even if you have previously resized the clip in Resolve.*

11. From the Sizing mode pop up, choose Node Sizing.

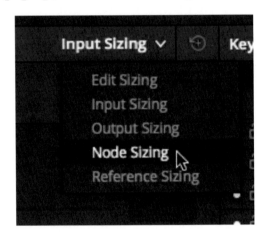

To resize the contents of a Power Window, choose Node Sizing from the pop-up.

12. In the Sizing palette, drag the Pan slider to the right until the Power Window covers the object completely.

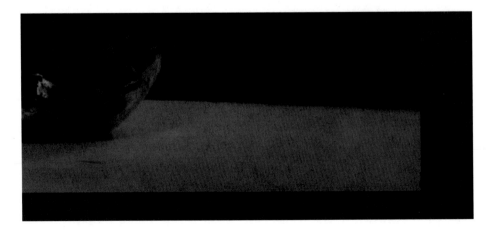

Using the Sizing palette, position the Power Window over the object to hide it.

13. Press spacebar to play the clip.

At this point you could return to the Power Window and refine the soft edges to blend the cloned area better. If the camera was moving, you could also track the Power Window to follow the camera move. If the object is more complex and there is no easy place to clone from, you could investigate using Blackmagic Design's Fusion software. Fusion is a visual effects compositing software that integrates with Resolve. You are able to launch Fusion directly from the Resolve timeline for more complex cloning and compositing work.

Caching in the Color Page

Like the Edit page, the Color page includes a Frame Indicator above the viewer that shows the playback frame rate achieved. However, in many cases the graphics card is over taxed when color grading, so the indicator is warning that playback is not at the true frame rate.

Frame rate indicator above the viewer.

To increase playback performance, Resolve has three levels of caching that can either work automatically or with your input. You can choose to cache the ungraded source media used in the timeline, the source media with the grades applied or just specific nodes of clip. If you don't want to have to think about caching the best setting is to choose the Smart Cache. If you want more control of what items are cached and when, then you choose User Cache. We'll choose User cache to learn a few basics about caching.

1. Choose Workspace >Viewer Mode > Enhanced viewer or press Option- F (OS X) or Alt-F (Windows) to display the Node editor.

2. Click back on thumbnail #08.

Select thumbnail #08.

303

This clip has a grade and two ResolveFX, so chances are your system doesn't play it back perfectly. Since we may still want to play around with the glow effect on the last node, we will use the User Cache to cache all the nodes leading up to the Glow effect.

3. Choose Playback > Render Cache > User.

TIP: *Smart Cache automatically caches complex grades including Noise Reduction, Motion Blur and OpenFX plug-ins.*

With the User Cache enabled, we can cache all the nodes in the Node editor except the one the glow on it. This can greatly improve performance while still giving us the flexibility to make changes on the last node.

4. Right-click over node 03 and choose Node Cache > On.

The node name or number will turn red to indicate it needs to be cached.

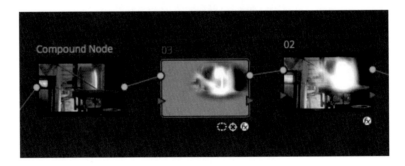

A node needing to be cached will have a red highlight.

The thumbnail timecode number will also turn red, as will a cache line above the timeline bar in the Color page mini timeline.

A thumbnail will have a red timecode number and a red cache line in the mini timeline.

After a set number of seconds of inactivity, the caching will begin. When the caching is finished, all the red highlights turn blue to indicate a cache is present.

5. Double-click the last node in the Node editor, then in the ResolveFX Settings, adjust the Shine Threshold down to increase the amount of glow.

    Changes to any node connected after the Cached node, have no affect on the caching. The Cache remains blue since the only change comes after the cache node.

6. Double-click the second node in the Node editor, then in the ResolveFX setting, adjust the Source Threshold down to 0.

    Changes to any node connected before the Cached node undoes the cache. Once your adjustment is made, the cache again turns red to indicate the change you made requires a new cache to be generated

Caching a Clip for Output

A more appropriate cache for when you are done with a grade and want to play it back without any plan to make changes, is the Clip Cache Output.

The Clip Cache Output renders the entire grade, in fact it renders every Version created for that clip as well. When the clip is cached, any change to any node will cause it to re-do the cache.

1. Right-click over thumbnail #37 in the timeline and choose Render Cache Clip Output.

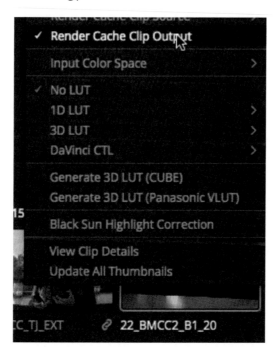

Choose Render Clip Cache Output to cache the entire clip , grade and all of the Versions.

The thumbnail timecode number will turn red, as will the cache line above the timeline bar in the Color page mini timeline.

Caching happens in the background after a period of inactivity. When caching starts, if you begin to move the timeline, click a button or use Resolve in any way, the caching will pause until you have temporarily stopped using Resolve.

2. Double-click the last node in the Node editor, then in the Primaries wheels, adjust the Gamma Master Wheel slightly.

Changes to any node undoes the cache. Once your adjustment is made, and the background caching time limit is reached, the node will automatically cache again.

Deleting the Cache

No matter how you create your cache files, they are retained even after you quit and open Resolve up again. At the end of a project you must delete the cache files manually, or else they remain on your hard drives, even if you delete the entire project.

1. Choose Playback > Render Cache > None.

TIP: *If Smart Cache is still enabled when you choose to delete the Cache, the clips or nodes will begin to cache again after the background waiting period is reached.*

2. Choose Playback > Delete Render Cache > All.

3. In the confirmation dialog, click Yes to delete all the cache files.

You are probably curious as to where the cache files are. If you remember back in chapter 1, we reviewed the Preferences for the Scratch Disk. The Scratch Disk is the first disk added to the Media Storage panel in the Preferences window.

Choosing the Right Settings

Now that you understand what caching is, and a few of the options available to you, we should take a step back and look at the settings for the cache.

1. Choose File > Project Settings or press Shift-9.

2. Click the General Options category in the Settings window.

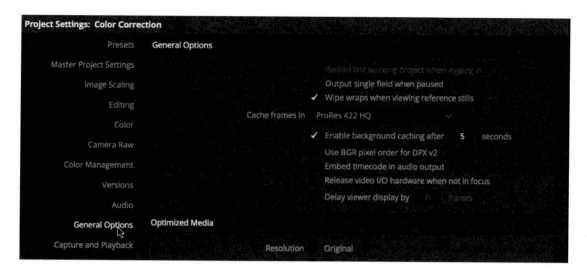

The General Options in the Project Settings window.

The General options includes two main settings for the cache. The first menu determines the format used to create the cache file.

3. Click the Cache Frame pop-up menu to view the list.

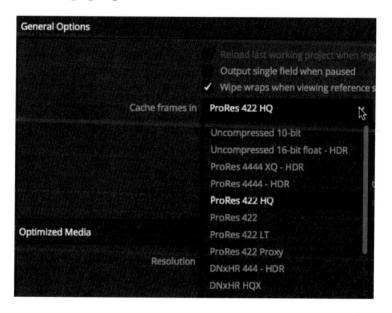

The Cache Frame pop-up determines the compression format for the cache.

If you plan on doing a lot of heavy grading and effects, you may want to choose a mastering quality cache format like ProRes 422 HQ or DNxHR HQ. It may initially take more time to cache files, but when outputting the master file, you will not have to re-render any of the effects which could save considerable time.

However, if you are on a laptop or using a more compressed file format like ProRes Proxy or DNxHR LB, then you can set the Cache file format to match the clip format and get better performance.

4. Leave the setting at its default by clicking off the menu.

   The next setting determines how quickly the background caching begins to process.

5. Enter 3 in the Enable Background caching field.

   Background caching will now begin after 3 seconds of inactivity.

6. Click Save to close the Settings window.

7. Choose File > Save Project to save the entire project.

You've completed the Color grading section of the book! Hopefully you are ready to start creating you own grades and making new, unique looks. This was a fairly detailed chapter so make sure you take the Test Questions at the end to see how much you have retained.

Chapter 14 Test Questions

Q1: In which toolbar palette is Stabilization located?

Q2: To stabilize a clip, what must be done after you press the Track Forward button to analyze a clip?

Q3: ResolveFX are located:

A) In the Edit page Inspector.

B) In the Color page OpenFX library.

C) In the Color page Gallery.

D) In the Edit page Effects Library

Q4: Which Sizing mode must be selected to clone an area of the frame?

Q5: Where are the selections for User and Smart Caching located?

Ch. 15: Outputting Files
Round Trip, ProTools and Custom Settings

When you are ready to get files out of Resolve for digital cinema, sound design or web streaming, Resolve includes a dedicated Deliver page. Although you have a large number of options, getting files out of Resolve is incredibly easy. There are preset choices for popular deliverable types, as well as the ability to create your own custom output settings.

This chapter will use the Premiere Pro XML timeline you conformed in chapter 11 to take you through the process of outputting three different files types. We'll look at outputting a files for audio sweetening in ProTools, returning the timeline with graded clips back to Premiere Pro and finally, we'll export a portion of the timeline for visual effects.

Switching to the Deliver Page

When the Deliver page button is selected, the timeline you currently have loaded in the Edit page or Color page, is carried over for output.

1. Launch Resolve and open the Color Correction project if necessary, then from the Edit page load the From Premiere timeline.

NOTE: *This project and timeline were created in chapter 11. If you have skipped chapter 11, return to it now and learn how to create the project and import the XML timeline.*

2. At the bottom of the Resolve window, click the Deliver button to see the Deliver page.

The Deliver page has settings on the left and a batch processing panel on the right.

310

The timeline runs along the lower half of the Deliver page.

Along the left side are the Render settings. Here, you can customize the parameters for creating an output file. At the top of the Render settings is a row of Render Presets.

Along the right side of the Deliver page is the Render Queue. The Render Queue displays a list of the files or *jobs* waiting to render.

Outputting Files for ProTools

A common workflow is to create media and an AAF project file for Avid ProTools. You typically send your timeline to Avid ProTools if you want to have additional sound design done by a professional audio editor. Each audio segment in the timeline is output as a separate file to give the audio editor flexibility when making changes in ProTools. The video is sent as a single file for preview and syncing, and an AAF file is generated for the timeline.

1. Scroll the Render Preset button list right, then click the Protools button.

Choose a preset from the row of buttons, for the type of file you want to output.

Once you select a button, the settings for that preset are displayed in the Render Settings window. At the top of the Render Settings is the basis for the file name and the location setting where you can choose to save the files.

2. Click the Browse button and choose a destination folder for the files.

Click the Browse button the set the location for the saved files.

When you click the preset button, the settings are configured for that preset, but they can be modified. Three tabs at the top of the settings are used to display and configure the video format, audio format and the file naming. One of the most common parameters to modify when outputting to ProTools, is the number of frames or *handles* you wish to add to the beginning and end of each audio segment.

311

3. Below the Codec pop up menu, click the Advanced Settings arrow.

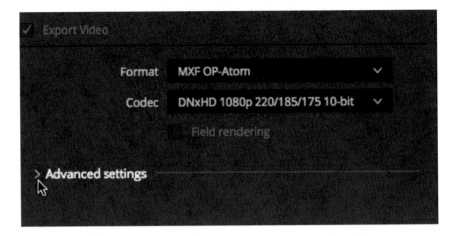

Click the Advanced Settings arrow to access additional parameters.

Since each audio segment is exported as a separate file when outputting to ProTools, it is helpful to the audio editor if you add a few extra frames on either side of each clip, incase they need to make any modifications when mixing the sound track. Each audio editor will desire different handle lengths, so it is best to check with them first.

4. Scroll to the bottom of the Advanced Settings, then enter 12 for the frame handles.

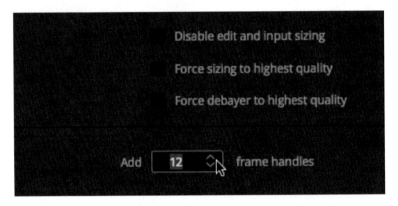

Add handles to audio clips when outputting to ProTools using the Advanced Settings.

Although adding handles to audio segments is the most common setting to adjust when outputting to ProTools, it isn't the only one to consider. In the next exercise, we'll add a watermark to protect our content.

Adding a Watermark

You can add a text based watermark, similar to a title, which overlays the video. Most often this is used for Don't Not Distribute text or to have a running timecode display. The watermark is created and formatted using the Data Burn-In controls on the Color page.

1. Under the Advanced settings, set the Data burn-in pop-up menu to Same as project.

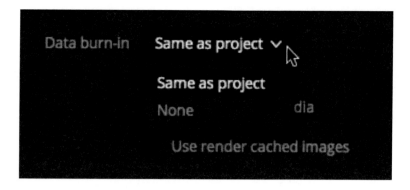

Choose Same as project from the Data burn-in pop-up menu.

2. Click the Color page button at the bottom of the Resolve window.

3. In the toolbar, click the Data Burn-In button .

Click the Data Burn-In button in the toolbar to display the burn-in settings.

The left side of the Data Burn-In settings includes a list possible data types to overlay on the video. Selecting the check box next to any option enables it.

4. In the list of burn-in data, click the Record Timecode check box to have the record timecode overlaid on the output movie file.

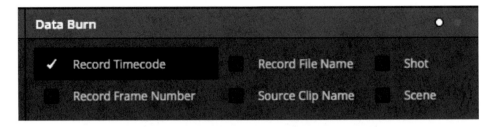

Click the check box next to any item to use it as a watermark.

5. Click the Custom Text1 check box to add a text watermark.

6. In the Custom Output Text field, enter DO NOT DISTRIBUTE.

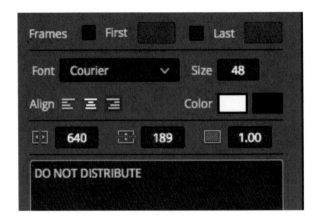

Enter and format custom text using the text format controls.

7. Drag the Size field to the right to increase the text size to 55.

The viewer displays all the changes to the Data Burn-In settings, as you make them. When you are finished configuring the burn-in text, you can return to the Delver page.

Adding to the Render Queue

With all the settings configured, you are ready to add this output to your Render Queue. The Render Queue is a list of jobs ready to be exported from Resolve. You can add as many jobs to the Render Queue as you need.

1. Click the Deliver page button at the bottom of the Resolve window.

2. Click the Add to Render Queue button, to add the job to the queue.

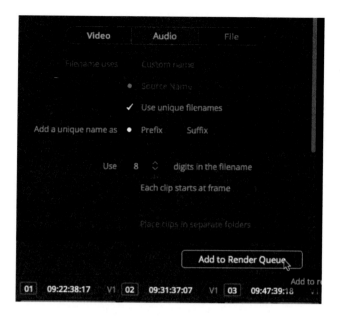

The job is added to the Render Queue once the Add to Render Queue button is clicked.

The job is now listed in the Render Queue waiting to be rendered. The Render Queue is a holding place for all your jobs. Nothing renders until you click the Render button. Before we render, there are still a couple of jobs we will add to the queue.

Outputting Back to Premiere Pro

This timeline was imported from Premiere Pro and in some cases you may want to return to Premiere with the new graded clips. That way, an editor can finish the project in Premiere. (Although, with the recent additions in Resolve 12.5 there are fewer and fewer reasons to do this.) These steps are for Premiere, but can just as well be used for outputting back to Final Cut Pro or Avid Media Composer.

1. In the Render Settings row, click the Premiere XML button.

Click the Premiere XML button to render the graded clips in the timeline for import back into Premiere.

Once again you should select a location for the output files, then go on to choose a video format and compression scheme.

2. At the top of the Render Settings, click the Browse button and choose a new folder that will contain all the rendered output files from this timeline.

315

3. From the format menu, choose Quicktime.

    Depending on your operating system, you will have different choices for Quicktime output. The primary difference is the ability to output Apple ProRes compression on OS X. Your selection should be the codec that retains the highest quality of your source material. Depending on the source material you use, you should do some tests ahead of your final delivery to make your decision.

4. From the Codec menu, choose ProRes 422HQ on OS X or DNxHR HQ on Windows.

Choose the highest quality compression that best suits your source content.

    Back in chapter 1, we created a timeline at 1280x720P resolution. So, for output we will want to match that as well.

5. From the Resolution menu, choose 1280 x 720 HD 720P form the pop-up menu

TIP: The Render at source resolution check box is only available when you render out individual source clips as we are doing here. It can be used if you have mix resolutions in your timeline and want to perform the resizing in Premiere.

6. Scroll down under the Advanced settings and set the Data burn-in pop-up to None.

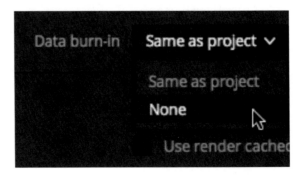

Disabling the burn-in for the setting does not disable it in the viewer.

Although the Burn-in is displayed in the viewer, it will not be in your rendered files.

If we took the time to cache our images at the highest quality to match our source material, we can use those cashed files instead of re-rendering our grades now.

7. Under the Advanced settings, click the check box to Use render cached images.

8. At the top of the Render Settings, click the File tab to display the naming options.

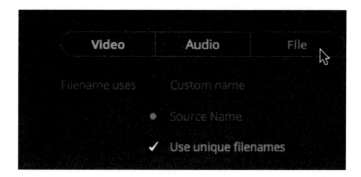

Click the File tab to display file naming options.

Since many segments in a timeline can come from the same master source file, naming them uniquely is incredibly important. Otherwise Resolve will overwrite one file with another, if they share the same master source clip file name.

9. Make sure Use unique filenames is checked.

10. Click the Add to Render Queue button to add this setting to the render queue list.

The Premiere Pro Preset will render out individual audio and video clips with the color corrections and grades you have applied. An XML file will also be generated that links to these new files. As we did with ProTools, you can add handles if you think you may want to trim, slip, or slide any of the segments in Premiere Pro.

Creating Your Own Preset

There are occasions where you want to output a single clip or a range of clips, instead of the entire timeline. The most likely situation is when you want to share a range of edits with motion graphics or visual effects applications.

1. In the row of Render Presets, scroll to the left and click the Custom button.

Click the Custom button to create your own preset.

The Custom setting doesn't pre-configure the Render Settings for any particular file format. It provides you with all the options, so you can configure your own settings.

2. Again, first select the location for the file using the Browse button.

    The next option to set determines if you output a single file or each cut as its own individual file. Depending on how the content will be used, you might choose either one. For our purposes, we'll choose a single file.

3. At the top of the Render Settings, choose Single clip.

You can choose to output individual files or one single clip for the entire timeline.

The next step is to choose the video format for output.

4. Click the Video tab to view the video format settings.

    We'll use the EXR image sequence, which is often used when sharing files with visual effects and 3D software.

5. Choose EXR from the Video Format menu.

Choose EXR for the format.

Next, you'll configure the file name for output.

6. Click the File tab to view the file naming settings.

7. In the Custom name field, type **First six cuts**.

    Now, you will set the range in the timeline for the area you want to output.

8. From the Render pop-up menu above the timeline, choose In/Out Range.

Choose In/Out Range to select a range of the timeline for output.

9. Drag the playhead to the start of the timeline, then press I to mark an In point.

10. Drag the playhead to the end of the sixth cut, just before the first interview clip, then press O to mark and Out point.

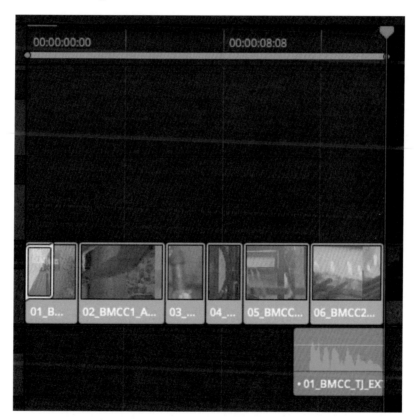

Mark and In point and Out point around the range you want to output.

There are audio tracks in the timeline that are not required for motion graphics or visual effects, so we can disable those tracks for the output.

11. Click the Audio Disable Track buttons for Audio 1, 2, 3 and 4.

Disable any tracks you do not want exported.

You could continue configuring the various settings to suit your output. In our case, we are ready to save this as our custom Preset, so we can use it in the future.

12. At the top of the Render Settings, from the Options menu choose Save As New Preset.

From the Options menu, choose to save the custom settings as a Preset.

13. Enter EXR Sequence as the setting name, then click OK.

The EXR preset now shows up on the left side of the preset button row, for use in a later project. Now, we have our own custom setting to use. We can add the job to the Render Queue and start rendering our three jobs.

TIP: *A custom preset will show up in every project, for every user on this local version of Resolve.*

14. At the bottom of the Render Settings click the Add to Render Queue button.

15. Select the top job in the queue, then hold the Shift key and select the last job.

Select all the jobs in the queue you want to render out of Resolve.

NOTE: *If you do not have enough free hard drive space, do not perform the following step to render out the three projects.*

16. At the bottom of the Render Queue panel, click Start Render to begin rendering all the jobs in the Render Queue.

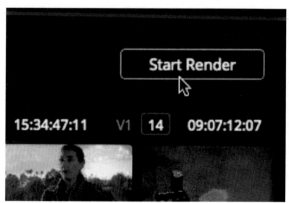

Click Start Render button to begin rendering.

When you start rendering the viewer updates to show you the frame that is rendering. A status bar is displayed at the bottom of the Render Queue to let you see the progress.

All About Data Levels

DaVinci Resolve gives you an incredible amount of creative power and technical control over image processing. With so much functionality, it isn't always obvious what is happening behind your back. Maybe the most overlooked feature that causes the most amount of problems is the range of intensity values used to process image data. This confusion often rears its head when you look at the output file of your project and it appears brighter/darker than what you monitored in Resolve. To clear this up we need a short review of terminology. Don't worry, it will be short.

It's worth repeating that all digital images in a computer are made up of bits. Your basic JPEG image floating around the web is usually made up of 8 bits for each color channel (RGB). This allows for each color to have 256 different intensity values.

0   255

Most digital cinema cameras capture 10-bit images. That provides each color channel with 1024 different intensity values, with the range going from 0 to 1023.

0   1023

This sounds pretty easy right? In a 10-bit image 0 is pure black and 1023 is pure white. Not so fast. Now we have to insert broadcast television standards into the mix. Your shiny new digital cinema camera might be able to capture 1024 discrete intensity values or *Data Levels*, but 10-bit HD broadcast standards will only accept 896 levels of intensity. This range doesn't start black at 0. It starts black at 64 and tops pure white out at 960. The range below 64 and above 960 are reserved for super blacks and super whites.

64   96

So now we have two data level ranges, which we will call Full levels and Video levels

- Full levels: 0-1023

- Video levels: 64-960.

TIP: *We are talking about image files here and not video signals. Video signals are measured using an IRE scale. The Full levels equivalent on the IRE scale would be 0-100.*

Having the incorrect data levels configured for your final output will produce images that are either darker or brighter than you see in either the Resolve viewer, or on an external monitor. Thankfully, Resolve does a very good job of handling this without any manual intervention from you. Still, it is important to know where and how data levels are set.

Setting Levels for Clips

When you read in a clip, whether data levels are set to Video or Full is usually not something you need to worry about. Resolve uses an automatic setting which makes that decision for you based on the file format you are reading. For instance, if the files were captured as ProRes or DNxHD/HR**, these files mostly use Video levels 64-960. If you are capturing RAW, like CinemaDNG from a Blackmagic camera or Redcode RAW from a Red camera, then those files are typically debayered into colorspaces that use Full levels 0-1023. It's the easiest part of the job. *You don't have to do a thing*. However, you can choose the setting if you feel Resolve has chosen incorrectly, which honestly it rarely does. Before you change it, just make sure you know how the clips were recorded.

To change the data levels of a clip:

1. Right-click over a clip in a bin and choose Clip Attributes

2. In the Clip Attributes window set the levels how you want the clip to be interpreted.

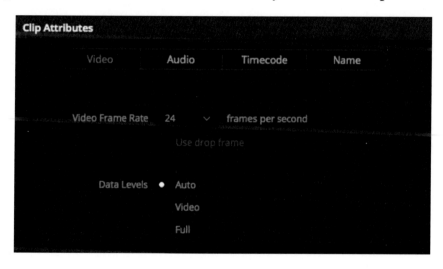

Clip Attributes automatically determines the range that should be used based on the file codec.

That's the first place that includes data level settings. There are other areas that cover monitoring and tape-based i/o but we will only look at file-based output.

Setting Levels for Output

For file based output, the Deliver page includes another group of data level settings. This is also set to Auto by default and again, I will repeat that *you usually do not have to change it from the default*. Depending on the output codec you choose, Resolve determines how the data levels should be set. However, like the Clip Attributes setting, you can change the Auto setting and manually configure the level range you want to use.

To change the levels of your rendered output:

1. Click the Deliver page

2. Select the video tab, then click the Advanced Settings disclosure arrow.

3. Change the data levels how you want the output file to be set.

Viewing Your Output in QuickTime

Quicktime is widely used on OS X to view movie files. Unfortunately, when viewing h.264 files, Quicktime applies a gamma curve which can make your images appear brighter than you anticipated. Comparing Quicktime and VLC with the Resolve viewer set to sRGB, shows the slightly brighter results when using the QuickTime player. Don't be fooled by the QuickTime player!

| sRGB in Resolve | VLC player | QuickTime X on OS X |

*** ProRes 444 and 444XQ use full levels, while all flavors of DNxHD/HR use video levels.*

You should congratulate yourself! You have completed the entire book. Although there is so much more to explore in Resolve, I sincerely hope the exercises in this book have given you a firm grasp on the basics of getting a job done. It's now time to explore on your own and figure out what settings, editing techniques and color grading tools work best for you. Good luck in your creative endeavors and mastering of DaVinci Resolve 12.5.

Chapter 15 Test Questions

Q1: How do you access the Deliver page?

Q2: What happens to the timeline you have loaded in the Edit page or Color page, when you switch to the Deliver page?

Q3: To select a range of clips you want to render, you must:

A) Choose EXR Sequence, because it is the only one that can output a range of clips.

B) Mark an In and Out point at the start and end of the range.

C) Go back to the Edit page and select the clips.

Q4: If you want to add a timecode water mark, on which page is that done?

Q5: True or False: You must click Add to Render Queue before you can begin rendering.

Appendix: Test Answers

Chapter 1 Test Answers

Q1: Media page, Edit page, Color page and Deliver page.

Q2: To import and organize media.

Q3: The Media Storage browser.

Q4: They remain in their original location.

Q5: False: A clip's colorspace is changed using the Project Settings.

Chapter 2 Test Answers

Q1: D) All of the Above.

Q2: A) Media page.

Q3: True.

Q4: Switches a bin to list view.

Q5: The Display Name column.

Chapter 3 Test Answers

Q1: True.

Q2: The source viewer is on the left and the timeline viewer on the right.

Q3: I and O.

Q4: A) Insert.

Q5: Overwrite edit.

Chapter 4 Test Answers

Q1: C) All of the Above.

Q2: C).

Q3: True.

Q4: Changes the speed of a clip to fit the marked range.

Q5: Click the frame in the viewer or press the keyboard short cut (2).

Chapter 5 Test Answers

Q1: D) All of the Above.

Q2: A) Deletes a segment in the timeline and leaves a gap.

Q3: The Link/Unlink button.

Q4: True.

Q5: Shift-Z.

Chapter 6 Test Answers
Q1: True.

Q2: B)

Q3: Choose Dynamic Trimming from the Trim menu or press W.

Q4: True.

Q5: C) The Project Manager window.

Chapter 7 Test Answers
Q1: To add additional sound, like music and sound effects, at the same timeline location.

Q2: Mutes and enables sound from the specific audio track.

Q3: Click the Inspector button or press Command-9 (OS X) or Ctrl-9 (Windows).

Q4: True.

Q5: False: If the Meters display yellow, the audio is falling within the reference range.

Chapter 8 Test Answers
Q1: Choosing Timeline > Add Transition, pressing Command-T (OS X) or Ctrl-T (Windows) or dragging a transition from the Effects Library.

Q3: In the Inspector.

Q2: Drag an edge of the transition highlighted area in the timeline.

Q4: True. The Smooth Cut can help repair a jump cut.

Q5: In the Project Settings.

Chapter 9 Test Answers
Q1: In the Effects Library.

Q2: True. Titles must be edited into the timeline before you can change any parameters.

Q3: A) Select a side of the segment to extend using a trim pointer.

Q4: The green wireframe represents the starting position and red represents the ending.

Q5: Right-click over the clip in the bin and choose Change Alpha Mode.

Chapter 10 Test Answers
Q1: The Change Clip Speed dialog. The Retime controls. The Fit-to-Fill edit.

Q2: True. Using Change Clip Speed will not change the length of the timeline segment.

Q3: True. Using the Retime control will change the length of the timeline segment.

Q4: Divide the clip, so you are able to set different speeds within a single clip.

Q5: D) All of the above.

Chapter 11 Test Answers

Q1: XML (AAF is used for Avid Media Composer).

Q2: Click the Color button at the bottom of the Resolve window.

Q3: The timeline carries over into the Color page. Nothing happens to it.

Q4: C) Shadows.

Q5: To organize or separate color adjustments on a clip.

Chapter 12 Test Answers

Q1: Right-click over the Still and choose Apply Grade or middle mouse click over the Still.

Q2: A) Applying Grades to multiple clips.

Q3: A Color Chart.

Q4: False. Shot Match can work on any clips.

Q5: True: A Smart Filter shows and hides clips in the Color page timeline based on criteria you define.

Chapter 13 Test Answers

Q1: To save and later, compare the different looks you create for a clip.

Q2: D) All of the Above.

Q3: To select a specific region (or create a mask) for an area in an image you want to color adjust, based on red, green and blue color channels, hue, saturation or luminance as well as standard green/blue screen.

Q4: True. Serial Nodes pass color adjustments from one node to another but Layer Nodes combine images.

Q5: False: Qualifiers and Power Windows are often used on the same node.

Chapter 14 Test Answers

Q1: The Tracker.

Q2: Press the Stabilize button.

Q3: B) OpenFX Library.

Q4: Node Sizing.

Q5: The Playback menu's Render Cache submenu.

Chapter 15 Test Answers

Q1: Click the Deliver button.

Q2: Nothing. The timeline loaded in the viewer remains the same.

Q3: B) Mark an In and Out point at the start and end of the range.

Q4: The Color page.

Q5: True. You must click Add to Render Queue before you can begin rendering.

Index